# Advance Praise for
# *Chimes from a Cracked Southern Belle*

"Using humor and a cast of zany characters, Reinhardt's book will have you laughing out loud and scratching your head, wondering what in the world could happen next!

I'm not a Southerner, but believe me when I tell you, Susan Reinhardt (bless her heart) has written the funniest damn novel about life in the South since *Gone with the Wind.* Wait, that wasn't supposed to be funny? Well, this book is. You'll laugh so hard you'll spit your grits out reading it.

In the Southern-fried voice we've come to love from her memoirs, humor columnist Susan Reinhardt goes for the jugular with hilarity and a touch of key lime pie sweetness in her first novel, *Chimes from a Cracked Southern Belle.*"

– Tracy Beckerman, syndicated humor columnist and author, *Lost in Suburbia: A Momoir. How I Got Pregnant, Lost Myself, and Got My Cool Back in the New Jersey Suburbs*

"Reinhardt creates such colorful, loveable and familiar characters. . . . She draws you into the narrative by scribbling the funniest lines outside the box, in a tapestry of a story that can only be woven with her passion for telling it, a deft wit and a true understanding of the outrageous co-existences of family relationships. The mystery of her impish magic rivals Rumpelstiltskin. Reinhardt has spun a new color of gold with this one."

– D.C. Stanfa, author of the award-winning *The Art of Table Dancing*, and co-editor of *Fifty Shades of Funny: Hook-ups, Break-ups and Crack-ups.*

"Susan Reinhardt's Southern roots show in her debut novel. Reinhardt can pass my personal litmus test for humorists—crying so hard you can barely breathe, then laughing so hard you blow a snot bubble with your nose."

– Robin O'Bryant, author of best-selling *Ketchup is a Vegetable and other Lies Moms Tell Themselves.*

"If you don't laugh out loud when you read about monkey shines and resuscitating squirrels, see your therapist immediately. Your sense of humor needs repair."

– JC Walkup, Publisher/Editor, *Fresh Literary Magazine*

## Praise for Susan Reinhardt's Other Books

### *Not Tonight, Honey: Wait 'til I'm a size 6*

"Susan Reinhardt takes the naked, honest truth and sets it on fire in a blaze of laughter . . ."

– Laurie Notaro, *New York Times* best-selling author, *The Potty Mouth at the Table* and other books

"She's like a modern-day, Southern-fried Erma Bombeck or Dave Barry."

– *Booklist*

### *Don't Sleep with a Bubba: Unless Your Eggs are in Wheelchairs*

"Susan Reinhardt is a riot!"

– Jill Conner Browne, *New York Times* best-selling author of the Sweet Potato Queens series

"Like hanging out with your bluntest, most mischievous friend, the one who never fails to crack you up."

– *Chicago Sun-Times*

# CHIMES
## FROM A CRACKED SOUTHERN BELLE

## *Acknowledgments*

This wouldn't be possible without the entire staff of Grateful Steps Publishing, the expert editing and devotion of Micki Cabaniss Eutsler, Lindy Gibson and the wonderful copy editors and designers for the skills and time they spent seeing this book come to light.

Thanks to past agents in New York for pulling for this novel during the time the Great Recession hit us all.

I'd also like to thank my children, Niles and Lindsey, and my wonderful husband for letting me talk about this novel for the many years it took me to labor and deliver the final product. Props to Randy Whittington who shot the photos and designed the cover. Thanks to Albemarle Inn for allowing us to shoot the cover photo there. Heartfelt appreciation to Joyce Dixon, my bookclub and friends. Finally, I couldn't do any of this without the generous support of my parents, Sam and Peggy Gambrell, who always root for me and slip me cash when the accounts are low.

Grateful Steps Foundation
159 South Lexington Avenue
Asheville, North Carolina 28801


Library of Congress Control Number 2001012345

Reinhardt, Susan
*Chimes from a Cracked Southern Belle*

Cover photographs and design by Randy Whittington.
Cover photo location: Albemarle Inn, Asheville, North Carolina

ISBN 978-1-935130-62-8 Paperback

Printed in the United States of America
at Versa Press, East Peoria, Illinois

FIRST EDITION


www.gratefulsteps.org

*To my mother, Peggy*

## Also by Susan Reinhardt

NONFICTION

*Not Tonight, Honey: Wait 'Til I'm a Size 6*

*Don't Sleep with a Bubba: Unless Your Eggs are in Wheelchairs*

*Dishing with the Kitchen Virgin*

*Only Hussies Wear Blue Eye Shadow*

SERIAL NOVEL

Contributor to *Naked Came the Leaf Peeper*

ANTHOLOGIES

*Fifty Shades of Funny: Hook-Ups, Break-Ups and Crack-Ups*
edited by DC Stanfa and Susan Reinhardt

*More Sand in My Bra: Funny Women Write from the Road, Again!*

*Twenty-Seven Views of Asheville*

*Southern Fried Farce: A Buffet of Down-Home Humor from the Best of Southern Writers*
Writers include Celia Rivenbark, Susan Reinhardt, Clyde Edgerton and Roy Blount, Jr.

*Women on Love, Sex and Work in our 40s*
All proceeds go to breast cancer education, research and access to care.

# CHIMES
## FROM A CRACKED SOUTHERN BELLE

*A Novel*

Susan Reinhardt

Grateful Steps
Asheville, North Carolina

# *Prologue*

Most often, people think the reason I married the best looking man in both Carolinas who turned out to be a complete psycho and near-murderer was because I was raised all wrong. The psychiatrists tried to mine the depths of a disorder that doesn't exist, thinking there must be some long-buried secret from my seemingly unblemished All-American past catapulting a girl from homecoming queen to intensive care via her husband.

Nothing could be further from the truth. A fairly normal woman can ignore the gigantic red warning flags if the evil of her choosing shows up wrapped pretty as a Christmas package and is so gorgeous on the outside she forgets to lift the lid.

"I'm saying this is the South. And we're proud of our crazy people. We don't hide them up in the attic. We bring 'em right down to the living room and show 'em off. No one in the South ever asks if you have crazy people in your family. They just ask what side they're on."

– Dixie Carter, better known as Julia Sugarbaker of *Designing Women.*

# *Chapter One*

**Wake up, Prudy. Rise and Shine:** *A man's courage can sustain his broken body, but when courage dies, what hope is left?* ***Proverbs 18:14***

**Mama's Moral:** *You may be living in an ugly apartment, but you have courage. And that in itself will bring you hope.*

EVERY MORNING OF this unsure existence begins with a phone call and a proverb from Mama, a moral always attached. I am not supposed to answer the phone when it rings, generally at seven o'clock, even on Saturdays, but instead wait and allow the machine to record it. That way, she says, I can replay wisdom throughout the day "on an as-needed basis."

Women like me need a lot of wisdom, she figures. Women like me who married hastily and poorly, extremely poorly, then ended up not just alone with two kids and no money—but alone and almost dead. Technically dead at least twice, according to several sets of official records and court testimony.

I wouldn't know. My mind chose not to remember most of the details, which infuriates counselors and doctors. The events of that premurderous day come to me in flashes, like strobe lights, and I've learned to effectively block them. Why remember something so horrific?

It wasn't even noon and already my mother was in my newly leased fixer-upper apartment, having written a check for the first month's rent, just to get me out of her hair and home.

"No more checks until you get yourself a job," she said, treating me as if I were still in college. "It's high time you secured honest and decent employment. This world stops for no one, sugar pie, and that includes women like you."

Like me. Lumped in a category and separate from the regular women who marry well—at least well enough to stay alive or unmaimed.

"They need makeup girls at Estée Lauder," she said, opening the curtains, a defeated gray material, once white, trimmed in a blue ruffle and torn on both ends.

I pointed to my scars, courtesy of Bryce Jeter, his church van and the tools in his glove box. "It pays minimum wage and you have to be pretty," I said. "These scars aren't going to lure many women into a vat of mineral makeup, now are they?"

"You're a beautiful woman. You could wear a scarf to cover that up—and nothing's wrong with minimum wage. This ugly old apartment isn't going to cost much anyway." She removed a curtain rod and snatched the frail cloth from the metal, wadding it up and stuffing the fabric in a huge trash bag she'd brought along. "These old things could be harboring insect eggs and all sorts of petulance."

"Pestilence," I corrected, accustomed to her mispronunciations. "I don't like the attitude of the makeup women." I rolled over and turned face up on my rented bed, which sagged on the left side. I wondered about the people who'd slept on this mattress before me. Were they happy? Did they believe the exchange of vows would bring them a strength and peace nothing could rip open?

The ceiling fan above clicked with the effort of old fixtures, trying to stir the musty air of this apartment, finally leased after two years of sitting empty while collecting dust and bug carcasses. "The makeup ladies are always talking about your big pores or ruddy complexion. They'll insult the hell out of you just to get you to buy a $70 jar of fortified mineral oil."

"Don't be bitter, Prudy. It's not becoming for ladies to say bad words and you know how I—"

"It's Dee, Mama. I hate the name Prudy. From now on, it's Dee, which is a form of Prudy when you think about it."

"I knew a lesbian named Dee, but forget it. You never listen to me, and acting all ugly isn't gonna get you a thing. So just quit cussing. It cheapens women. Just like putting a big cigarette in their mouths . . . or . . . I don't know . . . one of those fanny tattoos."

My mama walked back and forth like a frisky goat of sorts, her heels clacking against the worn hardwood floors. She was pumped with some kind of obvious mission, fueled with more caffeine than her doctor allowed. He had told her to cut the caffeine due to blood pressure and life pressure and all the pressures my bad choices had slammed her with the past couple of years.

Eleven months after she took the kids and me into my childhood home—this trio of disheveled and aimless people—the children and I had finally moved out of her lovely sprawling rancher with the giant American flag snapping in the front yard and a long rectangular swimming pool out back sparkling like a piece of the Caribbean Sea. These were to be my first steps toward independence. Renewed independence. Starting over again, not just from scratch but from near death and now, near poverty.

"I just don't understand," Mama was saying for the millionth time. "We were good parents. There's no tragedy in our family tree. How could you have married this . . . this monster? Your sister's husbands have all been fine men. I'm a good Christian woman and bake more macaroni pies for people with fallen bladders and whatnots, so why did this have to happen to—"

"Mama, I'm sorry but I really don't want to go into this again. And Amber's current husband has some issues in case you haven't been paying attention."

She shifted around, looking for a dirt-free place to sit. "He's got medical problems. That's different than mental problems. And he's not but 32 and rich as Bill Gates on account of his family's chicken franchises."

"They've been married less than a year and already he's had five surgeries."

"That's because he didn't have insurance beforehand, and there you have it. Some men, in case you never gave this much thought, marry for money. Some marry for the health coverage," Mama said.

"I just can't believe he didn't have coverage."

"Probably some preexisting condition. But to be quite honest, this one is on the feminine side anyhow if you ask me." Mama poked out her coral-frosted bottom lip, same trait my daughter inherited. "But even so, Amber's husbands have all been mighty fine men. None of them ever so much as laid a finger on her in a mean way."

I had tried to explain to everyone who questioned my marital choice since the incident, which shocked everyone because they'd bought into Bryce's nice act, that there are women, and I swore I'd never become one, who are perfectly normal and self-assured people until one day they meet someone and a string pulls, rewinding them like fast tops on slick linoleum until they've spun back into a state of complete dependence and insecurity. I used to feel sorry for these women, thought of them as invertebrates who needed to get a firm grip on themselves while growing at least a rudimentary backbone.

Without knowing what or how it happened, other than pure physical attraction that drowned the one or two weak warning signs Bryce emitted, I'd become one of them, a process that was so slow I never saw it creeping up. It was kind of like being one of those test frogs they drop in cold water and increase the temperature so gradually the frog never realizes it's being boiled alive.

Before Bryce Jeter I'd always had a man as a safety net, someone standing there and more than willing to catch the falling parts, make everything better with his gallant availability. But not now. The backbone I'd lost with him I aimed to grow back—one good choice after another—one vertebra at a time.

Mama began a slow pace, moving from one object to another and staring at my belongings with an unveiled disgust, with that expression telling a grown child she is teetering toward complete and total failure, a borderline embarrassment for a mother to bear.

She's been popping in at my new place at least once a day, sometimes twice, since I moved in a couple of weeks ago. She is afraid I'm dwelling on the second anniversary of my would-be demise. She doesn't say it in as many words, but I can tell by the way she jitters and huffs around the room that the anniversary of my ex's evil deed is on her mind.

"I wish you'd at least looked at that other apartment," she was saying, sitting along the bay window and scanning the older, charming homes of Maple Heights. This was a section of town in the center of Spartanburg, South Carolina, where each house, no matter its size, was an architectural blessing, not simply a box or rancher. Every dwelling in the Heights had character and style, and although some were getting older and run-down, they were affordable. And interesting. "You could have moved in The Oaks and the kids would've had a pool and central air."

"But I'd have had to pay for that air and chlorine," I said, rolling twice across my bed the way teenagers do when talking on the phone. "Here, the swirl of the fan is free. And heat in the winter is included in the rent. I like it."

"At least get yourself a new sofa. Let me buy you one, please. That old thing you salvaged has enough dust to sink a lung. You and those poor children are certain to come down with asthma or Legionnaires' disease." She was the type who thought all diseases and afflictions were out there waiting, focusing on people with a no-holds-barred hunger to infect. As if "catching" asthma was as likely as coming down with a cold. She was part of the clean and proper class of society, living in one of the better neighborhoods, Lakeside Park, in Spartanburg, South Carolina; or at least it had been until a development of stucco houses with imported tile roofs and a gated entrance had one-upped it a few years back.

Mama lived where landscaping was a must, where the mailboxes came to life with hand-painted cardinals or hummingbirds, and every Saturday morning the whine of mowers and blowers joined a neighborly chorus of yard betterment and beautification.

In Maple Heights, lawns ran the gamut from well groomed to growing wild. Most were in between: tangles of ancient shrubbery and scattered weeds, random flowers, along with the occasional meticulously tended beds. What I liked best about this neighborhood were the houses with white window boxes overflowing with geraniums. It was as if each window had a wide red smile, a way of sizing life up and figuring the good outweighed the bad. I'll bet the women in those houses were the cheerful, pie-baking types. Married to the men-who-don't-try-to-kill-their-wives-at-the-BI-LO types.

"You're 40 years old," Mama said, "and starting over, living like a college coed in her first pitiful apartment with discards for furnishings. I tell you, Prudy, it is way long overdue—"

"Dee. It's Dee now. And I'm 38." She loved to add years to make a point. At 25 she called me an old maid, and at 30, she decided I was a middle-aged woman frittering away her fertility and all but asking for a child with Down syndrome. "You and Bryce need to have children before your eggs go bad," she'd said daily, years before my ex-husband plunged into stark-raving lunatic madness. She'd mail me the most horrifying stories of maternal-age-related birth defects. All sorts of trisomies and broken chromosomes—cleft palates, intestines flopped outside the body, spines that didn't close, brains that failed to form—and she'd say, "If the Lord didn't want women to have babies early, he wouldn't have given them their periods at 12."

She licked the ball of her thumb and rubbed a smear of something from my picture window. "You're doing much better," she said, "so don't go getting me wrong. You've at least got a roof over y'alls heads, but I won't give it much more credit than that. I'll tell you, Pru . . . Dee, and I know you're tired of hearing this, but it's not good that you've skipped out entirely on one of the stages of healing. You've got to get mad at Bryce if you want to find wellness of mind. You've got to remember the ordeal from the BI-LO parking lot or you'll never be right in the head till you do." She took great pleasure in quoting my last and final therapist, the words on her tongue giving her authority.

Mama walked over to my vanity, the one decent piece of furniture I owned, and began messing with her hair.

"In addition," she said, trying to resurrect a flattened sprig of ash blond bang, "you don't seem to even want to remember that mess. I pray every night you'll face that day."

I try every night before closing my eyes to remember. All I can see is his face all red and bloated. Nothing comes into focus after that. Nothing but that scarlet face. That horrible sweaty red face and his right arm, high in the air, ready to strike, the weapon he clutched so small I never saw it coming.

Mama began emptying the garbage cans in the kitchen, den and bedroom. She was not one to sit still. "I want you to know that other than this here gloomy, semi-trashy rental unit, your poor old mother loves you and is proud of you as I can be. Just think about running over to Dillard's and seeing about the makeup counter job. At least you could get free mascara and all sorts of goodies. Whatever you do to make payments on this . . . this . . . dinky rental will be fine, I'm sure. I'll be proud even if you have to sell McNuggets, sugar pie. You just don't realize how proud you've made me and your daddy."

I thought about this carefully as I stared at the ceiling, noticing the brown outlines of past storms looping their circular calling cards in the plaster. Proud of what? That I could finally get out of bed and open a can of Campbell's by myself? That I could drive to the store and buy toothpaste and tampons or fill out the paperwork to rent an apartment, sign my children up for school? That I could, on most days, walk without a cane or even so much as a blatant limp?

She sighed, only with vocals, like a series of monotoned yoga groans. "One thing I'd like you to consider and get to quickly is the business of finding those kids a new daddy now that theirs is in prison till he's old enough for swelling prostrates, or however you say it, and clogged arteries, and for death, which I look forward to coming premature if you want perfect honesty. I know it doesn't sound very Christian, but that's how I feel and I can't help it."

She peered once more out the window, her eyes on the May sky, a diluted blue that seemed overpowered by the intensity of a South Carolina sun, a sun whose violent heat would hold us hostage from now through late September. I knew to let her keep talking; no point interrupting or it would take twice as long.

"Jay's nearly 7 and Miranda's pushing 4. That's two years with no daddy. Lord, I'd have thought you'd at least have a prospect, a decent respectable man to give those children an example. Even most widows I know only wait a year before getting back into the swing of things. The men widows are worse. They chomp around all lost and hungry, wearing wrinkled clothes and those fallen down faces. Not a month or two later, and most of 'em get a replacement wife before the first one grows cold. Remember Paul the fellow that runs the hotdog place downtown? He married Ann Trotter three weeks after Linda died. Did you know if a boy child grows up without a daddy, he could end up a homosexual?" She whispered the word, as if it were a sin just to say it.

I'd heard this for more than a year since the trial ended and my ex, the Rev. Bryce Jeter, got his 25 years and the kids and I changed our last names back to my original, which sounds so much prettier than Jeter. This was when I decided instead of being Prudence "Prudy" Jeter I'd go ahead and become Dee. Bye-bye, Prudy Jeter. Hello, Dee Millings.

Mama believed that once the proceedings were over and my injuries had healed enough, divorce papers signed and sealed, it was then proper and advisable to tiptoe back into the dating pool.

However, that did not include sexual relations, which she was dead set against before marriage. And quite possibly even afterward.

"Recirculate," she'd said, rotating her hands. "You're a beautiful girl, just like a Lane Bryant model before they started using those skinny ones. Lose a few pounds . . . or maybe not. Come to think of it, at least a few men find large fannies an asset. 'Course I keep telling you to cut off all that long hair you wear like you were an aging Hollywood star. I don't know . . . you have a lot to offer and at your age you can't afford to just sit around like deli turkey waiting to spoil. Every one of us has ourselves an expiration date. Be it with the Maker or in seeking out a proper mate."

I wasn't sure I was ready for a new man and figured I'd already tested fate with my expiration date. It was my goal just to live on my own again, get a job, find a program for Jay who just so happened to be a bona-fide genius. It was enough just to step out of a bed when the sun made its morning announcements, trying to be the best mother

I could under such extreme circumstances. Recirculating wasn't foremost on the agenda. A job was. And going to nursing school. How in the world I majored in psychology and still married a psycho is beyond me. Kind of rattles a girl's confidence in herself and future choices.

I needed to bring in $550 a month to pay for this rented roof over our heads and another $500 or so to feed the three of us and put gas in the car and electricity in the lights, water in the faucets. Oh, and hook up the phone, cable and Internet. Then there was the issue of spending money for entertainment and camps, maybe some new clothes.

Most importantly, it was my goal to get through a day with more smiles than tears and to be able to hold my children without breaking down and feeling I had failed them. Miranda may not remember the gruesome event, but Jay does. He has nightmares weekly, which I finally dealt with by letting him get into bed with us. Three of us. All in the same bed. I should have rented a one-bedroom apartment to save money, but Mama insisted it's against the laws of common decency for a brother and sister to share a bedroom and certainly against the laws of nature for a mama to bed down with her young children once they got past a certain age, say four months tops.

She slowly walked over to my yard-sale-bought chest of drawers, tapped on the wood, then wiped her hands on the front of her pale pink Levis of the dirt she imagined was accumulating in my "rental." What a striking woman she was. Even at 60 she had the same figure and bone structure of Linda Evans in her *Dynasty* heyday, even wore her hair the exact same way. Her nose was small and delicate, her face thin and cheekbones high enough to hold age at bay far longer than women of lesser genetic fortune. She stood 5 feet, 10 inches in bare feet and always wore modern and fashionable shoes that lifted her above most creatures walking this earth. She meant well. Only I wasn't well enough for what she meant.

"Your Aunt Weepie said there's a boy her husband met at work that she'd like to fix you—"

"Do you want some lunch, Mom? I've got some tuna or I could make a grilled cheese. I don't have to get the kids for another hour or so." Anyone Aunt Weepie knew I wanted nothing to do with. I wasn't in the mood to discuss a possible blind date, especially some guy my mother's funeral-crashing older sister had dug up from God knew where.

"No, honey, Weepie and I are going over to the Red Lobster for some shrimp. We like to go at lunch 'cause it's cheaper and we can get us a Bloody Mary. Actually, she's taken to drinking two of them. Last time we went she insisted on tootling over to the Red Cross, where she gave them a pint of her Vodka'd up blood and promptly passed out and threw up all over my new Town Car."

Soon as Mama got Weepie home she wouldn't let the poor woman in the house.

"Stripped me and hosed me down like livestock," Aunt Weepie had said, retelling the story about once a month. "Threw me a dingy—and stained, I might add—piece of shit night shirt to put on, then called 911. I'll never forgive her, I don't care if she *is* my sister. No woman wants to enter the ER in Mee-Maw panties and a housedress."

I led my mother out of the apartment and walked down the dark, steep stairs, gripping the railing, determined to keep from limping despite the shooting pains in my right leg. I shouldn't have taken a place with stairs, but the rent was affordable, provided one was employed in some capacity, and the rooms were huge, with high ceilings and thick plaster walls carved with built-in bookcases that I'd immediately fallen in love with.

I imagined filling the shelves with Brontë and Austen, all the classics on the upper shelves, newer authors in the middle, then all the books I'd try to read to my children—*The Absolutely Essential Eloise, Goodnight Moon, Where the Wild Things Are,* Shel Silverstein's collections and the science and solar system books for Jay. I would take them from the cardboard boxes and wipe off the dust, stack them with their straight and strong spines, and maybe I'd feel the same joy I'd felt buying them, the happiness of a normal and sane mother who had children without wretched pasts and daddies in prison.

In addition to the bookshelves, another plus for the apartment my mother believes is pitiful is the bathroom with its floor swirls of creamy pink tile and the grout surprisingly clean. Along the back wall, beneath a curtainless window I'd covered with a swag made from an old scarf, sits a clawfoot tub. A completely wonderful, big deep tub where I could escape for hours listening to Elton John or Allison Krauss, the Dixie Chicks or Miles Davis on the small Sony CD player I'd filched from home after the attack.

I could light a couple of candles, pour in lavender, ginger or jasmine oils and almost forget the rent was due and I was jobless. At least I was finally getting out of bed in the mornings. That was progress, I wanted to tell Mother. First let a woman learn to wake up and make oatmeal. Then she can worry about finding another man or a gig glopping on makeup.

The truth was I didn't want another man. It wasn't that I hated them, it's just I didn't trust my instincts after what had happened. *He seemed so normal.* How many times have I said this to myself and others? *Normal normal normal.*

***

For a while after the near-murder and the trial, I hid from mornings, slept right through them, until the wooden blinds in the bedroom offered nothing but a purpled dusk that eventually turned to blackness before I could ever move. I'd become nocturnal, the woman who awoke after dark with matted hair and a ragged, uneven hunger. I'd stuff a bowl of dry cereal into my body then wander into my children's room, crumbs falling from my damp T-shirt, and listen for their heavy, steady breathing, watching their eyes dance beneath transparent, vein-laced lids.

I'd touch their faces, cheeks always cool even in the bathwater air of a South Carolina summer night, and their breath would catch, then settle once again into the rhythm of a peace I couldn't find. Many mornings I'd wake up in their beds, clinging to them as if they were the mother.

Back then, I needed them; now they needed me.

***

Once we were outside the house, Mama turned and glanced at the place as one might stare at a filthy child. We stood on the sidewalk, the Carolina heat building while we said our goodbyes. She held out her arms and I hugged her, feeling the softness of her sleeveless summer sweater against me, inhaling the ammonia of her Miss Clairol hair dye, realizing she must have freshened her color earlier today. She gave me her usual wet lipstick kiss on the cheek and stepped back to check me over. "Your eye bags are better," she said. "They don't look like they've given birth to another set."

We both laughed, and I thought at that moment I could live through anything as long as she was alive, as long as she would appear on a daily basis or call with a proverb and tenacious willingness to lead me into a life I was trying like hell to invite back.

I knew she couldn't help herself. She was from the generation that believes a man would cure everything, and what I needed to get over this hump, this unfortunate tragedy of a very bad choice, was nothing more than a new and improved choice, a man with thicker wiring and no chance of short-circuiting.

It was now or never for me in the dating department, she and my Aunt Weepie would say, trying to be casual though the message was clear. At my age, according to all the magazines that scare us post-30 women to death, beauty begins slipping until it becomes a steady falling off, a sloughing of firmness, time cupping its cruel hands and blocking any sort of youthful glow.

Mama focused on two things: finding me another husband and paying back the first for the evil he'd unleashed.

"By the way," she said before heading toward her car. "I sent Satan's Twin another letter today." She hissed out the pet name she calls my ex. "Mailed it to his prison oasis on my way over here to this rented hovel. 'Course he left you penniless, every little dime he had going to God-knows-what but certainly not to God, to hear his congregation tell it."

She walked to her car, me following behind, and craned her long neck up and down the road, right, left, assessing. Always assessing. "A lot of good families grew up here before it became so run-down and full of hippies," she said, facing the house once again. "After that, the blacks began moving in, but lately, I've begun to realize they have much more class than most whites. You rarely see a black on Jerry Springer, not that I sit home and watch it . . . but you just don't. They have more couth than to stoop that low."

I ignored her comments on my neighborhood and the racial observations. I was thinking about her mean letters to my ex and all the threats she'd made to him the past couple of years. "You know those corrections officers don't give him your mail," I said. "You've been warned and warned."

"This letter wasn't so threatening. I didn't promise I'd rent a Greyhound and aim it right at him." Oh, but she would if she knew Bryce had been writing to Jay that first year post-rampage when we were still in Asheville, North Carolina, a mountain city about an hour or so from Spartanburg. She would if she'd seen the letter he'd typed and addressed directly to me shortly after the first anniversary of the BI-LO showdown. Thank God, the letters had stopped when we moved in with Mama, and now there was little chance he'd find us in this neighborhood. *Little chance. Please, God.*

Mama wrinkled up her pointy nose and unwrapped a piece of Wrigley's Spearmint gum that I could smell from where I was standing. "I simply clipped out a movie photo of Freddy Krueger. You know him? That hideous old creature with the blades for fingernails and that horrible face? I wrote down at the bottom, 'I'm on my way. Prepare yourself, you old wife killer.'"

"You didn't," I said, knowing full well she had, and I was grateful for every scathing letter she'd sent.

"I used an extra stamp with one of the old presidents on it. Gosh, I hope it was a Democrat 'cause I'd hate to desecrate a fine Republican. Well, anyhow I colored it red and black with horns and a beard and little pitchfork. Turned my 40-some-odd cents into a message from Hell." She smacked her gum like a bored waitress might, though she'd never chew gum in public, only at my trashy rental unit. She tends to adopt whatever type personality suits the environment. At the Spartanburg Country Club, she sits stiff as a queen, regal nose tilted just enough to let people know she's a woman of great manners and breeding. She speaks in a low, quiet voice, barely audible, and holds her shoulders as rigid as if they were encased in a brace.

Take her to Waffle House and she's an entirely different woman. Loose jointed and laughing, hee-hawing and even accepting toothpicks after the meal. God forbid.

Mama held her hands up, gazing at the manicured nails and rolled her head around, delivering her "Whatever are you going to do with your mama?" pose. She fluttered her fingers in a flirty goodbye wave, eased into the Town Car and slammed the door. I watched her fiddling with buttons and mirrors, rummaging around in the car's interior. It seemed to take her forever to crank the shimmering Lincoln and steer out onto the road. She reminded me of those women who seem to enjoy wasting half a day exiting a parking place while others grew restless waiting a full five minutes just to be 15 feet closer to the store's front doors.

***

Being on my own for the first time in so many years felt scary, and the last thing I needed to add to the mix right now was a man. Why is it some women seem to think a man is the best cure since the polio vaccine?

Women in my shoes, not that there are many, need friends, jobs and handlebars to the future. They need to rebuild, one small success at a time. They certainly don't need to hear the line of b.s. my doctor loved to spew.

"You know, Prudy, if you pick poorly once, statistically you'll do the same thing," my therapist was fond of saying repeatedly.

"I think that's a load, if you'll forgive my saying so," I told her. "I'm just not gonna buy it. To think I can't learn from a mistake is dooming me forever to live a life with no-goods and ne'er-do-wells."

"That's what'll happen if you can't or simply choose not to remember what you suffered on that awful day."

She was as upset as the other three therapists I'd endured that I couldn't piece together most of the details about the afternoon my ex tried to kill me with his church van and mini screwdrivers as he roared into the BI-LO parking lot like some kind of possessed Dale Earnhardt. But I see no point in reliving a death scene. None whatsoever, I told her, unless you're one of those freaks who must wallow night and day in the drama. I was glad I didn't remember everything. What I did remember was enough when combined with all that gruesome testimony, courtesy of on-the-scene BI-LO shoppers and gawkers.

"You need to remember what it feels like when death rings a doorbell," the counselor had said the last time I sat in her office.

"Some of us don't want to answer such a doorbell," I said.

"You aren't going to progress until you allow the full memories," she warned in a somber tone, thumping at one of her huge front teeth, freshly capped and so white I couldn't look at them.

"I'd rather find someone ten years my junior and take him to a pink motel for an afternoon," I said, knowing this wasn't nice. "Look, I know you mean well and I realize you're a lot smarter when it comes to the mind than I am, though I do have a bachelor's in psychology for what it's worth. The truth is, my mama's making me do this therapy stuff when I think shopping might help more."

She shook her head and sucked at those teeth, making sounds like hungry seagulls. "That's called temporary distraction."

Her body tightened and she held her arms to keep them from reaching for those new teeth her lips had trouble stretching to cover. She was growing weary of hearing this. She did what she always did when I wore her down and she ran out of answers. She removed a book from her shelf, another self-help book, this one called *Claim your Rage,* which I took with a smile and would never touch except to return by mail.

"Don't worry," she said, pretending not to glance at one of her hidden clocks. She took out her receipt book. "It will happen for you when you're ready. You've got a long way to go, Prudy. I'm really beginning to get worried about many things I'm seeing. Trouble's coming if you can't face that day. You can only bury something for so long, and then it will infect you and rattle your core."

She stood, my cue to leave. *How dare she stop the session with a cliffhanger: that she was beginning to worry about a lot of things? What kind of infection? What kind of rattling?*

How little she really knew. Cliffhanger or not, I wasn't going back in time. I could buy a nice tube of pink lipstick for my troubles or go sit in a cold movie theater and eat a giant tub of buttered popcorn, crunching all I wanted, feel my feet stick to the syrupy floor while enjoying two hours of mental relief. I wondered why more people didn't do that instead of sitting on microfiber tan couches, lost souls trying to dog paddle their way across life's great waves and riptides.

"Fleeting affairs are never the answer," she said in parting.

That's all I want, I felt like saying. String a few temporary distractions together and one could avoid her own slipping down state for quite a while. One could pretend she wasn't growing older with no prospects, two fatherless kids, a bad leg, an ever-widening ass, a trashy apartment, a crazy mother, her nut-job older sister . . . and worse . . . no employment, not officially. But I had an idea.

Since moving into the pathetic apartment, I had a plan for work: two jobs, if only I could convince the people to hire me. One of them, I prayed to God, would be easy. The other was nothing but a bit of office work to supplement the bills. Being the wife of a preacher certainly teaches a girl to type—all those church updates and announcements—and smile sweetly.

# Chapter Two

**Wake up, Prudy, Dee, whoever you are. Here's today's bit of holy wisdom**: *Teach a child to choose the right path and when he is older he will remain upon it.* **Proverbs 22:6**

**Mama's Moral:** *Ha! I believe I tried to show y'all the right path but only the dear Lord above knows why you decided to veer off and wander. Get back on it, sugar. It isn't too late!*

IT WAS MY mama's idea to name me Prudence, something she chose as extra insurance toward chastity and long-lived virginity. Pair Prudy with Jeter—Prudy Jeter—and you are left with an abomination of syllables, an alphabetic car wreck. Why couldn't she have named me Judy or Heather? Well, at least now on this gorgeous morning I'd awakened legally as Ms. Dee Millings, leaving Prudy Jeter far behind and buried. Prudy Jeter made bad choices, but Dee Millings was brilliant in that department. She'd never stumble in the land mines of male charms. She'd look for substance or nothing at all. She'd secure employment and earn her own keep, get her children some dental coverage, maybe even try to connect with some other moms and play groups and who knows . . . dial up a few old friends from high school and see how life had treated them in the last 19 or so years. Surely they will have remembered her. She was Miss Spartanburg High School and the homecoming queen. She knew she got those awards because the blacks and rednecks liked her more than the inner, hard-to-penetrate circle of snoots, the super cool girls never won because the "in" clique was so limited.

It would be so nice to have a friend, someone to talk to other than Mama and Aunt Weepie, and yet where would we be without those two?

I waved as Mama prepared to drive away this morning, her second visit in as many days, she pretending to want coffee and conversation but the true reasons for dropping by nothing more than thinly disguised spy missions to see if I was out of bed, had drool on my tattered robe, witch hair and fuzzy teeth. She was searching for the paleness of a woman who won't face sunlight or acknowledge her beating heart.

She rotated her hand through the window, imitating her old beauty-pageant wave, sure to leave behind a guilt trip and another assessment of my all-but-housing-project existence. "I'll be home by three to take you all to the zoo," she said.

"I really don't have time to—"

"Prudy, you gotta show those children some pleasure and fun in life. Now, we're going to the zoo and that's all there is to it. They got four new monkeys according to the *Herald-Journal*. They were on some kiddie TV show 'bout ten years ago and I want to see them in person. I'm sure the kids do, too."

"I was going to see about a job today."

"I told you to go on over to Dillard's or Belk and get on with the makeup people. I could use a discount on my Estée Lauder and it wouldn't hurt you to spruce up some either."

With that she drove away, hand stuck out her window in a final salutation.

I once again trudged upstairs, sat alone in the kitchen, drank coffee and later, forced myself to eat a plate of chicken salad she'd delivered, chewing mechanically, not really tasting anything but swallowing because I was told it would keep me alive. Eating now because for almost a year, I couldn't unless it was sweet, hence my extra weight.

I breathed in the smell of piled up decades, that mix of musty scents that stir and settle in buildings over 100 years old. The white plastic clock splattered with grease ticked annoyingly. The hands, the longer one broken at the tip, showed it was getting late and I needed to hurry and pick up the children from school. Maybe there was enough time to dial up an old friend or two. Could be they won't be home, that maybe they have children to retrieve, and then I wouldn't have to actually talk to them. I could leave a message, the ghost of me, which means investing nothing emotionally into life's system of relating to others. I could be a caller who searches for friends when I know they won't answer. I would leave my name and number and see if they called back; this way there wouldn't be awkward conversations that made my heart beat all weird and my throat constrict. The possibility for rejection would be reduced by putting the ball in their court.

I searched an unpacked box for the old phone and address book I had pre-Bryce. Opening it, smelling the dust and age of something long forgotten, I wanted to kick myself for not getting in touch with these once good friends. I'd let them go, year by year the calls dropping off, until not even a Christmas card arrived in the mail anymore.

I had no one to blame but myself. Bryce and his world had swallowed my own. I'd turned into one of those women I couldn't stand who live for their men and kids and never take a moment to remember who they were . . . still are.

I flipped through the book, sneezing, and the pages settled on my former best friend in the world. Claire Hopping, only the Hopping was crossed out and replaced by Boyle, the name of the frat boy she'd married our senior year in college.

I picked up the phone and dialed. What would I say? How long had it been? Four years? No, five? The ringing triggered a panic, and I slammed down the receiver. I'd try later. Maybe. Probably not.

"It's a start," I said to no one, grabbing my keys and purse and walking into a postcard-blue afternoon to pick up Miranda and Jay. Miranda at the upper-middle-class preschool paid for by my parents where the other mothers wore clothes from the Lands' End catalog and flat leather shoes and spawned children they dressed in linen and oversized bows and who never got terribly dirty or mucusy. Junior League mothers. The wives of oral surgeons and corporate attorneys. Women who had their nails done on Fridays, their hair on Saturday mornings, and worked out each day the sun rose. How would I ever fit into this world?

If examining the situation in full honesty, I'd have to admit I didn't want this world of pretense and soccer games and ballet lessons, a world of normalcy played just like the game of Life. I wanted the zigzagged roads of spontaneity, a carefree path that came with mismatched tags of joy and laughter. I knew exactly what I wanted—the very thing Bryce tried his best to stop me from ever having. Independence. Every breath-drawing creature on earth deserved it.

The pickup line bustled with shiny hair and the slick paint of Mercedes and BMW SUVs. Most mommies wore their gym clothes and happy faces, many getting there early to secure the best spot in line. Some read books, but none that I could tell ever had the music going. Nobody waved, but then again, I didn't wave either. It seemed as if each life was perfect from the perspective reflected through my windshield. They probably went home to husbands who adored them, or at worst, absolute worst, ignored them. I'll bet none of them had displaced children staying at grandma's while their mother struggled for life in the intensive care unit, flat-lining twice.

These women in the car line were nice girls with shining bobs and straight white teeth—girls who didn't have that sort of life. That was the kind of life reserved for people like me—the bad choosers. The women, according to my therapist, "who don't love themselves enough to choose better."

How could she keep saying that? Every time she did I felt enraged and began to sweat. I love myself. My parents love me. God loves me, so the Bible says.

Why haven't I ever felt like I fit in this world? How hard could it be? Maybe these women who were all alike on the outside, were in fact, completely different inside and wore and said and did conforming things because that was the only way they could comfortably live.

Maybe I should follow their rules and pretend to enjoy domestic bliss and it would come. Pretend life is smooth and unmessy and thus it shall be. Maybe I could drive past the line, park the car and get out one day. I could walk without my cane and try my hardest not to limp as I picked Miranda up early and waved to the other mothers in line. Then they'd see me. They might ask for our number and Miranda could have a play date. She would stop whining every day and telling me she had no friends. The women would see I was clean and normal looking (from a distance) and wouldn't notice the scars if I wore the right clothes. They might even invite Miranda to Chuck E. Cheese for birthday parties and prize tokens. How hard could it be?

One day I would do this, but today I didn't care whether they waved or stared ahead at nothing. I inhaled deeply and unwrapped a few Hershey's kisses for Miranda, placing them on a paper plate along with two carrots. If she ate the baby carrots, she could have the chocolate. Bribing works so well with kids.

I couldn't take the quiet of this line because that's when all the noises could really get in and mess with a person's head. I flipped on the CD player and cranked up the Dixie Chick's singing "Goodbye, Earl," a therapeutic tune for all survivors of the planet's most misogynistic men. Miss Capped Teeth therapist says it's not good for me to keep playing "Goodbye Earl," and I said to her, "But you're the one telling me to get mad or I won't get well." And to that she says, "Getting mad *directly* is what I'm after. Not your living out anger through a bunch of song lyrics."

One would certainly think if she married a man of the cloth, her husband could have at least asked for some divine intervention before following his wife in the church van, burning rubber and scratching his sorry self into that parking lot to mow her down in broad daylight, for God's sake.

Aunt Weepie says most preachers are fine people but every now and then there's one who's a worse sinner than regular folks.

"They go into the business 'cause they got something bad to hide or chase off," she said. "Remember that Jerry Falwell? That Jim Bakker? That's why I married a mechanic. I know if he comes home with his hands clean, he's had them up some hussy's skirt. A man would wash himself of Castrol before caressing a young slut's thigh."

My mama, who takes every commandment as seriously as if God were living in her back bedroom and keeping a constant eye out, has wanted to attack the Rev. Jeter every day since the tragedy. She used to visit the prison, drive all the way to Charlotte, N.C., with her 9mm loaded in the glove box, bumping up against the New Testament and her road maps. She was willing to forgive just about every sin on earth except what her son-in-law had done to her daughter. No guard ever let her inside. They had seen her marching about near the entrance, shouting her plans of revenge and how she had a new Town Car with its engines revving and ready to roll the reverend flatter than a highway possum.

A restraining order from Bryce's lawyers plus a year's supply of Zoloft had toned her down a hair, with the exception of the regular letters she sends festooned with the horned and pitch-forked presidents, Democrats if she can locate them.

The anger she emits has been beneficial. Every time she expresses rage she absorbs it in her very bones, releasing and almost bleeding my own pain so I can concentrate on healing, on getting out of bed to eat a sandwich. So I can read a bedtime story to the kids and not collapse in tears when I get to the Happily-Ever-After part.

So that I can drive a car down the road and honor the hands of a clock, the days on a calendar, basic ticks and squares of life I once couldn't follow.

For many months they ran together, a melted pudding of hours and days. The segments and increments were parceled and meaningful for others, for those who could get out of bed and eat their Grape Nuts and wheat toast, check a watch and obey the sun and the light. Normal people who went to bed at eleven, fell asleep during the news. People whose alarm clocks buzzed at seven. Not people who writhed in damp sheets and stale pain, people who couldn't tell one day from the next.

***

The Dixie Chicks had finished up with Earl and his wrongdoings and were now singing about the Sin Wagon. I must say those girls were helping me much more than therapy and were right on the money with their word choices. They understand a woman's pain, you can just tell by the way they sing.

*Praise the Lord and pass the ammunition.*
*Need a little bit more of my 12-ounce nutrition.*
*One more helpin' of what I've been havin'.*
*I'm takin' my turn on the sin wagon.*

Most of us need a good ride on the Sin Wagon, and if I were to meet a man who was better looking than say, Yoda, I might treat him to some Serta hospitality. I'd like to have said this to Mama but could not because she is certain that a real Southern lady doesn't enjoy the business at hand. She does her duty while considering what kind of vegetable to serve with spaghetti and meatballs. Once her husband's finished, she's got the whole menu figured out in addition to ensuring his good mood for the next 48-or-so hours.

My mother, the keeper and preserver of morals, a woman who can barely bring herself to even say the word sex, is a piece of work, a piece of pent-up, sexually fearful work. She is gung-ho on virgins. Thought they were about as godly as anything on earth. If I hadn't been born, if my sex-kitten sister had not followed two years later, I would never have believed my mother capable of taking off her clothes and doing such a thing.

She can't stand to see it on the nature channels. She fusses at the poor old TV, calling the humping lions "hussies and harlots" and punching the OFF button with exaggerated drama and grunts of disgust.

"I'd feel better if they were at least married," she once said to the darkened picture tube. "Those nature shows are one undulation away from total pornography. I hope you don't let your young children watch this filth."

I smiled, turning down the Dixie Chicks as I got closer to the line of waiting children. I leaned back and felt the sun beating through the car windows, warming my forearms as they rested on the steering wheel, forgetting skin cancer warnings and enjoying the heat. Lolling in this daze of thought, I heard a car honk behind me, signaling it was time to move forward in the line. I gazed at Miranda's feet, enormously large in shoes a size too big, Mama's idea as a way to save money. I placed our assigned number in the window and worked my face into a cheery pucker of animation and delight. Happy mother. Semi-happy, semi-healthy, semi-normal mother of two, living in a fine albeit ugly-ass apartment in a culturally diverse part of town. Mother with no sex life, no prospects, no job or money, but with a wide, plastered-on smile stretching endlessly with optimism.

Miranda hopped into the car, her hands full of crafts, including a construction paper sunflower made from an empty Bounty roll, her picture right in the center. I tried hard to ignore the yellow devil horns coming out of the top of the flower, as they did on most of her artwork. We ate our Kisses and carrots, then drove to TCBY and had the sugar-free parfaits that were on sale, slowly eating until it was time to pick Jay up from big-boy school.

"I hope you aren't gonna drink beer cans," Miranda said right out of the blue.

"Beer? How do you know what beer is?"

"The people from drug addicts came to school and said it's bad if your parents drink beer cans. Don't ever drink no beer."

"Any beer. It's any, and no, I don't plan to."

Miranda had always been old. She was born a grandmother. An ancient and wise soul. She could lecture like a Catholic school nun and was the family's youngest moral enforcer. She takes after her Mama Millings, both of them sitting in judgment and ready to pass on bits of wisdom via lectures to prevent sin. I dare not put a glass bottle into the regular trash. Miranda can go on a half-hour tangent if people litter or don't recycle. Lord, the things the preschools teach children these days. In my day, we had a commercial featuring an Indian, back when we were allowed to say Indian instead of Native American. He was standing on the highway and a single tear rolled down his perfect face when he saw someone had littered the countryside. That was the saddest commercial of my entire life. Hard to imagine what that poor Native American would think if he saw my garbage when Miranda wasn't watching—bags and bags of plastic, cans and bottles that weren't separated according to materials. How can you explain to a 4-year-old, grandmotherly nun-child that the recycling man is $30 a month and we don't have $3 for one lousy Happy Meal?

***

I glanced to see Miranda, as if reading my mind, gathering bits of stray paper in the floorboard of the car and dribbling them into her backpack. "It's not good to litter or you could go see the jail."

I nodded. I've learned to accept this Mother Theresa of a child and love every fiber of her vocal enforcements. "Like Daddy. Isn't Daddy in the jail, Mama?"

"Yes. Yes he is, honey, but that's not our fault."

"I know. He got the flu in his brain. Some people get the vomit bug in their tummies. Mama Millings said his brain got all sick."

"That's right. You're a very smart young lady."

She took out her colored pencils and began to draw flowers with human faces and clothing. I imagined they'd have devil horns soon enough. "Do brains throw up?" she asked.

"His did."

I started laughing and thank God she did, too. I wasn't sure where this conversation was going. This had become our routine. Sometimes as we ate, the child would talk a mile a minute and asked questions about her daddy. Other times she'd stare off into space, as if juggling a thousand problems on her mind.

I wondered how much this had affected her. How much she remembers. What had she overheard as the grownups talked into the night about whether or not her mother would live, and if she lived, what kind of shape would she end up in? Whether it would be more merciful for God to go ahead and take her mama than leave her all wrong in the head or laid up with her limbs twisting and withering in bed the rest of her life. All of these questions had been thrown into the heavy air and batted around, along with the hostility and heartache a son-in-law's sudden and inexplicable rage had caused—the destruction of an entire family in eleven minutes' time.

"Your flower's beautiful," I said, wiping chocolate from her moon-round face. "Great job."

"No it isn't pretty. It's not 'posed to be. This here is Daddy. See there?" She lifted the flower by the newly drawn set of horns.

"Well, that's okay. One day you'll get tired sticking horns on everything, sweetie."

"No I won't. Mama Millings doesn't. I see her drawing a million gabillion horns a day and all night, too." I reached for her, rubbing her sun-drenched head ringed in curly dark hair. "I saw her drink a beer can, did you know that, Mama?"

I considered this and knew it couldn't possibly be true. "You'll have to tell her it's not nice next time you see her, babe."

We turned into Jay's school, a place for young geniuses where we lucked up and got a scholarship. The clientele here was different from Miranda's place of preppy moms and dads. The parents of genius children, I've learned, are quite the diverse group. Some are earthy and wear Rastafarian dreadlocks and smelly crochet hats, their infrequently washed skin soaked in Patchouli. Others are rich, some dirt poor; then you have the trust-fund moms or the flat-out rednecky types. You name it.

Jay sulked out in the May sun with his head down, eyes on the cement. He opened the car door, slung his book bag onto the rear dashboard and said nothing.

"Did you have a good day?" I asked, all fake in my chirpy good mommy voice. "We're going to the zoo with your grandmother. How about that? They have four new monkeys."

"Monkeys suck," he said. "I hate the bastards." Mercy. I made a mental note to get him back in counseling.

"You don't need to talk trash."

"You sound like Mama Millings. She sucks, too."

"Watch it, bud. That's your grandmother."

"Every single person on the planet Earth all the way to Pluto sucks, so there. And by the way, Pluto isn't even a planet anymore."

The air hung over this corner of the South Carolina Piedmont like an electric blanket, so still and stifling; not a single leaf or flower petal so much as fluttered. It was hot as August and I realized another unforgiving summer would soon arrive. "Y'all both watch your language and manners," I said as we steered the car—my Dad's old Honda Accord—down the cul-de-sac to fetch Mama. It seemed to me people who lived on cul-de-sacs led far happier and more normal lives (at least on the surface) than those of us who lived elsewhere—on streets that bled, merged or changed into other streets.

We drove the 12 miles chatting about mindless things like the best Popsicles on the market and the new Groovy Girl bed. By the time we pulled into the gravel parking lot of the Spartanburg Celebrity Zoo, I had a pounding headache. I looked in the mirror and cringed. The heat had enlarged my pores and caked my makeup. My eyes had that tired look even though I'd slept nine hours. The more I slept, actually, the worse I looked.

"We're here," Mama chirped. Her voice had never been higher or more operatic. She was beaming with either a caffeine overdose or her ultra-strength prescription of change-of-life hormones. "Did y'all know they have animal movie stars here? They get all the old has-beens that used to be featured in TV commercials or movies. All the elephants and primates—a primate is a monkey, Jay."

"Duh. And we descended from them."

"We certainly did not. We were made in the image of God."

"Well I guess God's a monkey."

"Prudy, you've got to do something with this child before he," and she mouthed the last part, "turns into his daddy."

She took out her church fan. "Lord have mercy. Anyway, sweeties, they've got 'em some rhinos and tigers and all sorts of animals that went from New York to Hollywood and ended up in good old Spartanburg. Aren't we lucky to have the poor things?"

"Papa Millings drinks beer cans and we learned at school it will make you kill people with your cars," Miranda said.

My mother momentarily stopped chewing her gum in order to process this shocking statement. She shook her Diet Dr. Pepper and took the last sip before popping the spent gum into the opening.

"Your granddaddy's one of the finest men on this planet, honey."

"Beer cans make your brain sick. Is that what happened to Daddy?"

"You stupid freak," Jay hissed. "It's not beer cans, you just say beer. The cans have nothing to do with it."

"Listen, this is enough. Let's just go see the monkeys and all get along, okay?" Mama said. She made her typical noise of disgust and judgment, a short and deep grunt, then opened the car doors as we stepped into what felt like the inside of a dragon's hot mouth.

"I really need to be out hunting a job," I told Mama as she paid the $12-a-pop ticket price so we could all enjoy a stroll in the heat and smell of hot beasts and their excrement.

"These children need sunlight, Dee, or whoever you are today. You can go hunt you a job later. It'll be too hot to visit this place in June, plus I heard these monkeys do all sorts of fun tricks and I aim to show my grandchildren a good time. As you can see, I'm the one paying the admission so you can at least act grateful. That's all you have to do, if you can manage it."

We wound around the perimeter of the zoo, visiting sleeping and depressed llamas, camels and more varieties of goats and sheep than I could count. The chimpanzee cages lined the south end of the zoo and signs with black stars and painted movie cameras led the way. Below each cage a podium and plaque told the story of this or that animal and what its claim to fame had been. Most were in short-lived TV shows and commercials for pantyhose and rental cars.

We stood for at least ten minutes watching chimps and orangutans, baboons and other monkey types, screech and howl, pound the bars, cut flips for peanuts. Jay laughed for the first time in a week, and I wasn't about to pull him from this small peephole of light shining on his troubled little soul.

"Look at their butts," he said, and Mama hissed for him to hush and not say words like that.

"Fanny," Miranda corrected. "You're 'posed to say 'fanny.'"

"Ass," he said loud as he could, and Mama shook her head and lifted her hands to the heavens as if to say, Lord, I give up.

"I'm calling the therapist," I whispered. "Don't worry."

The monkey show was all a great hoot until one chimp decided to treat himself to exhibitionism and pumped his hand furiously at the little thing between his hairy legs. I sat frozen in fascination, having never seen any creature do such, and here was this monkey, mouth open, grinning as if saying to all us humans, *"See this, dumb people. Stick around. Don't leave till I finish my show. Y'all don't know what you're missing not doing this in public. It's twice the fun."*

I led my children away, though Jay jerked from my grip and rushed straight back for the cages. I tried to interest Miranda in giving the baby goat a bottle and saw that Mama had also stayed behind with Jay, her eyes transfixed while the monkey finished what he'd started.

"What's he doing?" Jay asked, but before Mama Millings could answer, the monkey reared back his arm and flung his results at her, coating her coiffed hair with primate sperm and setting off in her a wave of screams that had the whole zoo at her side.

She had swooned and collapsed on a wooden bench and everyone was fanning her, paper-toweling her hair and bringing her water as she kept rolling up her eyes to the sky and saying, "Oh, lawsy. Oh, have mercy on my soul. What, pray tell, did I do to deserve this? What kind of perverted place is this?"

Jay had his hand over his mouth and his bony shoulders shook. I knew he was laughing and I tried hard not to join him, but the pain of the past two years seemed to drop like dead skin from my body and I fell to the sidewalk in waves of unstoppable mirth. Tears streamed down my face, I laughed so hard.

"Prudy!" Mama screamed, calling me the old birth name. "Have some decency and take your children away from here. Where's your sense of motherhood?" She turned to the zoo staff. "You people are going to read about this in a Letter to the Editor. If you can't get your monkeys to control their urges, you oughtn't have such filth for my grandbabies to see. Why, I never even knew monkeys had . . . had . . . well that sort of thing between their legs or that they could do such a thing."

"Oh, yeah," a man in a jungle-print official zoo shirt said. "They are smart as we are."

"You think that's smart? Is that what you teach your—"

"Ma'am we're so sorry about all—"

"Prudy, take the children away now. Go get an ice cream! Will you please get me some fresh paper towels so I don't have to go home with sin caked in my hair? You will be hearing more from me about this, I can assure you."

By the time Mama got in the car, she wasn't talking, but her face was puffed up and pink. She folded her arms over her chest and kept emitting that grunt. A grocery bag covered her entire head, held together like a turban with a Scrunchie.

I drove along in silence, letting the children carry on about the zoo, all the while trying to placate my mother with occasional pats on her knee and offerings of Juicy Fruit gum. She had chewed and spit out three pieces by the time we turned into her subdivision, the glare of late-day sun blinding.

"Mama, watch out," Miranda screamed. It was too late. I felt the small body of a something hit my tire. I slammed on the brakes. "Mama! You kilt it."

I pulled over and saw a squirrel lying in the road, pawing the air, its tail swirling like a helicopter. "It's not dead," sweetie. "Hold on, okay? Mama, watch the kids, hear?"

I got out of the car and scooted the squirrel to the other side of the road with my foot. It was still moving, but didn't seem to be breathing. One leg was at an odd angle and blood ran from its foot. I crouched over its little body and made a small O with my thumb and index finger. I placed the O over the squirrel's little mouth and blew two small puffs of air into its lungs, alternating this with two-fingered chest compressions. No sooner had I begun my rodent CPR did Mama fly from the car and start yelling.

"Get away from that thing right now! Are you crazy? They carry rabies. Prudy, I'm not going to sit here and let your children see this spectacle. What in God's name is wrong with you?"

I removed my mouth from the O and stared at Mama. "Get back in the car, please. I know what I'm doing."

"You could get rabies. I didn't raise you to French kiss road kill. This is the most embarrassing and—"

Both kids had by then freed themselves from the car and crossed the street to watch. "That is so cool," Jay said.

"Gross, Mama," Miranda said. I continued my CPR and chest compressions until finally, the little animal began to breathe on its own.

"Look, y'all, he's breathing," I said, spitting onto the road and wiping my mouth with a Kleenex. "Run to the car, Mama, and get that empty box out of the trunk. I'll put him in there."

"I won't do any such a thing. I'm taking you home and you're going to wash your mouth out with Listerine and scrub those lips with Ajax and Lysol. Now let go of that filthy old thing and get in this here car. I've had an awful day and we could both use scalding showers."

Jay had fetched the box from the car's trunk and lined it with straw and grass, small twigs and even a rock. He was really such a sweet boy, just needed some guidance. "Here, Mom."

"Prudy, I'm not about to go home with—"

"It's Dee now, Mama, and I'm not about to let this animal die. I'm taking it to the vet so you can either walk home—it's only two streets down the road, you know—or we'll be happy to give you a ride."

"I am not getting in the car with you after you've been to second base with a nasty old squirrel. You leave those children with me. I'm wondering about you, Pru . . . Dee. I know you've always loved animals and can remember you bringing lots of injured creatures home, but this takes the cake. You're losing your mind."

I thought about this as I loaded my revived rodent into the car, up front so I could keep an eye on it. "Mama, for the first time in two years, I'm actually getting my mind back." The kids jumped in the car with me. Not because they loved me better but because they thought they had a shot at a pet if the squirrel lived.

"I love you," I said, waving just like she did as I drove from the scene and toward the emergency vet's office, not even thinking about how I would pay for this squirrel's treatment. "Enjoy the long walk home."

"Don't ever call me again!" she yelled.

The news was good. And it was free. Other than a broken leg and a few missing teeth along with a case of shock, the prognosis called for a full recovery.

"It's okay, Gracie," I said to the squirrel. "Not many people have all their teeth, either."

"Gracie?" Miranda inquired.

"Yeah. That's her name, kinda like your middle name. She's a girl the vet said."

"Can we keep her?"

"We'll see."

***

When I got home there was a single message flashing on the answering machine.

> *Hey, Prudy. It's your Aunt Weepie calling. I'm excited about seeing your dinky apartment. We'll make it pretty, sugar. Listen here, hon. I'm going to a really sweet funeral tomorrow and I know the family in a distant but distinctive way because a long time ago I had love relations with the deceased's second cousin, so I think we'll be a shoo-in for going on over to the house afterward for all that scrumptious food. Call me, darlin'. I got a big surprise for you, too, hon. Aunt Weepie's found you a man!*

I settled the children with apple slices and fruit juice, grabbed a glass of tea and returned the call. It rang about a dozen times.

"Hey, Sweet Prude," she said, drawling out the words slower than any human being with a heartbeat. She sounded sleepy. "I was having me a little nap up under my bed. It's so nice under here and nobody comes and asks me to fix them a meal." She literally sang the word "meal," giving it three separate and distinct syllables.

"You said something about a funeral?"

"Oh, hon, it's going to be some good eating," she yawned. "I knew the old bat slightly. She was mean as hell. I went to high school with that cute little old second cousin of hers and got to know him in a way that—shall we suffice it to say—entitles me to chicken and a bit of all those yummy casseroles. It wouldn't be a problem easing in and then getting a bite afterward. Your mama quit going with me. Said I embarrassed her to death a few months ago and got all uppity about it."

I tried to remember what Mama had said about that particular funeral, but all my aunt's antics had run together. "Are you sure you don't want to come over here? I could make us a sandwich and we could rent a movie. I have $6.32 until I get a job."

I heard a rustling sound, like a dog trying to get comfortable in its carrier.

"That's why I keep getting married, Prudy—sorry, I meant to say Dee but keep forgetting. I keep myself married so I don't have to get a job. When you gonna learn? Look, this is about the only funeral I can honorably make this week. I have scanned the obit pages through and through and can't justify hitting any of the other services unless I drive over to Greenwood and that's way too far, even for a good squash casserole or homemade pecan pie. You know there has to be a trace of a connection to the departed before I'll go, and there's no point attending the service if you don't get the go-ahead to come on over for the food afterward. It's just a waste of good mascara."

Aunt Weepie refuses to wear waterproof because she said that defeats the purpose. "They need to see the grief and anguish on your face. Only then will someone feel bad enough to ask you to the covered dish."

"Hmmm. Right."

"Come on, go with me. Your mama acts too proud to crash funerals for the food. She oughta live with Tony. She oughta have to eat the things he serves that look like big old hairballs."

We call Tony the saint behind Aunt Weepie's back for what the man puts up with. "Sure, I'll go. Might get my mind off things, like trying to find a job, which if I don't do in a matter of 24 hours we'll lose our roof."

"To hear your Mama Lucinda tell it, it ain't much of a roof."

"It's fine for us. I love it. Old charm. Old dirt. All it needs is paint and a few warm touches."

"You can always come stay with me and Tony. I'll sleep under the bed and you and the kids can sleep up on top."

"So who's this guy you've dug up for me?"

"That's the surprise, honey. He's a little fella from Tony's garage who saw your picture and had a fit. He's handsome, if you like the sort, and smart, too. Got him an associate's degree in something or other besides brakes and mufflers."

"What do you mean, if I like 'the sort'?" I asked.

"Oh, I don't know. I'd say he's on the odd side of the fence, but who isn't? He jerks his long old body in a knot when he talks to attractive women and gets his words completely mixed up. But like I said, he's got a degree or two and Tony bragged the station is just a stepping-stone for him. He's got plans to do something I ain't ever heard of and is enrolled in school *again* for what must be the third time. Look, I'm bringing him to the planting because he's pole-cat skinny and could use a home-cooked meal."

"You are setting me up at a funeral?" I couldn't believe it. Or rather, I could.

"Better'n a bar, Prudy."

"Well, I'm not sure if it's a good way to meet a man. First date and all."

"Oh, it'll be great. He can't make it to the funeral, sug. Y'all gonna hook up at the graveside. I can't think of a better way. You've got food, people all around on their best behavior, mood music—you know I've always felt the death songs the organ ladies play have a sexual undertone to them if you're in the right frame of mind while listening."

"They don't have organs at gravesides."

"Wrong you are. The family is insisting on it. Going to wheel it out on a truck and play three selections. The old woman had a will listing about 12 songs to play at her great send-off and no one would sit in a church for that long hearing organ music. It's too hard on the digestive system when you got your mind on a honey-glazed ham and yeast rolls."

"This guy . . . does he know he's gonna meet a strange woman at the funeral?"

"You ain't all that strange," Aunt Weepie said, laughing, snorting into the phone. "I swannee, girl. Just meet the fellow. He has a clean criminal history 'cause Tony ran a check on him before hiring him at the station. Only thing on his record was a rash of indecent exposure charges at an elementary school, but that was two years ago."

"AUNT WEEPIE!"

"Hon, I'm only kidding. Relax. You're gonna like him. And even if you don't, that old dead woman's people make the best fried chicken in the Carolinas."

Where my mother's anger at Bryce was the bandages, my aunt's humor was the balm. Going to a funeral with her couldn't be all that bad. Might expedite the recovery. Hard to be down about one's personal maiming when the woman staring face up from her satin pillow, the stiff figure slathered in pancake makeup and pursing beige lips, was in a far worse fix.

Of course, that is debatable.

# *Chapter Three*

**Rise and Shine, Pru-DEE:** *Work brings profit; Talk brings poverty. If you love sleep, you will end up in poverty. Stay awake, work hard and there will be plenty to eat.* ***Proverbs 14:23 and Proverbs 20:13***

**Mama's Moral:** *I know you like to sleep and wallow in your misery, but my dime's about up and you need to get some kind of employment pronto. I'm not going to cook another meal for you until you produce proof of valid employment that doesn't involve nudity, liquor or a compromise of morals.*

A LETTER POSTMARKED FROM Charlotte, where Bryce is incarcerated, with no return address lay like a flat weapon in the mailbox first thing this morning. With shaking hands and a stomach threatening to empty, I ripped it open, thinking it had to do with Bryce's sentencing or fearing it would contain the word PAROLE.

A heat spread over my entire body, and I sat on the porch steps and fanned my face before unfolding the plain piece of white paper inside the official prison envelope. Why had I even bothered getting the mail? It had been three days since I last checked the box, and it contained the usual "Welcome to town" coupons and fliers for a variety of home improvement services and restaurants.

The letter was typed but I couldn't focus on the words just yet. I folded it and placed it back in the envelope, thinking instead of Mama's words about employment, anything but what that letter might contain. I wasn't mentally strong enough to face what I figured it held: word about good behavior and a reduced sentence or transfer to another prison, one even closer to us. Surely they wouldn't consider paroling a man who came so close to killing his wife.

In the kitchen on a kitty-cat note pad, I scribbled out a To-Do list, something I never started making until last week. Unless I put it in writing, I figure it won't get done. First, I planned to put on all my makeup and a decent dress, Spanx included. Next, after dropping off the kids, I'd show up at two places of potential employment and wow them. Or at least beg. And third on the list, I'd call Claire whatever her last name is now and see if she'd like to go . . . what? What is it people do together who don't have husbands or play bridge or tennis? How does a woman reintroduce herself into a world that tried to take her out, reacquaint herself with former friends or the very sex that wanted her dead, the dating pool that never gave her much more than swimmer's ear and lungs full of water?

Why hadn't I said yes to all the good boys and men I'd dated? I could have been happy with any number of them, and yet I chose Bryce, thinking he stewed in goodness, all because of his lavish courtship and stance at the pulpit. All because I thought he could banish my secret sin. If only I hadn't let my parents' opinion steer me from the one great love of my life, my high school sweetheart, Croc Godfrey.

Amber didn't lure the psychos. Lucinda didn't collect psychos. Aunt Weepie didn't get psychos. Where did I go wrong?

Maybe I could invite Claire to come over for some coffee and catching up . . . no, not at my apartment until I made it more presentable. I remembered only mismatched coffee cups, one that says Mission Hospitals on the front, a little souvenir from my eleven weeks in Intensive Care. I made a mental note to figure out where all the thrift stores are in this town and the local Goodwill so I can scrabble some necessities together and open cans without using a hammer and table knife. You'd think I'd have more nice things, being a minister's wife, but while I was clinging to life, Bryce had his family members wipe us out, clean out the parsonage as if no one would ever return. Guess they thought the only décor item I'd ever need again would be a headstone.

Mama had given me dishes and flatware, but for some reason, no coffee cups or a can opener. Just when I prepared for domestic duty, I'd boil the pasta and realize I had no way to grate the cheese.

Little things. Don't make a big deal out of little things, my therapist kept saying. Too many people get knotted in vines of misery because they let stupid minutiae such as not owning a can opener or getting a new stain on the carpet bother them. Who cares if a person possesses a fleet of ugly coffee mugs? *This is solvable,* I said to myself. All these small things can be taken care of. It's the big stuff worth the sweat and concerns. Jobs, children's well-being, the return of joy and meaning in life. These are the biggies.

If I just do what normal people do in life, then the sun will have set on a positive day. "Baby steps, Prudy," my therapist said. "One at a time, and before you know it, you're walking back into the world of functioning women. You're strong. Take a step. Keep stepping."

I reached again for the prison letter sitting on the table like a stick of dynamite, feeling it like a ticking bomb in the palm of my scarred right hand, the one I used to shield the blows from Bryce's screwdriver. I still dared not read the words.

I wondered what in the world the prison system needed to reveal at this stage in the nearly two-year ordeal. I should have placed such a letter aside, knowing there remained more important matters to tend, such as beseeching corporate heads for employment opportunities that I'm certain I don't directly qualify to receive, given my degree in psychology, given the fact I didn't go ahead and get a master's to go with it.

Standing in the kitchen, wondering if I should light the gas and try to make pancakes, I tapped the letter on the table, stared off into space and thought about how in the world the prison system found us here. Who would have given out the address of this run-down but secure haven I'd found?

I checked on my still-sleeping children and rubbed a hand across each one's brow. Jay frowns as he dreams. Miranda laughs in her sleep. If this sorry prison system thinks it's going to ruin my day and chances of providing my children a roof, decent clothes and the occasional Happy Meal, they're wrong. Baby steps. Just keep moving. "You'll get there, Prudy," the therapist promised. "You will but only if you remember and release the pain."

I shoved the letter in a drawer, awakened the kids and fed them Rice Krispies with sliced bananas, then perked a half a pot of coffee and was dressed and ready to go in less than an hour.

In the car, I stared at my children from the rearview mirror and was jolted into reality by the condition of their clothing. Certainly they were clean, the clothes fresh from Mama's washer and dryer. But my brood didn't look as well cared for as they did last year when Mom and Dad and all the aunts and uncles loved all over and up and down them, buying every new dress or pair of slacks on the racks. Now that it's been awhile, the gifts stopped, but the kids kept growing and needing, creating a vacuum of never-ending tending.

They were like furnaces on a train. One continually has to shovel coal to keep running.

Jay needed a haircut, the hem of his jeans was not only frayed but rose an inch above the tops of his Nikes, part of the rubber curling from the shoe itself. Miranda hadn't fared much better. She had refused to let me comb her hair for a week, screaming wildly at the very sight of a hairbrush. Her dresses had grown tight around the middle, and her tops barely covered her navel.

As we drove across town, past these ancient houses made of enormous stones or featuring thick Corinthian columns, and toward the newer neighborhoods, I sipped the bitter coffee from my hospital mug and tried to figure out which bills would arrive first: the phone, electric, gas, cable, water? I couldn't remember which ones were already included in the rent, but it wouldn't look good to have bill-paying trouble during the inaugural stage of one's new life as a renter, and I'd promised my family I was ready to reenter the world and workforce.

All the more reason to hightail it to WUSC radio station and convince them I can type 100 flawless words a minute. Mama would be a bit dismayed at my secretarial "career" but she'd have to get over it or we'd end up back in her home, penniless.

An acquaintance from high school worked as the assistant general manager and morning show host, and I thought he might put in a good word or two once he heard my fingers dashing like Mozart's across a computer keyboard.

Next, I'd go to the nursing home where I'd worked in my younger days and apply for a job doing whatever they needed: mopping, serving meals, even giving enemas if that's what it took to get my foot in the doors of a medical career.

Before I met Bryce, I had qualified and passed the test as a certified nurse's assistant, though I'm sure this eligibility had expired. I'd worked in the local hospital, taking care of the elderly, most of whom had incurable cancers and diseases. I had also enrolled in night classes to become a registered nurse, but quit soon after I married.

After dropping Jay off at school and promising him a trip to the Discovery Museum with my first paycheck, I stopped by Mama's and reminded her she was supposed to sit for

Miranda while I attended business and later the funeral with Aunt Weepie, which I was dreading, knowing about my aunt's wild shenanigans from my mother's outrageous recountings.

"Don't forget I'm going with her to the funeral as a favor to you, Mama, because you swore up and down you'd never go again as long as you drew breath."

She sipped coffee, and I could tell by the open packs of Sweet'N Low she was on her third cup, which meant she would be crazed with caffeine. "Your aunt is a mess, and I told her she'd taken this funeral attending thing way over the top. You should see the drama. It's downright beyond embarrassing. You'll see. And all for a free piece of cold chicken or lump of green bean casserole. What that woman will do for a meal she doesn't have to cook is nothing shy of prostitution. Going to funerals of people she doesn't even know, for heaven's sake. I can't wait till she gets caught. Hope they tote her off to jail, arrest her for Larceny of Macaroni Pie. Soliciting Food from the Dead."

Miranda tugged and clung to me, and I tried to reassure her half a dozen times I'd be back soon, that it was all right and that Mommy always came home. "It's okay, precious," I said, kissing her beautiful, full moon face. "You'll have a great time with Mama Millings." She held onto my leg and pressed her wet mouth and nose into the places doctors had pieced back together. I heard muffled cries, but was used to them and the pros had told me they would gradually stop. The separation anxiety at her age was common and made even more so by what she'd been through with her parents while too young to understand.

"I'd rather be called Nana," my mother said, a big turban covering her head as she drained her Maxwell House poison. "It sounds so much more refined."

"We tried that. They didn't catch on. I'm sorry but it's Mama Millings. Sure beats Mee-Maw, though if you'd rather us call—"

"You don't need to go sassing me," she said. "What in the world are you so dressed up for? You look like a hooker with a large fanny."

"What is that thing on your head?" I asked. "You look like you're headed to Iran to give a Sunday school lesson."

"The monkeys," she whispered. "I put Purell in it and am still fumigating my hair and scalp, Miss Priss. Look here, you need to invest in an exercise regime and whittle down a few of those pounds now, Prudy, I mean Dee. Dee is a thinner name, anyway. I'm just being proactive because you'll be entering the dating scene and it's best to be as marketable as possible."

"Lighten up about my weight," I said, knowing a size 12 wasn't thin, but nowhere near gastric-bypass-qualifying obesity. "Truth be known, I thought there might be a need for such full-figured tarts down at the Econo Inn."

She set down her coffee cup. "Prudy, you've always walked sin's tightrope. I won't have any such business in my house. Now, why are you all hussified?"

"Mama, for the hundredth time, I'm going to get a job. Got a lead and need to look nice."

She considered my face, peering around to check it out from all angles while Miranda blew her nose in my silk skirt and ran off in the playroom to search for her dolls and her granddaddy.

"I see," Mama said, smiling. "You sweet girl. You are going to Dillard's for the makeup job. I knew it. You know when your Mama's right. You even blended your base so well I can barely see the scars on your neck. Your blush is on the heavy-handed side, though, to be quite honest."

I smiled and told her I was sorry but she was wrong about the job.

"I'm going down to WUSC radio and check out a possibility," I said.

"WUSC? The rock station?" She thought rock music made people lust for sex and guns and heroin and was the melody by which Satan stoked his fires, readying his den for new arrivals. "You mean that station where Chuck from Spartanburg High works?"

"Right," I said, trying to wipe off some blush.

"What could you possibly be trained to do there? Isn't he the boy that tried to get you to drink a slow gin fizz when you were 15?"

"Mama," I said, kissing her soft cheek and smelling something lethal leaking from her turban as if she'd also soaked her head in ammonia and vinegar, "he tried to get everyone drunk, not just me. Don't worry, the station has a secretarial position open because I read it in the classifieds. Since I know Chuck, I have an in, so to speak." The look of horror on her face kept me from going on, ruining her day with the shame of her college-educated, nearly murdered daughter becoming a clerk, though quite frankly I thought it was a sure-fire way to make money. "Mama, relax. I've got options and ideas. You'd really be quite surprised. Wish me luck."

"But you have a degree. A college degree! Look at your father. He went to college on the GI Bill and made a great name for himself in the textile industry. He did so well he retired early and only has to take on consulting work. He did so well, in fact, that I never had to work at all. That's what finding a good husband can do for a woman. Since you don't have that husband, you can just use your degree we paid thousands for you to get."

"It's in psychology, Mother. And you need a master's to make it worth a dime. My degree isn't going to pay my rent right now, understand?"

"Well, why'd you have to go and take up with that piece of road kill? I told you to send it to an animal rehabber. You don't think that squirrel's going to cost you a fortune?"

"It doesn't matter, Mother. If it brings smiles to my kids' faces it's worth every dime. The vet comped the bill, anyway."

"By the way," she said, following us out to the car, "I noticed Jay walking funny, like his shoes were too small. I can't abide by that, Prudy, Dee, or whoever you are. I'd just as soon get a job whipping up biscuits and burgers at Hardee's than have my grandchild's feet turn all deformed due to lack of proper shoe fit."

"I'll find him some at the thrift store, Mother. Please, I'm trying. You need to lay off."

"Lay off? I'm just wanting you to get back into the routine of regular living is all. Look at me. I'm baking two pies and a green bean casserole for a couple of women in my church who right now at this very minute are in the hospital having parts removed and tossed into the garbage. I may not work a regular job, but I never stop moving. That's the key, honey. You just can't stop moving."

I waved as nicely as possible, slid into the car and backed away slowly, the way one does when facing a predator, making it half-way down the drive before she came running out screaming, "Wipe off that blush, it's way too dark for day. Blend, Prudy, blend, blend, blend. I've taught you to blend since you were 16 and you never remember. Blending is everything,"

"You already said I'd blended fine," I shouted, turning onto Dogwood Avenue, passing four houses, all with flags and perfect lawns. This was "I Love America, Support the Troops" country, and if a Democrat lived among them, he or she surely hid that party affiliation the way a witch hides her little jars and potions.

I made a right onto Fernwood Place and out of her perfect world, sun blinding from the east, the direction of the station, the direction of my future.

***

When the church van struck, I did not feel pain. Didn't know my tibia bone protruded in shards from open, jagged skin. Or that my hand was crushed where I'd used it to protect my head and chest, not wanting another screwdriver jabbed into my neck.

The noise of the church van I remember most and can still hear, as if it were a plane revving its engines and building enough power for take-off. I felt myself airborne and then falling onto the concrete, crashing into BI-LO's plate-glass window advertising hams and chuck roasts. I remember seeing Bryce's beef-red face as he tried to finish the job of killing me with his set of Philip's screwdrivers. Then I shut down.

I am blocked. I don't know another way to live right now. I know the facts from what people tell me, what I heard in the hospital, in court, yet it is almost as if they are talking about someone else. I wouldn't have believed all the horrific things they said had I not seen the wounds and gouges, the marks of madness all over my body to show for it.

They say when you hover at the hem of death, when tubes and machines, ventilator and prayer are the only things keeping you alive, you can't hear the voices in the room. You can't know they are writing you off as dead, you can't feel the urgency in the hands holding yours, the tears falling on the bedsheets and your own wounded flesh.

They are right. For the most part.

But on a rare occasion or two, moments of clarity arrive and senses sharpen like new No. 2 pencils and you want to scream out but can't because a breathing tube is stuck down your throat and you're trapped in a subconscious state, frozen and immobile.

You can hear them. The grief and pity are as real as the cold air in Intensive Care rooms and the harsh lights and doubts that go round and round through your head.

People in ICU, if my case is any indication, those listed as critical and given less than five percent chances, know the odds of dying are real. We lie tied and tubed, a chest tube removing air from a punctured lung, braces and brackets, sutures and clamps holding our splintered bones and clavicles, our torn ventricles and diced bodies. We may hear doctors fretting over whether death will come from pericardial tamponade—the pooling of blood around the heart—a sudden embolism, or if one of the injuries might brew up a fatal infection.

"It's a miracle to me," one doctor said when my eyes opened and he sensed an audience, "a real miracle the weapon didn't kill her when it hit her heart."

But it had, I wanted to say. It most definitely had in a metaphorical sense.

That same doctor had held my bandaged hand for one of the nurses. "See this," he said. "The weapon went nearly clear through, but this hand probably saved her life. She had it over her left breast. Still grazed a ventricle but could have been much, much worse. Had that screwdriver been a couple inches longer . . . had her hand been anywhere else on her body . . ."

***

I remember the first time I woke up a few days after it had happened, seeing my Mama in a chair with her head flung across my bed, pressed into the railings, into prayer, into a hope she'd never abandon.

I reached for her strawberry blonde bob and held tight. She looked up, saw my eyes, my good hand moving frantically, a game of Charades. Guessing the need, she handed over a piece of paper, rummaged and found a pen and wrapped my stiff, blood-stained fingers around it so I could write.

It took awhile for my brain and hand to connect, but eventually they had.

*"My kids need a mama,"* I wrote in fairly illegible print. I wanted to tell my mother not to let the doctors give up.

But that wouldn't be necessary. She's always fought for life over death. Even when my grandmother posted the Do Not Resuscitate sign in her chart at the nursing home, my mother, acting as power-of-attorney, changed her mind when a heart attack hit the old woman midday and demanded doctors, "Give it all you got." The poor woman, bruised and battered from the paddles and CPR, lived an extra year thanks to my mama and was able to enjoy another Thanksgiving, another Christmas turkey and the feel of grandchildren, even great-grandchildren in her lap, before she died peacefully in her sleep, timing it where no one could yell Code Blue and whip out a crash cart.

I pushed the note toward my mother. Tears fell from her eyes and face, and she clasped her hands and said loudly, "Hear that, Lord? My baby isn't ready to go yet."

Bryce sat in the county jail while my body slowly repaired itself, as did the torn ventricle, broken bones and slashed and pounded neck and chest. My leg was all that still hurt, a patchwork of rods and screws looking like a genetic misfiring. All told, it took nearly three months and many close calls, but I was finally out of the hospital, out of rehab and back into the Cape Cod because the church insisted I stay in the parsonage, though it had been stripped of most furnishings thanks to the Jeters' buzzard mentality. The church members took charge with their love and warm food and ever-present babysitting services.

It was moving and heart-wrenching how they stood by us, giving me much more faith in Christian ways than hearing some phony at the podium. These women were real. They came in perfumed and pearled to vacuum and scrub the tub and toilet, all while telling stories of their own pain and horror: a daughter who beat one of the women, sons who hadn't written in years, breast cancers and other diseases and afflictions—of both body and mind. Seemed few people in this life ever had it easy.

They saw me all laid up and battered and didn't mind letting their secrets fly. They were so sweet, allowing us to live there rent-free, or practically. I paid the church a small donation when the disability and accident insurance kicked in but it wasn't what you'd call a real "rent."

A few times, we even visited the church on Sundays. We wore what we wanted, not the neatly pressed and starched clothing when the stage belonged to the Rev. Bryce Jeter, but jeans and Dockers for Jay, Mermaid and fairy costumes for Miranda and the big, ugly purses she enjoys carrying around. I wore long skirts, even in the hot months of late August and September because I didn't want to draw attention to the purple scars and shattered leg. I swallowed Percocets like M&Ms, downing those pills so I could walk without wincing, so I could take my children to Disney World and the mall, to Ocean Drive Beach, South Carolina, Six Flags Over Georgia and all over the Southeast where for a certain price a woman and her children could distract themselves enough to believe they were happy. We fell asleep in motel beds beneath fake-wood-framed prints and found ourselves tired enough to sleep without dreaming, without remembering.

That's how we lived in the early months after my recovery. Going from site to site. Sprinting from the memories always threatening to outrun us, running out of money instead.

When the trial came up, I managed to get through that ordeal, the mezzanine of hell, by taking two or three times more pills than the doctors recommended. I thought it was the only way I could face Bryce's defense lawyers, his parents, even Bryce himself and worst of all, taking the stand.

The state gave Bryce 25 years without parole, and Jay cried his eyes red and swollen many, many nights. Unless we were on the road and I was rambling about Star Wars or roller coasters, planning beach excursions and then cramming those days with crabbing and fishing, museum touring and a schedule that would all but kill a regular family, he sobbed and shook as if electricity coursed through his veins.

It was easy with Miranda; she was still a toddler and forgot her daddy a week or so after he was gone. I thank God for that tender mercy.

Everything in our lives motored on shock and autopilot during that first year post rampage. All the distractions were a blessing; the paperwork alone for hospital bills and police and court mess would have consumed the energy of three.

"I don't know how you're doing it, Prudy," Mama said. "Please let me or your daddy come up and help. You kick us out after two days every time we come."

"We're managing, Mama," I'd say. "I really appreciate everything, but I have to learn to make it on my own now, and I can't if I have you for a crutch."

And then it happened: May arrived. The first anniversary date, which passed uneventfully, or was about to, until the cards from Bryce began arriving in the mail. Most had been benign American Greetings or Hallmarks sent from his prison in Charlotte, North Carolina, and had all been handwritten and addressed to Jay. I handed the mail to him after I'd first screened and approved it. I even paid for a book of stamps so Jay could send his daddy mail in return. One therapist told me I was a fool to allow such a thing ever, under any circumstances. Another told me to follow my heart.

In all, that first year, Bryce sent seven cards to Jay with brief notes about how much he missed him and how he wished everything could be different. And Jay matched him card for card.

It was strange but Bryce never addressed Miranda and never wrote or mentioned me. And then the letters quit coming. Relief washed me like a hot shower.

***

This latest letter, a huge and awful surprise, lay on the passenger-side seat as I drove to the radio station and was the first prison mail I'd received in a year. It was addressed to me directly, and as I picked it up, waving it around a couple of times, I figured whatever was in it had some heaviness attached—if not by weight, then emotion. At least it was typed and not written in Bryce's meticulous penmanship. I don't know what I'd do if I got a letter from him personally.

***

The radio station was six miles out of town in an ugly section of Spartanburg where nothing but mobile homes and factories, a few convenience stores and lots of gas stations lined the state highway. It was located in the middle of a piece of raw, red dirt, towers rising behind it, the tan brick and cream shutters giving the station the appearance of someone's house in the middle of nothing.

The call letters were out front, on a sign and across the entrance. I was nervous but had my spiel and pitch ready to go. Two hours of rehearsing and the moment was now. I pressed my lips, making sure the lipstick was still there, tucked in my blouse, adjusted the double-pearl choker to hide the bulk of scars and opened the door. Bells jingled, and I was greeted by an older woman who looked like she could have been related to Joan Jett. She was still trying for that Journey, Foghat groupie look.

"Could I help you?"

"Yes . . . well, I'm actually . . . I don't have an appointment but went to high school with Chuck and if he's here, that'd be great. I'd like to apply for the receptionist-secretary position."

"We call them personal assistants. The terms 'secretary' and 'receptionist' have a condescending ring to them."

For a while after her remarks, she said nothing, just stared for what felt like forever. "Is he expecting you?"

"No. He's not, but like I said, we—"

She punched the phone and said, "Chuck, could you come up front your next break, someone's here from your past, darling."

She hung up and told me to have a seat. I could feel her eyes on me, probably wondering about the slight limp and the urgency of my request to see Chuck, though I'd tried to be cool.

Chuck arrived ten minutes later looking exactly like he did in high school—tall, slump-shouldered, long-haired and a cross between a hippie and a computer geek.

He gestured toward me, offering three kinds of Tootsie Rolls as if I were a kid. "Come on back, Mrs . . . Ms . . ."

"Chuck? It's Prudy. Well, I mean it's Dee now, but I was Prudy. Prudy Millings from Spartan High?"

His face sort of dipped and rose, all the features in almost an ocean-wave movement. "Good God Almighty," he said. "It is you. I read all the stories. Jesus Christ. Jesus." He continued shaking his head and eyeing me up and down.

"Chuck, listen. I know we weren't the best of friends in high school and maybe you thought I was a little snooty when I didn't ask you to be my homecoming escort, but all that aside, I'm desperate for a job. And anyway, Mama wouldn't let me ask you to be my escort 'cause she knew you drank." Why couldn't I just shut up? Why did nerves cause me to spout every irrelevant bit of information from the plaque of my quivering brain?

"I'm back on the air in 20. We're playing a long set. If you zip the lip, feel free to sit in the studio and we'll talk until I have to go back on the air and work my magic. Can you dig that?"

"Yeah. Consider it dug."

I took a seat in the studio and faced Chuck who unapologetically lit a Kool cigarette and blew the smoke right at me. "Gotta maintain my gravely voice," he said. "So. What can I do you for?"

I knew this wouldn't be easy. I should have been nicer to Chuck in high school because you just never know where the losers of yesteryear might end up. I mean here I was, the belle and homecoming queen of Spartanburg High, now sitting in front of the "loser" ready to beg for a job. The irony of it all.

"I need a job and saw the ad in the classifieds." My hands tingled at the fingertips, as if zero circulation could find its way to the edges of my body.

"Well, you and a thousand others," he said, putting his feet on his desk, being the hotshot he thought he was. "I don't remember us doing much together in high school. What I remember is I'd ask you out and you'd make up some excuse. 'Course you were a cheerleader and I was one of the outcasts, as I remember everything."

"Look, I have to confess that since my accident or whatever you want to call it, I'm having to rebuild my entire life from scratch and could use whatever position you have. I'm groveling. How does that feel after all these years?"

He roared and coughed. "From what I recall in high school, you couldn't type your way out of a trash bin. Wasn't it 20 words a minute?"

"I just need a job. I'm a fast learner, can type like crazy and have two kids with shoes too small, and the bottom line is I'm broke. I have nothing else to tell you, Chuck, except if I didn't date you in high school, that's no reason to penalize me for the job, is it?"

Chuck Roland stared at me as if I were my own road kill. "I'm sorry," he said. "We got candidates much better qualified than you for typing and shit . . . but you know, there is something we're wanting to try out, but I don't know . . . a new segment on the show. I'll call you. Leave a number with the secretary and we'll see."

"Please, isn't there anything I could do now?"

"Well, we do need a maid. Sorry, I think you call them housekeepers or domestic servants these days. How about

I put you on evening toilet patrol, say two days a week? Shouldn't take long to clean this joint and the pay's pretty good. Like $200 or something."

Chuck Roland, smug, pompous and offering me a maid's job. I saw in my head the bills stacking up like a concrete wall I had little hope of scaling unless a rope dangled soon.

"Sure, I'll take it," I said and stood up, trying not to wince as pain shot through my lower leg. "Thanks for your time. When can I start?"

"Tomorrow evening if you want. Check you later," he said. And that was it.

I walked out into the muggy South Carolina sunshine and wiped a tear before it fell. I planned to hold my head up high and clean every toilet necessary if that's what it took to put food on my children's table and buy decent clothes that fit them, shoes that weren't coming apart at the soles or so tight they caused blisters.

God help me. That's all I'll ask for now.

The letter. I still hadn't opened the letter.

# *Chapter Four*

**Rise and Shine, Prudy. I know it's not 7 in the morning, but it's my guess you are napping yet again, so I'm sending an afternoon message for a change:** *Don't repay evil with evil. Wait for the Lord to handle the matter.* ***Proverbs 20:22***

**Mama's Moral:** *Prudy, the above proverb hollered out to me this afternoon as I was reading my Bible and rewashing my hair. It's my own moral to myself. I'll try to heed it and quit sending mean mail to Satan's Twin.*

**Here's yours for the day:** *My son (daughter), how happy I will be if you turn out to be sensible! It will be a public honor to me.* ***Proverbs 27:11***

AUNT WEEPIE'S PICKING me up for the funeral at any moment, though I expect she'll be her usual 15 minutes late and smelling of two ounces of Beautiful sprayed all up and down her glorious body. She said she had a surprise, and I told her it better not be that man, that a funeral is no place to bring a blind date.

Aunt Weepie's the one with whom to discuss the letter, men, sex and anything else for that matter. It's hard to believe that crazy woman and my very own mother share the same DNA.

Weepie's joys in life are two funerals per week (purely for the food), sex most days (even when she says she can't stand her husband another moment) and martinis taken extra dry while settled beneath the wooden slats of her mahogany four-poster, where she's constantly adding a blanket here, a pillow there, a reading light and various junk food. That's where Aunt Weepie goes to drink, sleep, snack, escape and solve all her problems.

Mama, on the other hand, won't discuss sex and claims total chastity prior to marriage.

"We kissed," she said.

"With tongue?" I asked.

"Of course not. That would lead most girls into other things. That and the fact the boys always thought if a girl performed wet kisses, she'd then let him paw her." Mama was against Frenching, pawing and anything but upright dry kissing prior to marriage. After marrying my father, a man who loves shocking her with off-color remarks brought on by bourbon and water, I tend to believe she remained either in a state of total frigidity or was the hottest little housewife on earth.

My sister, Amber (who hit the jackpot with the popular name, the thin gene and the rich husbands), was never pounded with the "sex" lectures I received. While Mama was instilling the values of sealed canals to me at 16, my hot little sister with the stripper name and body was out riding on the sin wagon with a boy who looked like a frog with his big bulging eyes and his green football jacket.

Aunt Weepie says we're all wrong about Mama, that she's putting on "her pathetic virgin act," when she's really one scorching mama beneath her ice-blue packaging.

She sure looked the part. My mother, Lucinda *"Never call me Lucy"* Millings, was a first runner-up in the Miss South Carolina pageant two years before I came into the world. While in her late teens and early 20s, she had the annoying habit of spouting off her beauty-pageant battle cry—"I'M A VIRGIN!"—at every opportunity.

Aunt Weepie said, "Your mama told the judges, 'I am firmly against sex before marriage,' and they ate that right up. I swear she'd have won, but she couldn't sing a lick. Everyone was roaring. She stood there on stage and started howling and warbling up real high, all this fake opera she made up as she went. Nothing Italian about it. Just pure dog-wailing jibber-jabber."

Mama's still got her beauty queen figure and wears her hair the exact same strawberry blond shade of Kathie Lee Gifford, though she really doesn't like the woman, thinks she's a closet fornicator with untamed urges. My mother can still swing it, too. She can throw those skinny hips out and wiggle around town like some kind of pin-up for Social Security.

She dresses in the fashions of the young and hip except on Sundays when she completely transforms her style into that of an ancient old spinster in floral print. She walks in the sanctuary, gliding down the aisles and toting three different Bibles, "in case the minister or someone else in the congregation doesn't think one of the versions is as

'Christian' as the others." She makes certain all the biblical bases are covered.

As for a mother's duty to teach her daughters the facts of life, Mama sheepishly handed Amber and me a Disney book on the subject.

"Y'all take this to your room and read it in private. If you have any questions, I'll try my best to answer them."

And that was the extent of our sex education via Lucinda Millings.

***

*Please, Aunt Weepie, please be on time,* I begged, sitting along my bay window, watching the clouds as they appeared to float up from nowhere, bumping together in the sky, a couple of them already turning a threatening gray.

"I will, hon," she said when I phoned her. "I'm too hungry to be late; you know that." But she was late, and I was counting the minutes.

Free time, idle moments aren't favored or savored at this juncture, and I was tapping my good foot, twitching and jiggling with jangled nerves in the humid apartment, feeling myself melt between my breasts as I watched the clock, then the street, looking for that gold Mercedes 450 SL.

I tried to remember the last funeral I'd attended, but as always, a vision of Bryce Jeter in his burial blues raided my head, him preaching all serious and voice sonorous, nothing at all like his rowdy motioning and pounding during regular Sunday services for the living.

I was thinking of all the people at my trial, and how if I'd died, only a few of them would have come to the funeral.

Everyone turned out for the legal lynching. They were all too happy and eager to sit in the courtroom and watch the drama unfold. This was, after all, a smaller Southern city where scandal was the bread and gossip the butter on which many dwellers thrived and fattened. I remember looking out at the "audience," where people had to stand in the aisles and against the walls for a peek at the plaintiff and defendant. That's how it was. You were much more interesting to them if you survived what few could. A freak, almost. People have always been drawn to the freaks and I'd become one. I should have told Chuck Roland I was a freak now, too.

***

The church was fairly full and Aunt Weepie and I were barely seated before the first song, a piped in version of Enya's "Only Time," emanated from a hidden speaker system, which I spent the better part of the first ten minutes trying to find.

Aunt Weepie purely oozed sexuality in a black rayon dress that fell to her ankles, but not before catching every single curve on her body. She wore a pair of spectator pumps in black and red and carried in her hands a red handbag, a fake Chanel. She sported her faux Gucci watch and her sunglasses with the Chanel logo on the sides. She'd obtained all her accessories from a friend who goes to New York twice a year and hits the knock-off markets that sell their phonies on the city streets.

She was wearing too much foundation, and I could see the orange line where she'd either forgotten to blend or didn't bother. This is the very reason I always put on my makeup at the kitchen table. Only natural light will show a woman what others will see. I leaned over and tried to blend it for her, but she swatted me with the program as if I were a large mosquito.

"Stop it, Prudy. I'm concentrating. Let's not talk until I'm in the zone." Mother had told me a few times that Weepie sat stiller than the dead themselves when she was getting into "character," preparing for her throwdown of despair as insurance for the invitation to the big meal afterward.

She opened her purse during the first preacher's meaningless words, the warm-up preacher who'd probably never met the deceased before in his life, a ghost-faced man who was saying this and that about her being a wonderful mother and the salt of the earth. They all said salt of the earth unless the departed was in the Junior League, or was a prominent man's wife. Then they called her "a vibrant and irreplaceable member of society." Aunt Weepie rustled in the bag, pulling out a tube of fire-engine-red Chanel lipstick, a compact, and finally, the pack of pink tissues, already opened, one peeping out and ready for the taking.

She took a practice sniff. Then another until she'd managed to produce some sort of fluid in her nasal passages. She sniffed repetitively and then began dabbing at the corner of her still-dry eyes with the first of many tissues she would use. We hadn't been seated twelve minutes when the first stab of agony hit her and she let rip an audible and melodramatic gasp of anguish, so loud half the church turned back to see who in the world was crying her eyes out over the death of a 92-year-old woman who for what we'd learned so far was salty and had a great love of crocheting and turning toilet paper rolls into frilly commode décor.

The organist played a song and another soloist, this one a man who appeared hung-over and in need of a stiff drink, began a deep baritone rendition of "Bringing in the Sheaves." Aunt Weepie was not about to be upstaged by a bellowing drunkard. She began to wail to the beat of his baritone. I wanted to crawl under a pew. I managed to slide down far enough that it would not seem I knew her, and when I did so, she threw off a mean look. I noticed her mascara had begun its first estuary down her suntanned Estée Laudered face.

I inhaled deeply, smelling the flowers of death and a hovering cloud of old lady perfume, an intermingling of all the ancient scents Estée Lauder hides behind its glass counters for women over 70.

Weepie's shoulders rocked and her whole body began a series of convulsions. She put her hands over her eyes and let it all out, moaning here and whimpering there, tearing out her pain and throwing it like confetti at the other mourners. The man hurried through his song on account of Aunt Weepie ruining it, and she lifted her head toward the cathedral ceiling and released the mascara'd tears turning her skin into black tiger stripes. She was completely torn apart by this Mrs. Pearlie Mae Corn's departure. Everyone at the funeral *except* Aunt Weepie was well aware Mrs. Corn had suffered and withered to bones in a Hospice cancer ward. Goodness gracious, all Aunt Weepie had to do was read her program and it said as much right there in italics. *The family of Pearlie Mae Corn would like to thank Hospice for all their care during this most difficult time.*

When it was all over and the final preacher had surprised even the hardcore Baptists by issuing an altar call at a funeral service, asking sinners to come repent and get saved, Aunt Weepie actually stood to go down the aisle.

I yanked her black dress. She whipped her head around and growled, that mascara making her look like a character out of a horror movie. "Stop it, Prudy."

"You can't go down there," I whispered. "No one sane gets saved at funerals." But I knew this to be untrue. Rev. Bryce Jeter, Satan's Soulmate, had led 26 men and women to salvation during funerals. I always thought it strange that a preacher would issue a call for live souls while trying to send dead ones off with a reverent bang.

"I've done it many times," Aunt Weepie said and turned her ample body sideways and sashayed down the aisle like a broken-hearted bride in black. She sniffed and sighed. She daubed at her face. She paused at the old woman's coffin and curtsied, then threw her arms across it for a full horrifying 30 seconds. The reverend pried her loose and she managed to stand before the mourners, accepting whatever the man was offering. Salvation. Redemption. The last ticket to eternal life. A better shot at a three-bean casserole. A pint of tears emptied onto her face.

By then I had managed to switch sides and was sitting near a stained glass window far away from Aunt Weepie's Chanel bag.

"Who's that woman?" the lady in front of me whispered to her friend. The other lady shrugged her shoulders and both of them laughed so loud they had to bow and pretend they, too, were crying. That set off a chain reaction of similar laughter masked as grief, and by the time it was all over, all the pews were shaking to one degree or another.

After the service Aunt Weepie found me hiding in the funeral home bathroom.

"Where have you been? We're going to miss the graveside."

"There is no way in the world I'll go there, Aunt Weepie. I had no idea you put on such a show. Mama never told me the extent of your actions."

"That's the furthest I've gone. It's progressive. I'm getting much better. What's wrong with you, anyway? I used to could count on you for all kinds of fun. You gotta put that evil deed behind you and find your fun again. Get it back. Life's too short to be all uptight like your damned mother."

My mother would not have lasted the first three minutes, much less remained seated for the entire 28, and believe me, I was counting every minute, every mortifying second. "I think I'm not feeling well. Do you mind if we skip the graveyard service?"

"Are you out of your mind? You are going nowhere, Miss Gloom. I've had four people give me directions as I was hunting for you just now. They *want* me there. Once you make it to the hole in the ground, you are good to go for the covered dish. Only those who watch the dead go down get the buffet afterward. It's the reward for attending, sweet Prude, and probably the only one you'll get, since I couldn't bring that man for you. He canceled at the last minute, damned fool."

Thank God for small miracles.

No matter who you are or how decent your life, if you live in South Carolina and die in the summer, it's going to thunder and lightning and rain at your service unless you are buried before noon. Most people would have to schedule death months in advance to get the a.m. appointments. That's why you see so many tents popped up at say, 2 or 3 p.m., everyone huddled like long lost friends, never mind they're trying to spare themselves an electrocution.

Aunt Weepie unleashed her Jones of New York umbrella, which I knew came from Stein Mart, the store closest to my near murder. Though all my relatives promised they would never in a zillion years go there again or BI-LO, I knew Aunt Weepie couldn't resist the store's 12-hour sales.

The rain soaked us as we made our way through soggy grass toward the big green tent. Every few steps, Aunt Weepie had to stop and pull her heel from the mud as if she were being partially swallowed by burial dirt. I had worn flats, have done so since the mowing down, and will continue doing so unless I think sex is in the offing, which has not been the case in 24 ½ months and counting.

We managed to slog our way to the tent, and it would have been my assumption and to my great relief had Aunt Weepie chosen, as she had at the funeral, a seat near the back.

Under the blue tent, six rows of fold-out, velvet-draped chairs sat unsteadily on the wet ground, and the wind blew the rain in at angles, soaking anyone who sat on the side. The chairs up front, as is typical, were reserved for family and the closest of friends, or perhaps a devoted Hospice nurse. There were three empty rows in the back and a few seats up front, where most decent people who aren't relatives of the dead refrain from claiming.

I wondered if I had died that day in the BI-LO parking lot, would more than this dwindled crowd come to my service. I certainly hoped so. I wondered, too, if and when Bryce was going to send someone to kill me, or would he do it himself once released from prison. *Please God,* I prayed quickly, *don't let that letter be about him getting out of prison.*

Rain sure will send mourners home, especially if the individual in the coffin was due his or her appointment with death. It seems kind of unfair how the older you are, the fewer are in attendance for the grand day, but I guess by this age, most of one's friends have passed as well.

While I didn't want to be seen with her, all heads and eyes were feasting on Aunt Weepie as she wriggled her way one row back from the coffin. I couldn't believe it. She had planted her bold self right up there with kith and kin. She settled into her seat and shook the water from her umbrella onto the lady's legs to her left, oblivious to all but herself. She pivoted her head about like an owl's and flashed a movie star smile and full shot of her glorious Raquel Welch figure. Her dress was tighter than a girdle, and she wore it as well as any woman a fraction of her age.

The preacher was unfamiliar, a third for this Pearlie Mae Corn, and he had a mighty hard time yelling over the thunder and lightning, thus he gave up and mumbled, giving Aunt Weepie his full attention, forgetting blood kin altogether. He hurried so fast Aunt Weepie was unable to produce but one decent long-winded lamentation and a mere mouse squeak of sorrow.

To make up for it, when we all stood to say the Lord's Prayer at the end, she staggered after the "Amen" and fell partway into the burial pit, hollering "Pearlie Mae!" for great effect. Four big men in black had to haul her out, and the old ladies in hats and clutching wadded tissues gathered around and offered her rides to the family's home where the food was on its way out of ovens, bubbling in Pyrex containers and CorningWare, which held the heat for hours.

Aunt Weepie managed to nail six invites to the covered dish dinner where we stayed for an entire two hours, Weepie gushing and pretending she was happy as a clam to see "so many familiar faces after all these years."

People appeared confused as she greeted them, her plate sagging with deviled eggs and fried chicken, meat loaf and green bean and squash casseroles, pecan pies and congealed salads.

"Good to see you, sugar," she'd say and the old folks would offer a wobbly, watery-eyed smile, then their faces fell and eyes went blank, probably wondering if they'd been struck with Alzheimer's. I swear two of them were baffled enough by her line of bull that after they'd eaten I saw them in the living room frantically working crossword puzzles, which my daddy does because he read it would prevent dementia.

As we were leaving, the hostess, owner of the home, approached my aunt, and I knew that was it. We were history, caught like thieves with chicken grease on our hands.

"Winifred?" she said, trying out Aunt Weepie's God-given name. I guess someone finally told the woman who my aunt was. "It was nice of you to come. I had no idea you and Aunt Pearlie Mae were that close."

"Couldn't have been a better woman," my aunt said and sniffed. "Salt of the earth. I got four of her little potty dolls."

"How nice. Well, you know we're burying her sister, Icy, tomorrow. It's been so hard on her. They were twins as you know, and Icy just gave up. Here, let me give you directions to the service. I'm sure Pearlie Mae would have wanted you to be there." The smile on Aunt Weepie's face, like that of a cat getting ready to swallow its prey, was as cunning as any I'd ever seen. She opened her little daybook and wrote out all the particulars, giving me a clandestine wink. I sure as snow in Maine would not be joining her again. On the other hand, as far as entertainment value and good eating, she really was onto something. That squash casserole was to die for. I also spotted a really cute man in the dining room. Not that I was looking. I mean who goes to funerals to meet men? Though Weepie says funerals aren't really about the dead.

"It's about emotion, sex, food, hedonism, friendships and love. It's everything in life all boiled down in one event with musical accompaniment. Can't beat it, Prudy. Come on, be my partner. Your mother turned into a dud after the second round."

We made plans to send Icy Corn off to the eternal yonder, but I wasn't certain I'd actually have the nerve to go for Round Two. Weepie said if I brought a big enough purse, I could easily slip in enough food to feed the kids later that night.

"Eliminates one of life's more miserable chores," she said. "All it costs is a bit of emotional effort, but don't worry. You're a natural. All you gotta do is conjure up some of that shit Bryce did to you and the tears will pour. We'll get all kinds of invites back to the kin's homes and hearths. It's called the Put your Pain to Good Use Plan, Ms. Prudy Dee Millings."

# *Chapter Five*

**Wake up, Prudy. I know you plan to sleep all day**: *Teach a child to choose the right path and when he is older he will remain upon it.* ***Proverbs 22:6***

**Mama's Moral:** *Ha! I believe I tried to show y'all the right path but only the dear Lord knows why you decided to veer off and wander. Get back on it, sugar. It isn't too late! The bed will bring you nothing but poverty and misery. Get up!*

BEFORE TURNING IN for the night, after tucking in the children, having given them baths, funeral chicken, and forcing them to brush their teeth, I picked up the letter again, this time deciding to read it.

I carefully unfolded the plain white paper and felt myself get sick after reading the first couple of words. *Oh, God.* I rushed into the pink-tile bathroom and leaned over the toilet, hacking and dry heaving, but nothing came up but acids. Sweat beaded like tiny ants along the back of my neck and forehead.

The words on the page weren't from the prison officials.

They were from Bryce.

The room swayed and this time, as I flung my head over the commode, I wretched all of the ill-begotten funeral food.

*Dear Prudy.*

*You're marked for life, like a brand. All mine. No one will ever touch you but me. Don't think you can move somewhere and not be found. Don't think I don't have people watching you. It's pretty amazing what a prison preacher can accomplish. We are the iron gods, and there's nothing the good old boys here wouldn't do to help a man of the Lord out, if you get my drift? There's lots of free time in prison and lots of the guys spend it working out, lifting weights. They must think their brawn's going to get them somewhere. Not me, Prudy doll. I'm every minute of every day possible studying the law and searching the Internet and have found more loopholes to jump through than I could ever need. I plan to take a big leap, sweetheart. You be ready. When I get out—and believe me, I will get out—you'll be the first I come visit. Have the coffee ready. I take it black these days. No sugar.*

*Yours in Christ, Bryce."*

I sat by the toilet for an hour, hot tears pouring from my eyes, but no sounds, no sobbing or wracking shoulders like Aunt Weepie produced. How did he find us? That's what I needed to know. That's what I had to find out in order to survive.

***

Jay woke up in the middle of the night, delivering a high-pitched howl, a sound that most human beings don't have the capacity to make unless strangled with fear. I hurried from my bed, having lain awake for hours, and crossed the hallway, the webs of crusted tears instantly wiped away by a mother's ability to bolt upright in any given set of circumstances when her children are involved.

Once in the hospital, after a C-section and Percodan, I awakened as if a caffeine IV bag had been dumped into my veins. Right then and there I hopped out of bed, stomach stapled and oozing and rushed to the nursery to find my newborn Jay crying and unattended, a blanket bunched and blocking his mouth and nose, all the nurses in the hallway gossiping, unaware my baby was about to smother. A mother's instinct is as real and strong as any feeling I've ever had, and I've never once doubted it.

As I now reached for Jay and held him in my arms, he thrashed and squalled. He was soaked with fear, partly from the nightmare, partly the humidity a ceiling fan only manages to stir and spread. It took a few minutes to rouse him, but soon his large brown eyes searched mine. I'd never seen such terror. Not even when I was dying in the hospital and they had brought him in to meet the chaplain did Jay act like this.

"Daddy's coming back," he said. "He's going to get us, Mama."

Not again. Not the nightmares, which for the most part had stopped by the time we moved to Spartanburg last year.

"Sweetheart, your daddy's not getting out. He's a very sick man and did a very bad thing. He loves you but he's got to get some help. You don't need to worry, sweetheart." Lies poured from my mouth the way new milk fills a mother's breast without effort.

Holding Jay was like sitting on the hood of a cranked car. He was hot and vibrating with a fear that wouldn't relent.

"He's coming."

"No, sweetie, he's not."

Jay reached under his mattress and handed me two envelopes, white business letters with no return address but that same Charlotte postmark that sent an electric shock shuddering through me, a hot sting along my spine and neck.

"How did you get these?" I asked, taking the letters, thinking of the one I'd received this morning.

"I got the mail before you did a few days ago. They brought it up to the side porch. The man handed it to me and I was scared to show them to you. I only opened one. It was real mean."

"No, I mean how did he know where we were, sweetheart, our address? Did you write to him? Remember, I told you he couldn't write for a while?"

Jay began crying. He buried his chubby boyish face into my chest and choked on his grief and fear. "I didn't, Mama. I swear I didn't write him."

"It's okay. Shhhh. It's going to be all right, sweet child." I ran my fingers through his thick hair, color of Atlantic Ocean sand. Just like his father's.

"I miss him, Mama," he said, sputtering. "I love you, but I miss him, too."

"It's all right to miss him, sweetie," I said, knowing my little boy was so hungry for that lost love, even the letters were better than nothing.

I tucked the mail underneath my arm and rocked him back and forth while his body and breathing slowed and returned to normal. "You want me to make up one of my stories? How about the Pink Crow in the Crowconut Tree?"

He laughed through salty tears and a running nose. "I love you. I'm sorry, Mommy," he said, coughing. "Can I have some water?" As soon as he had a few sips, he fell back asleep. As easy as that.

For the rest of the night, I was up pacing, heart pounding, trying to figure out how this could really be happening. More abuse, more mental torture, only this time from behind a steel fence capped with razor wire.

I walked with a forced calm into the kitchen and climbed onto the washing machine to reach a shelf where I hid the matches from the kids. I struck one and held it to the corner of the envelopes, the single flame stretching as if trying to ignite the words through its own will. I stared as the fire slowly consumed the typed threats. Afterward, I flushed the ashes down the toilet.

I washed off all my makeup, put on the threadbare pink nylon gown I'd lived in for a year and climbed back into bed, knowing this was the worst thing possible. I reached for the phone.

"Mama, you'll have to get the kids in the morning. I have the flu or some kind of bug."

"Prudy, it's 4 in the morning. You aren't telling me the truth and I'm not going to sit here, roused from my sweet dreams of Jesus and—"

"Mama. Please. Just this one time." I hung up the phone and writhed in the sheets until the world darkened in my mind.

***

This is the last time, I told myself, I'd allow a day in bed in the pink gown, and the next morning, after Mama reluctantly picked up the kids, I took the same book of matches, ripped off the gown, and let it burn to a putrid smelling ash.

After the letters, I felt myself shut down, like a button going click and then by mid-afternoon of my day in bed, I turned it back onto auto-mommy pilot. Nothing complicated. Just one flipped switch. Baby steps. Just do the next right thing, the therapist had said. "You can only eat an elephant one bite at a time."

I'd also called Aunt Weepie and canceled Icy Corn's funeral and big spread of luscious foods.

***

In the months after the incident, before the first anniversary of the "event" and prior to living at Mama's, the world had seemed to stop unless the kids and I were traveling and running from the memories. The phone would ring and it would be the PTA needing a volunteer to work the dunking booth, and I jumped right in with my plastic cane and plastered-on grin. The doorbell chimed and I received visitors, writing them all thank-you notes and returning each and every casserole dish. I worked and mothered and tried to be the absentee father until I finally collapsed and couldn't get out of bed. This was about two weeks after we'd had our whirlwind tour of oceans, amusement parks and the string of trips and motel pools.

I taught Jake how to work a microwave and warm Miranda's bottles, even though technically, pediatricians all said a cup was in order at this age. At two-and-a-half, at least she was potty-trained.

"Warm them on 15 seconds only," I told Jay one morning as I stumbled out of bed to pour him some Apple Jacks mixed with Grape Nuts, a nutritional compromise we'd made. "Don't let her out of your sight. Don't let her put a thing in her mouth. Do you know how to call 911?"

I spent hours cooking meals and putting them in Rubbermaid containers and plastic baggies, scrawling phone numbers, everyone's but Mama's, lining up edibles, movies, activities all in arrangement for Jay with written instructions. He was a genius, bona-fide, and had been reading since he was 3. He could handle this for a day or two, I told myself. Just till I can sleep this off, just till I can stand up again. Twenty-four hours. Forty-eight, tops.

I gave him the phone list and the responsibilities of someone more than twice his age.

"All right, Jay, sweetheart. Mommy's going to bed for a little while, but you get me if you need me." I felt so guilty that I didn't shut the door, left it wide open so my children could slide into my bed, the physical form of a mom giving them a hint of comfort when my hands couldn't put food on the table or pour warm water over their bodies, work shampoo into their hair. I would sling an arm across them and mumble, pulling them close. I wanted to love them, but an oppressive mental fatigue pushed any maternal instincts clear to the bottom of the waiting list.

Every morning I crawled into bed after pouring their cereal and cutting on the TV, snuggling deep where the sheets were cool and meanness was just a memory. It was June, 13 months post incident, and luckily, school was out.

Two weeks later, down to skin and bones, hair like a haint's, children having been passed to and fro like a football—from one church lady to the next—my mother got suspicious and appeared.

She wasn't alone. She had Weepie and Iris, her two sisters, by her side, as the entire Aunt Brigade packed up the house of what I allowed to be removed or what the Jeters hadn't filched—my clothes, kids' things, and other essentials that would not elicit nightmares. Most of the furniture, what the Jeters hadn't robbed me of, I left behind, and by nightfall on the day of their arrival, the aunts packed us in Mama's car, pulling a U-haul of our life behind them.

I had lost almost 20 pounds and was a mess. I don't remember getting out of bed but a few times during those weeks, zombied trips to the grocery store, buying milk and cereal, a new can opener so Jay could feed himself and Miranda, too.

"Filth," my mama said, driving down the mountain, a 70-mile path to her home, my old hometown, Spartanburg, South Carolina—70 miles that made a world of difference as far as heat and topography—even type of people.

"You smell like something rotting, and those poor kids' nails are dirty, noses crusty, they look . . . well . . . all of you seem neglected," she said as she drove down the mountain. "All I can smell are dirty scalps probably festering with lice and scabies. I don't know why in this world you didn't tell me you weren't a functioning woman, Prudy. For a while you seemed to have it all together, though I wasn't fond of all that traveling y'all were doing. It certainly ate up all y'all's finances."

I pretended to be asleep.

"What she means," Aunt Weepie said, craning her head back at us, "is that you look like you were pulled from a Dumpster at a homeless shelter."

"Don't go trying to make her feel any better," Aunt Iris, who lives in Florida, said, her voice edged in sarcasm. "Think about what she's been through. Who among us could endure this type of hell?"

"Both of you hush," Mama said, suddenly going from critical to defensive. "The child at least finished all her important business, got herself well enough to show the children six month's worth of good times before she shut down and took to her bed. If that Jenny friend from church hadn't called, who knows what would have happened to them. Look, look back there at those three, would you?"

Iris turned to view us. I saw her from the corner of an eye I opened a tiny crack out of curiosity. "You're right, Lucinda," Iris said. "They sure need some TLC, and you know, I was thinking not long ago how very few women could have taken it as long as poor Prudy did."

"I wouldn't have lasted a night," Aunt Weepie said.

"That's for sure," Iris said.

"Okay, that's enough," Mama said. "We're going to take care of these three pitiful orphans for as long as we need to. Iris, search her purse for those pain pills. They'll be the first to go. Throw out all but about six so I can detox her gently. Oh, Lord, have mercy, I should have trucked up here for them months ago. I should have known it was coming. Prudy sure put up an Oscar-winning performance as the 'Recovered Woman,' there for a while, now didn't she? She wouldn't stand for it, kept on saying, 'I'm fine, Mama. Couldn't be better.' Bunch of sorry lies . . ."

Mama pounded the steering wheel, hands open and flat, her diamond wedding ring catching the sunlight. "Y'all listen up," she said to my aunts. "I can't do this alone and Parker's not going to be a whole lot of help. He gets to drinking that bourbon and it can go either way. He can get all warm and feel-goody or he can get on a revenge trail I don't want to see him ever ride again. You all remember what he did in the courtroom, trying to jump Bryce? We can't count on him. So it's the three of us. Deal?"

"Deal!" they all shouted, as if we were a project and this was a long, uncertain road trip. I curled into my seat and fell asleep, my head against Miranda's velvet-soft thigh. I never wanted to wake up again.

***

A year later and I'm here, in this old apartment, forcing myself to see the charm in the very things my mother deems flaws. Chuck Roland won't hire me for anything decent, but that's not the end of my journey. This is the beginning. No more pink gown. No more letters because I plan to call the prison and report them. Of course, that didn't stop him the last time.

Maybe Mama and Aunt Weepie were right. I should get out, mingle, meet friends, maybe even a man, God forbid.

# Chapter Six

**Good Morning, Pru-Dee:** *Don't tell your secrets unless you want them broadcast to the world. God puts out the light of the man who curses his father or mother.* ***Proverbs 20:19-20***

**Mama's Moral:** *I know you're probably applying for unemployment today or government cheese or 40 acres and a mule, but remember it's not necessary to hang all your pitiful business on the line. Please, Prudy, remember I have my bridge biddies to face. Use some discretion. I want your light to shine a long time, sweetheart. We aren't the types to go on the dole. Try, honey, try, to get a real job.*

AN EAGER AND bleached Monday-morning sun flaunted its Cloroxed summer light directly into my window. It was the mother's hand that rouses a child from sleep, the bold announcer that another day has come and I've lived through it. Like it or not. Many times since moving to the apartment a couple of weeks ago, I've thought about rigging enormous black sheets to the bay window, blocking the inevitable, the day I'd have to face, whether at 7 a.m. or at 10 or noon or even 2. No matter how much darkness the old self craved, I knew the dangers of giving in.

*Get up, get up; Prudy, get up,* I chanted in my head. If you get up, you can always go back to bed. Give it three hours. Feed the children. Don't make them eat Pop-tarts and watch videos while you hide in the shell of a bed, underneath twisted covers that smell of depression and dead dreams. The letters from Bryce. Forget about the letters. Too much to do today. A life to get back on track. Brave fronts to put up for the children.

I pushed the pastel sheets off my bare legs and stood on the cool boards of the hardwood floors. I liked the firm feel of wood beneath my skin. Bryce and I had wall-to-wall carpeting, and these floors, while scarred and worn, had a surface that hid nothing. What you saw, was all that was there, nothing lurking in fibers or padding, nothing but skin against wood.

Across a small hallway, in the other large bedroom, Jay and Miranda slept in single beds, hers a white canopy with a butterfly spread, his a trundle, the sheets and comforter swimming with a sea-life pattern. Their beds and my antique vanity were the only furniture I had taken from our old house in Asheville. A few things remained that I'd left behind. But not their beds. They had to have some semblance of the old life, vestiges from the flawed but familiar to hold on to, some childhood continuity offered by the pink butterflies and the blue angel fish.

Seeing them asleep, at complete peace with themselves and their lives, I could imagine anything. I could pretend they hadn't lost a father to a mad and murderous mind. I could pretend they had a daddy who had moments earlier kissed their sleeping faces then rushed out to operate on the poor and lame in an inner city clinic, a gentle Labrador of a man who would be home later that evening to share fascinating stories of ruptured appendices and who would tell me how delicious the lasagna tasted and how blessed he was to have this family, these two precious children. He would tell me how thin and pretty I was, seeing in his forgiving eyes a size-8 woman and not the 12 who'd join him later in bed.

I could look at the innocent flushed curves of my children's cheeks and imagine that such a life might be possible. Might still be possible. They were young. Miranda did not even remember her father. They would have other chances. But only if their mother got out of bed, made them oatmeal and combed their hair and took them to school, opening doors of both opportunity and laughter. And only if she didn't date losers or marry potential killers. I put on a pot of coffee, staring at the new magnets Mama had put on my refrigerator the week before. The coffee maker gurgled and spat, finally trickling hot dark fluid into the decanter. Mama and her magnets. She'd found a couple at Spencer Gifts, that naughty store in the mall where she claims "trash gathers," but couldn't resist. I read them every day, every time I get hungry or thirsty.

PICK A MAN THE WAY YOU WOULD A MELON: SNIFF FOR FRESHNESS, THUMP FOR RIPENESS, AND SLICE TO MAKE SURE BOTH HALVES ARE FULLY SEEDED.

Next to it were other magnetic enlightenments she'd purchased and slapped on the fridge:

> A NERD IS AS GOOD AS HIS WORD –
> AND HIS PLATINUM VISA!

And then this:

> YOU'LL GET A DATE TO MATCH YOUR BAIT –
> DRESS LIKE A TRAMP AND BRING HOME CROTCH CRICKETS!

I believe she lied when she said that last one came from Spencer's. It looked more like she made it herself during one of her ceramics classes she can't seem to get enough of. Usually it's frogs and owls. Now this.

I grabbed a cup of coffee—poured in one pack of Equal and stirred with a fork—taking it into the living room for my morning stretches on the woven rug Aunt Weepie had given us. Moving my body this early in the day sent daggers of pain through my right leg, the one Bryce mangled with the church van, but I had to do this, the routine of stretches and strengthening exercises. I refused to use crutches or a brace, even when doctors advised it. My children had enough inner scars. They didn't need a daily reminder in the form of a mother who limped and scritch-scratched along on crutches or a walker. They certainly didn't need Miss Percocet for a mom.

I leaned forward as a yoga tape played, a gentle voice telling me I was a survivor, "a warrior," as I stretched, feeling the pain. For the next 20 minutes my body tested its limits and responded to the will behind it.

A light band of perspiration dampened my neck as I walked through the apartment my mother hated and I adored. The ceiling fans chopped the early morning air enough to send chills along my hairline. I drank a second cup of coffee while staring at the kitchen, a white rectangle with white appliances, the paint chipped in spots, and a gas stove that still frightens me every time I light a match and hear the whoosh, see the sudden dance of blue flames.

The owners of the house, a couple who had years ago upgraded to a newer neighborhood but couldn't bear selling the place, had left it partially furnished. In my case, this was a good thing. Since the beds and my antique vanity were all I could bear from the old life, the rest of what few objects I owned, chests of drawers, a sofa and chairs, I'd picked up at Goodwill in downtown Spartanburg, and after cleaning and buffing the chests and lining the drawers with contact paper and sachets of lavender, they were almost as good as if I'd bought them new. No smells lingered from former owners.

This morning, as with at least half our mornings, Jay woke up grouchy and didn't want his Honey Bunches of Oats and said he didn't care to eat a hoagie at his summer camp because the meat smelled funny and had gristles and could I please pack him a Lunchable.

Miranda decided she'd wear nothing but her monkey-print pajamas and wool poncho in 90-degree weather, topped with a straw hat, and completed with a pair of pink snow boots for her half-day at the private summer preschool. All the Junior League sorority snoots I'd gone to high school with and who'd heard about my tragedy back in Asheville will think she's neglected and pitiful and that I'm too mired in my own mess to care for her, all their Gymboreed mini-me's in bows and Mary Janes, my Miranda in chipped glitter nail polish and a giant pocketbook that once belonged to my grandmother, to whom she owes her strong-willed personality and the jet-black hair she had at birth, hair so black Bryce swore up and down she was Mexican and I had cheated.

***

No matter how much dignity you try to squeeze into your life, some things keep resurfacing, like coffins in swollen, flood-ravaged cemeteries. The way to live fully is to hold the floodwaters back and keep buried all things of no benefit. So the letters from Charlotte have returned, my personal coffins, resurfacing from the swollen, flood-ravaged cemetery of my past. That doesn't mean it's time to go six-feet under and let Bryce get the best of us.

Today was huge for the future of my career, my chances beyond housekeeping, and all my hopes hung on this interview I'd scored at the nursing home, the same place where I once volunteered as a young woman and would now seek a paid position. A step closer to being a real nurse. A step closer to new dreams.

I spent a lot of my young adult years at Top of the Hill Manor, which isn't on much of a hill at all. It sits on a hump of land, surrounded by dogwood trees and white pines, but for Spartanburg, a hump is considered a hill because most of our city is on the flat side. I first became affiliated with Top of the Hill 17 years ago when I walked through the doors, tears in my eyes, begging for a bit of volunteer work to ease my troubled and guilty conscience.

Nursing home duty is what a Baptist-bred girl does when she slips up and sins, especially if the busted commandment lined up for balancing has something to do with a man and one's desires for some gratification in the Sealy/Serta department.

Lots of sinning going on in college, which is when I first discovered the joys and conscience-easing salve of servitude via Top of the Hill. Plenty of girls could up their sex-partner totals way into the double digits and not even bat an eye, but not me. The one thing I promised myself in the sweeping age of the Sexual Revolution was this:

*Have some fun if you must.*
*But never, ever dip into the double digits.*
*And always balance fornication with service work.*

I managed to graduate college with only seven lovers, and reach age 30 with only 12 or 14 (two may not count due to impotency on their part). But, of course, if anyone asked, I always said *four.* However, my totals could have been as high as my friends' had I not invented a method of partnership management called "Recycling."

A smart girl knew the value of recycling, and I rarely nailed new boyfriends, just dusted off the old ones. Not only could a woman remain relatively satisfied between serious relationships by recycling, but she could keep those totals down in the single digits for as long as possible.

Mama said a girl's reputation was all she had and virginity was a must. Twelve to 14 wasn't bad for a girl with a body like mine. It may be on the large side now, due to genetic rear-end expansion and passage through the Big Mac and Breeding Era, but from 1980 through 1995, I had myself a fine figure.

Aunt Weepie always said if you slip up, and crack open a pot of major sins, one better bake someone a pie (this from a woman who hates to cook) or sew doll clothes for the foster kids in the county system, which she has done for years regardless of sin tallies, or better still, darken the doors of a nursing home and get your hands dirty and soul clean.

Thus began my long association with nursing homes, Top of the Hill, in particular. Every time I'd fall off the virtue wagon, I'd rush down the corridors, ducking into patients' rooms and changing Depends or polishing the horn-like nails of some poor old lady's yellowed toes. I'd let the old men cuss me out one minute and try to feel my boobs the next, tongues hanging out and coated in Ensure and old age.

Today I wore a gray and blue dotted dress that fell at my ankles and had capped sleeves and a high neck, even though it was hotter than August outside and unbearable for early June. I didn't want the scars on my neck and chest to show. Sometimes I didn't care, but today I wasn't up to answering questions about them.

My appointment was at eleven o'clock and I arrived with two minutes to spare, enough time to reapply lip gloss and brush out my long hair. At 11:05, I was waved in by a stocky woman with brassy blonde hair and a face straight out of a Mary Kay makeover session. She shook my hand, hers sticky with lotion that smelled like grapefruit, and said her name was Theresa Jolly, director of Top of the Hill, and to please call her Theresa or Tee.

"What do you want to do, Prudy?" this woman asked after she'd gone through the small talk.

"Please, just call me Dee. I decided Prudy sounded kind of cold and stiff."

"Well, now, you've helped us so much over the years, or so I've been told, so why don't you just tell us how we can help you."

"Anything, really," I said. "Mama used to be a beautician and taught me how to give perms and wash and set hair. I can do basic trims, manicures, pedicures. I can bathe patients and feed them. I got my nurse's assistant certification one summer back in college and was taking classes for my RN before I got married. The assistant certification's been expired for years, but I still remember most of it."

"We can train you, Dee. But I must say, it's not a lot of money, even though I see here you have kids, so I could offer you flexible hours at the very least."

She stood from her desk and shut the door of her office. I heard her hose rubbing as she walked, and I wanted to reach out and hug her. She was offering me a job and her inner thighs met just like mine did. This sweet, stocky, barrel-chested woman was giving me a chance to work in a field I needed and one I truly believe needed me.

"I may be out of line, but we are all aware of what happened to you and are terribly, terribly sorry." She waited for me to elaborate, everyone wanting more than they'd read in the papers or heard third-hand. I never could deliver much more because of the fuzzy memories.

"I could start with three days a week," I said, "and see how my leg does. It's usually fine, held together with metal, I'm afraid, but other than that, I mean my other injuries, they've all healed."

"Bless your heart." She shook her head and scanned me for other scars. "Don't you qualify for disability?"

"Technically, yes. But the truth is I'd rather not label myself disabled. I couldn't get up in the morning if I had to admit my husband made me incapacitated. I may not have a complete leg bone, but I still have a backbone." I laughed nervously at my stab at humor. "I'm ready to work, just tell me how I can help."

"This resume says you have a degree in psychology."

"Yes, but not a master's. It's kind of like having dentures without the adhesive." I let off another laugh. "Little good it'll do you."

She winked and inhaled deeply. I also took the opportunity to grab a deep breath, having held mine during the "interview" portion of our meeting. The room smelled like Lysol and a Glade Solid air freshener, floral scented. In most nursing homes, I could smell urine, but not in her office.

"In here, a psychology background will do you a lot of good," she said, walking to a fake marble counter and pouring from a half-filled Mr. Coffee maker. "Would you like a cup?"

"Sure. Thanks. The coffee I make at home tastes like motor oil." I took the hot coffee as Theresa Jolly settled back behind her desk, stirring the sugar with the tip of an ink pen. I liked her; she wasn't pretentious. I thought I was the only woman alive who stirred milk and sugar with pens and pencils, forks, chopsticks, even hairbrush handles.

"I was thinking . . . a lot of our people . . . they could use your good company and counseling. You wouldn't believe the number of residents who don't get a single visitor. It'll break your heart." She placed a hand over her left breast, each fingernail vivid red and filed to perfect rectangles. "Listen here, we have no budgeted position, but I think the 'miscellaneous' account will allow me to pay you $250 for the three days. I'd also like you to come in and do hair, plus the visits and counseling. I could get you more money for the extra work. Now, this would be three full days to start. If you could arrive as soon as you drop the kids off at school?" I nodded. "Let's say around 8 or 9 and stay till at least supper. Oh, and we eat real early around here, so you can help feed if we need an extra hand and still get out by 5 or 5:30. I tell you what, if there are leftovers, you can wrap them up and take them home to your kids so you won't have to cook."

"I'm so grateful, Mrs. Jolly," I said, making a mental note to ask Mama or Aunt Weepie to watch the kids those three days after school. At least Chuck was allowing me to bring them to the radio station for my cleaning gig.

"Don't mention it. Remember, call me Theresa. These little old men and women are going to love you, especially if you treat them like real people and not children or invalids."

She told me I could start that week, the day after tomorrow, and that my regular days would be Mondays, Wednesdays and Fridays.

After my interview at Top of the Hill, I stood and clasped Theresa Jolly's hand. She paused, then reached up to hug me. "I read all the reports," she said. "You are the bravest, strongest woman I've ever had the pleasure to know."

*Ah, little do you really know,* I wanted to say.

"There's another one like you here," she said, lowering her voice and whispering even though the door was closed. "She works on the East wing. C.N.A. level II. Husband shot her in the head. It's a miracle she can walk or put two thoughts together since that bullet's still somewhere in her brain. I'll want you to help her out. She can train you as far as the job, but you can help her with her memory and the lifting.

"Oh, listen to me. Are you able to lift and do such heavy work?"

"The plates in my shin work better than the bones ever did," I said and drank the last of my coffee, the bitter part, the hardest sip to swallow. "I can't thank you enough. You won't be sorry. I'll see you Wednesday."

I added the money in my head, $1,000, plus the $200 a month at the station, knowing we'd barely make it, but it was a good start. My only backup would be to break down and take the money Pauline Jeter, Bryce's mother, was always trying to mail us to ease her own conscience. Mama and I decided to rip the checks in half every single month, though lately, I've begun to wonder if we shouldn't reconsider.

At least Mama had sold Bryce's Mercury while I was in the hospital and paid for our living expenses when we were with her. By refusing Jeter dollars and donations, she felt justified in keeping them from their grandchildren, except at Christmas and birthdays when there was a supervised meeting between Pauline and the kids, my mother lurking in the background, Dr. Jeter stewing back in Virginia, their home state, and refusing to visit.

Bryce's church raised enough money for the children's health insurance for a couple of years, setting up a small trust for them after the tragedy. It gave me new hope in the Baptist faith, that they would side with the victim and not the man in the pulpit. Yet one or two of the crazy old bats thought the entire incident was brought on by my actions, which vicious tongues decided were far from proper and churchy.

Bryce had been accusing me of cheating off and on for most of the marriage, but especially the last 18 months as his craziness and irrational behavior escalated. I couldn't even look at a man without him swearing up and down that I'd slept with him or wanted to. It started with the accusations that I'd given birth to a Hispanic baby girl, him thinking my trips to my favorite Mexican restaurant were more out of lust than desire for good salsa and ethnic food.

Every other day I drove to El Chalupa's and pigged out on tostados and enchiladas, tacos with guacamole and pico de gallo. The smell of sizzling fajitas drove me crazy with cravings. The chips, the hot, spicy salsa and the fresh chopped cilantro the waiter always brought as a special favor. Bryce thought I had a thing for this one waiter who would bow and very boldly say, "Senorita is *muy bonita,*" as he delivered my cilantro in a miniature cast iron pot. Bryce did not like that at all, though he begrudgingly grinned his preacher man smile and plunked down a meager 10 percent gratuity at the end of the meal.

We had eaten at El Chalupa two hours before my water broke on the fourth stair of our home, and we rushed to the hospital, my contractions beginning with fury and immediacy.

I was in labor only three hours, squawking and begging for an epidural, being told it was too late by the nurse and that it "wasn't God-like" by Bryce who relished in my suffering, that pompous anus.

They gave me a shot of Demerol, which did nothing for the pain but made me see double of Bryce—as if one of him weren't bad enough. Mama was in there scampering about, pointing her video camera at my open legs.

"Close your legs, Prudy," she'd say, darting around the doctors and nurses. "I'm seeing more than I probably should."

"For christsakes, Mother, I'm having a baby. I've got to open my fuckin' legs." She and Bryce gasped. I was cussing up a storm because no one had ordered the $1,200 epidural. If they were going to keep me in the most intense pain of my life, this prying apart of the human body, one muscle, one tendon at a time, then I was going to cuss enough to split their eardrums just as this baby was splitting me.

"Cross them, Prudy," she demanded, two frown lines perfectly parallel above her nose. "I don't want to see that ole black curly pubic hair in my birth video."

"I can either push a baby out of my ass or cross my legs," I screamed through the pain of a contraction that had dilated me to eight centimeters, meaning I was in what they call "transition," the most excruciating and productive stage of labor. I was shaking like a drunk coming off 10 days of fortified wine. I was throwing up and looking like Linda Blair in the "Exorcist."

Mama came around to the side of the bed and pointed the Sony in my face. "Prudy, tell everyone about the name you've picked out for the baby," she said in her narrator's voice. "Tell us, hon, about this precious little girl on her way into the world."

Pain seared and threatened to rip me in half. Bryce was in the corner, reading the Bible and taking furtive peeks at my privates, which mama kept draping with the sheet, much to the doctor's utter annoyance. "We need to see what's going on and check the progression," he snapped at Mama every time she tossed the sheet over my region.

"What's this angel's name, Prudy?" She took the camera from her eye, made an odd face and fanned the area near her nose. "Lord, child, what have you been eating? I'll bet these doctors can't even focus on you with that oniony vomit breath you're blowing in their faces. Here, have a few Tic Tacs—you should have thought to suck one while all this was starting. It's the same as with church breath and—"

"STOP IT! I CAN'T TAKE THIS!" My eyes were on a telephone. I figured if she didn't hush her mouth, I could hurl the phone onto the floor to get her attention. Before I could do anything, she'd stuffed a few white Tic Tacs into my mouth at the exact moment another contraction tore through me, a pain so wretched I shrieked as if in a slasher movie, choking on one of the little mints. The birthing team jumped up and then shut the door so other women delivering babies down the hall wouldn't pack up and go find themselves a vacant ditch for their births. I wasn't good for business. I was the live animal being torn apart limb by limb.

"What's her name, Miss Prudy?" Mama asked, as if nothing had happened, oblivious to the hollering and anything but my breath, pubic hair, and the name of the baby because we hadn't quite settled on one yet. "What's this angel from God's blessed little name?" She peeped around her viewfinder and grinned. "You can get closer to me now, Pru, because the breath mint has started to work and I . . . oh, what's this precious little tot's name going to be, hon?"

"Her name is . . . is . . ." a contraction plowed like a backhoe. The sheet Mama had once again thrown over my necessary birthing parts was askew and she was frantically trying to cover me up as I writhed and shouted. "Her name is . . . ohhhh . . . shit . . . it's Vageena," I yelled. "It's spelled just like one of these," I said, tossing the sheet and pointing downward, "but we are going to pronounce it differently."

I was, quite simply, possessed by the pain. I tried to jerk the camera from Mama's hands as she was erasing "Vageena," from the birth video. "Help and get her out of me!" I grabbed the nurse's teddy-bear print coat before she could run out of the room. "Get her out NOW!"

Jay was an easy delivery. I went in, had an hour of tolerable pain before the doctor announced he was breech and they numbed me up and performed a C-section. Nothing to it. No legs spread or exposed privates for Mama to fret over. Nothing but a tasteful laying out on a gurney and a few choice slices through the abdomen and uterus, and then it was all over, and I had given birth to a genius with a perfect head, having not squeezed him through the birth canal.

My sister's firstborn had a squid head and red splotches and welts for two months. He looked, to put it mildly, chewed up. She toted her Bratwurst-headed boy to every portrait studio in town, proudly propping him up and causing a few horrified yelps among young inexperienced photographers at Kmart and Olan Mills, people who hadn't seen coneheads and storkbites of that magnitude. My Mama waited till his head shrank and the red patches faded, around the child's six-month set of photos, before she'd put one on her fridge or show her bridge biddies her new grandbaby.

"Time to push," the doctor said, while mother jockeyed for a place near my outer thigh in order to get a documentation of the birth that wouldn't earn an X-rating.

Bryce held my hand with one of his, the black Bible in the other. He said things like, "Breathe, in the name of Jesus," and Mama would say, "Give her another mint, first," and I was ready to haul off and knock both of them out cold. Half an hour later the most beautiful child I'd ever seen came squirting and sliding out of my body, her head hardly squidy at all but her coloring as brownish red as any minority baby born on the ward that day. For a second I thought she was part black and wondered if Bryce had any African Americans in his family.

Everything grew quiet as the nurse plopped the ethnic-looking baby on my breast and allowed us a quick bond before she cleaned and weighed her. My child started rooting and nursing immediately, and Mama turned off her camera because a shot of my nipple, stretched to the size of a small satellite dish, simply wouldn't do, though she was all gung-ho on breastfeeding because she read it would increase IQ. She had seen the results of nursing Jay the Genius who hung in there for two years, though Mama said it ought to "be outlawed to have one hanging on the teat for more than six months."

"But the American Academy of Pediatrics recommends a full year," I'd said back when Jay was a little over a year old and they were all fussing about his need to keep nursing.

"They don't have class and decency," she said.

"They're a bunch of flaming liberals," my father had shouted from his bourbony perch in the green recliner.

***

After a while, they cleaned and bathed my daughter, Miranda Grace, the name Miranda all my choosing and Grace coming straight from Bryce, though I did find it lovely and appropriate. She was gorgeous, my sweet 8-pounds, 4-ounces of love, and they'd dressed her in a little white T-shirt that had built-in mittens to cover her sharp little fingernails. I was immediately smitten.

Not my in-laws. Not the Jeters who drove from Virginia and arrived later that night.

They brought me a single rose, one pathetic little flower from the hospital gift shop that cost $3 and wasn't even in a vase. They eyeballed my baby and poked around in her bassinet, then turned to Bryce.

"Son, we need to see you in private."

They left the room and shed one lingering frown at my baby's bassinet, not even bothering to say goodbye. When Bryce returned, he was alone and droopy-faced, all sagging in on himself, not like those old baby cards from the '60s where it shows a man's chest swelling with the pride of fatherhood and a button popping off.

"What's the matter?" I asked. "Where are your parents?"

He turned red and clenched his teeth. His fists made two white balls by his side.

"Gone home."

I was shocked.

"Prudy, that isn't my baby," he said. "You've had yourself a . . . you've gone off and given birth to a . . . a . . . wetback."

I glared at him like he was crazy, then I laughed and couldn't stop laughing. Tears rolled down my face, and it felt like my bottom was going to open up and deliver another child.

"A what?" I wiped my cheeks and reached for Miranda Grace. I lifted her pink-knit hat and stared in amazement at the loads of jet-black hair she sprouted. No one in either of our families had hair that dark or thick except my grandmother on my daddy's side. And no Jeters had met Grannie because she died a few years back. The proof was in the cemetery. Lord, we'd have to find some old photos of Grannie. My own hair coloring was a mystery. I hadn't seen anything but the roots since I was 15, product of growing up with a mother who was a beautician without a parlor.

Bryce peered into the bassinet where Miranda was trying to get a mittened hand into her mouth, those beautiful bow-shaped lips puckering. He touched her hair and recoiled.

"Look at her," he shouted. "She's a Latino of some sort. She's as much a Mexican as any I've seen from that restaurant you've been frequenting. I knew you were going more for the illegal immigrants than the food."

"Go home. Go on. Get your thick-headed, prejudiced self home and don't come back. Mama's coming after a while with Jay and I don't want them to hear your filth."

"Prudy, you know you're breaking several commandments as you speak. You need to get right with the Lord and—"

"I'm going to lay you out on this hard floor if you don't get out of my room and away from us."

It took an entire month for Miranda's jaundice to clear up, and three more months for her skin to lighten from brownish orange to olive and for her black hair to fade to a softer brown. I will admit she did, indeed, appear to be Mexican. But that's no reason for a husband to accuse a woman of cheating. He ruined the birth. Up and ruined it.

There were lots of things he ruined, actually.

***

Mama was going to be thrilled I'd found some gainful employment. She and Dad had said they'd help out in a pinch, but that's not how I was operating anymore. No more charity, either in the form of possessions or over-attentiveness. If I stayed in that apartment any longer than necessary it would all come back. Too much spare time isn't good for people with tragedy on a leash.

What had happened in Asheville after the trial could happen again. I might stay in bed and not be able to get up. The sun might reach in, nudging with its blinding wake-up call, but I knew how to crawl deep, far away from the light and from anyone or anything. Bryce Jeter and his threats and letters would not have that hold on me any longer. Not if I could do something about it.

I walked to the children's room, fell into Miranda's pink butterflies and closed my eyes. The day, though it was only noon, had pressed like a lead coat, but if I just curled up on the corner of my daughter's canopy bed I could sleep until time to pick them up for the afternoon. Just a bit of sleep. Not the kind like last year, the long, fretful slumbers when I couldn't get up for days and days, weeks and months.

Not like when the Aunt Brigade took over and would brush all three sets of teeth at night. They'd hop from bed to bed, saying prayers, though for the longest time, my children slept with me, my son's arms clutching me as tight as a child has ever held onto a teddy bear.

This, I told myself, holding the pillow to my chest, was a garden-variety nap to refresh the mind. A small, innocent nap of the sort that normal people who haven't been dead off and on might take midday.

The sunlight slipped through the plastic blinds and turned the wall into a pattern of slats, like those from a grill. Like those from steel bars in a prison cell. I took my hand and touched each shadowy stripe, like a child who plays with her mobile before drifting into the uncomplicated sleep of babies.

I would not, under any circumstances, dream about Bryce or think about the letters and how they got to our address. Nor would I relive the months in the hospital or the various ways I could have made it all different by leaving sooner. I will not touch those places, nor the physical ones—the indentations along my neck, the holes in my chest and shoulders that made my skin appear like land that had been dug and tilled, readied for new life.

I wouldn't reach down and rub my foot and leg, feeling the hard edges of plates and screws, a rebuilt lower leg that hurt so bad at times I wanted to hack it off with my bare hands.

My last thought before sleep's sweet ease was of my two children, and how those babies are the very reason I'm alive. The only reason. Without them, I'd have died on the sidewalk at BI-LO in front of the display windows advertising chuck roast, windows my airborne body had shattered.

# *Chapter Seven*

**Hey, Pru, I Mean Dee:** *It is better to live in the corner of an attic, than with a crabby woman in a lovely home.* **Proverbs 21:9**

**Bonus Proverb:** *A constant dripping on a rainy day and a cranky woman are much alike! You can no more stop her complaints than you can stop the wind.* **Proverbs 27:15-16.**

**Mama's Moral:** *It doesn't pay to be a crab. You'll never get a good, decent husband.*

EARLY JUNE IN South Carolina can be one of two things and is typically a combination of both. This time of year every shade of pink a girl could envision blazes throughout the greenways and meticulous lawns as the dogwoods, redbuds, azaleas, rhododendron and impatiens turn the town into visions sweet enough to take minds off the building heat.

We can almost forgive the relentless South Carolina sun if we gaze long enough at the Upstate's generous beauty, as dolled up as if the whole region took itself to the Merle Norman counter and asked for the works.

Daisies, wisteria, jasmine, peonies, butterfly bushes and the front porch favorite—geraniums—all thrive in the state known for heat and storms. Its people, incidentally, are a replica of the weather and flora.

One minute they can act sweet as honeysuckle, and the next caught breath they could very well fire up and rage like an August sky.

This is how it is and the price one pays for living in a place of four seasons, mild winters and women who are, for the most part, about as lovely and painted as the spring and summer blooms.

But even with their quirks and misguided priorities, South Carolinians are warm and gracious, typical Southerners who will give neighbors everything out of their cabinets or gardens but won't wince if a time comes that a neighbor must be properly put in her place. Vengeance is as alive as repentance, and quite often the two hold hands.

During this time of intolerable heat and floral loveliness, the tree for which our people is known—the great majestic magnolia—spreads a perfume through its wedding-white blossoms that no designer could bottle. Every child with an ounce of energy climbs up in the magnolias, generous with their stair-stepped branches and propensity to shed romance on most any situation. While the Palmetto is officially our state tree, few pay that hybrid palm much mind. Quite frankly, the only places I've ever even seen one is along the coast.

The coast is what we live for, is how we get through the long, hot summers. The South Carolina shoreline is a stretch of sandy paradise where we often flee when the rest of our state becomes a stifling, breath-robbing burden. We're like a bunch of crazy people flocking to the Atlantic, bumper to bumper, as if trying to outrun a lava flow.

This is the time it all starts, when the sun's burner is cranked to high and when the strong hint of another unbearably long season blows a hot yawn down our backs and across our faces. Some evenings it's like walking inside someone's mouth, even as late as dusk when I stroll Miranda in the neighborhood or play basketball in Mama's driveway with Jay and Daddy.

At least it's not Columbia, I tell myself. There's no place on earth hotter than Columbia, South Carolina. That town is the foyer of hell, all its pretty flowers just vases of color to decorate the entrance.

Spartanburg, an hour and a half away from Columbia, may be only a few degrees cooler, but those degrees are of life or death importance. People get mean in the heat, start mouthing off, even killing each other for nothing. I once knew a girl in high school who suffered a tragedy during a family reunion held in Columbia on an ungodly July afternoon some 20 years ago.

One day at lunch she sat across from me, opened her milk carton and slipped in the straw. Calmly and matter-of-factly, she said, "My uncle killed my aunt this past summer."

"Do what?" I said, uncertain I'd heard correctly.

"He asked my aunt, said, 'Hon, could you get your guitar out and sang us a purty song?' Aunt Faye was a' fanning herself with a big old flap of cardboard and told him, 'I'm too hot to move,' and he picked up his shotgun and blowed her right off the porch and up to Jesus."

My friend took herself a giant bite of peach cobbler soon as those words fell from her lips, as if it were simply a matter-of-fact, steamy South Carolina showdown.

It wasn't as bad in the mountains of Asheville, where I'd absolutely fallen in love with the gorgeous views, vistas like wave after purple wave and temperatures mild and relenting. Even though Asheville wasn't but an hour or so away, it had a completely different climate, and I suspect I'd still be living there if my husband hadn't held his private Revelation in a parking lot. As it was, when we lived for a year in Mama's rancher in the upper-middle-class suburbs on the right side of town, we were blessed she had a pool where we could swim off our heat and bad moods every afternoon and evening.

Since we moved out last month, I've sure missed that pool, and there's no way we can afford a membership to one of the private clubs. This is why I've decided to surprise the kids. When they get home from their summer enrichment programs today, I'm going to have them the nicest plastic pool money can buy. I saw them at Kmart, complete with built-in molded sliding board, separate deep end, and an object through which water will shoot like a spray of exploding fireworks.

I put on some jeans, my padded Miracle Bra—that quit providing miracles after I breastfed my last child for 18 months and my assets turned into two long trout—and sat by the bay window to put on makeup in the good, natural light.

Lord, my face was puffy. I wet some paper towels and put them in the freezer, took them out after two minutes and applied the cold compresses. Seems as soon as I turned 35, I began swelling for no reason. It didn't have to be PMS time for me to retain water like some desert camel loading up for a long, broiling march across half the globe.

Everyone says, "Drink eight glasses of water. That will help." I'll tell you what happens when I drink eight glasses of water. This. This puffy-eyed, upper thigh, fat-ass and stomach swelling. I've also noticed that if I stand up a lot, or I'm doing a lot of walking, say at a county fair or the mall or a street festival, I'm lucky to manage a trickle, a mere two ounces of tee-tee.

I can go all day without eating so much as a Slimfast or half a sandwich, but if I'm required to stand, the heaviness sets in. I can leave home weighing 140, and then I come home, having not eaten a fly's serving, and weigh 145. Seriously.

Not that 145 is swamp-sow material, considering my height of 5 feet, 8 inches, reduced after the Murderous Rampage and subsequent foot and lower leg surgeries to just under 5 feet, 7.

A frozen Bounty paper towel always works its magic within a few minutes; then I'm able to put on my makeup, which, most days, includes the full arsenal of cosmetics, another South Carolina trait most of our women have clung to since the state had its first contestant in the Miss America pageant.

I pour on the foundation, then act like a crop-dusting plane with the powder and spread on liner, eye shadow, mascara and, the most essential of all cosmetics, lipstick. My personal motto is, "There's nothing in the world a new tube of lipstick can't make better." I went through three tubes during Bryce Jeter's five-day trial.

My all-out favorites are the pinks and peaches, especially the frosts, which may sound trailer-park trashy to some people, but if you can swallow your false pride and buy a tube, prepare for a flood of compliments. Something about the glimmer of the frost wipes five to 10 years from the face. I put on two coats of Shimmer Pink every year at the State Fair and the midway man never guesses my age. This is how I easily win my kids nice stuffed animals that smell like B.O. and cotton candy.

By the time I arrived at Kmart, it appeared plenty of other mothers had beaten me to the pool selection. Those left were lined up outside and propped against the building, along with the swingsets and gas grills, the Miracle-Gro potting soil and a few rickety patio sets and umbrellas. The pickings were slim, every mother in town buying $30 worth of blue plastic relief.

I pulled up right as a woman was leaving, her pool strapped to the roof of her car, a smug smile on her perspiring face. I aimed my car at the angle best suited for pool loading, and within a few seconds a purposeful young man in his standard red Kmart vest skipped to my car window, boogying to tunes playing only in his head.

He was jumping and jiving, trying to be all pumped about his sidewalk job, but I could tell the heat and mothers had whipped him to worn-out shreds with the rush on kiddie pools.

"Can I help you, ma'am?"

"First, you can drop the 'ma'am' business," I said, and lowered my black Ray-Bans so he could see my clear and unpuffy, Bounty-blessed eyes. "I appreciate your manners, but save those ma'ams for the vast numbers of unfortunate and unattractive women you are most certain to come across today." *Oh my God. Who is this woman saying such things to a man? Could it be I've grown one or two vertebrae in my Bryce-induced spineless back?*

"Yes'um. I mean, okay." He cast his eyes down and grinned a sly smile. "You here to get you a pool?"

"Well, I'm not here for a facial. How about that big one there? You think I could cart it home on top of my Accord?"

"I reckon I don't see no problem there. I got some string and we'll just tie her up there and say a prayer or two."

I went inside and took the ticket, paid for the pool and bought a tube of Preparation H because I read somewhere it would get rid of wrinkles and bags, which is definitely a must if you are post-35 and find yourself with no husband or prospects and likely morphing into a five-humped camel due to massive water retention.

When I returned, the Kmart man-boy was already hopping around my car like a red-vested crow, had both car doors open as he tugged and tightened, trying to get the pool snug and secure on my roof minus a luggage rack.

"She's good to go," he said, and I wondered why men always had to call objects "she." Why is a plane a she, a car a she, everything but their precious and highly over-rated wee-wee a she? That's the one thing they'll call Mr. Big or the Blue-jeaned Bass. I once had a boyfriend who called it his "Heat-Seeking Missile." He was a big Gulf War enthusiast so what could one expect?

I offered Mr. Pool a sun-sapped smile and a dampened dollar bill that I'd had wrinkled in my hand for the past 10 minutes. He took it and put it somewhere in that red smock, said thank you, and then pogo'd away, playing air guitar, one skinny leg straight out in front of him.

Typically, in Spartanburg, a gentle breeze is not one of our amenities. We get strong winds during killer thunderstorms; otherwise, the Upstate saves its breath to brew up deadly tornadoes that take the tops off everything but homes and buildings constructed with bucks and stamina.

Today, for some reason, call it Murphy's Law, the wind picked up just as I was easing onto I-85 to cart my load home. I had gone about a quarter of a mile down the highway before I heard a noise, a loud banging on the roof and thought any minute it would cave in. I checked the side mirrors and saw a flash of blue. Good, the pool was still up there.

All of a sudden the wind gusted, lightning flashed, thunder cracked and roared and my pool copped air, rising from the roof, higher and higher, the slack rope tightening as if I'd caught a Marlin. I heard a loud pop like a gun going off and checked my mirrors, noticing a huge line of cars backed up behind me, the dropped jaws on the drivers' faces, their horns blasting and their frantic hands motioning for me to get off the road. I searched for blue. It wasn't there. The pool was gone.

*Oh, shit a thousand times. I'm just trying to be a good mother.* I'd gotten a note from Jay's teacher on Friday saying he was "acting odd," sulking and wouldn't play with the other children at recess, that he wanted to stay inside and read books on dissection and that I might want to address these "issues" during the summer vacation. She had given me that old teachery glare and said, "Why does your kid want to know about the inside guts of every living thing on earth?" I guess she had a point.

At home, too, Jay was behaving strangely and had been for the past week, though when pressed, he told me, "I'm fine, Mom. Don't I look fine?" and made a monster face, showing me all he had in the tongue and tonsils department. He had been doing fairly well since I got him back into therapy and, all things considered, including the letters, left me to wonder: *How can progress unravel? How can an entire year of therapy and tenderness and stepping as carefully as if one were on a bed of spears reverse itself in a few weeks?*

I made a mental note to watch him closer, but for the time being, I could at least buy my fatherless, heat-sapped children a cheap plastic pool. We could pretend to be a happy family. We could swim and splash and make believe we were like everyone else, that Daddy, the inner-city surgeon with Labrador eyes, would be home in time for supper to tell us about the orphans from Nicaragua he had spared from disease and deformity.

Until I can find this make-believe dream man, I'm aimed to let my kids know that their mother can do things most daddies do. That a person can be both Mom and Dad. I understand now why some single women feel the need to overcompensate after their divorces. Add to that mix a woman who's trying to make her children believe that it's really okay to have a daddy in prison for trying to kill their mama, and that it doesn't matter that their mother is on the verge of bankruptcy or a major mental breakdown, according to Dr. Capped Teeth therapist, who I quit seeing months ago, damn her and those stupid predictions.

If a swimming pool would take their minds off the "Where's Daddy?" questions I've had to field for two years, then, by God, I'd get them the biggest plastic pool money could buy.

A car horn blasted behind me and wouldn't relent. I slowed to 20 miles an hour, rolled down my window and let the driver go by.

"You fuckin' idiot," a man shouted as he eased past me in the other lane. "Crazy ass bitch of a woman!"

I stuck my teeth out like a mule's and shot him a bird, even going as far as pumping it a couple of times, though Mama would have disowned me and said only trash shot birds. Who was I to care? I was no longer a minister's wife, so I did not have to put on a sorry-ass public front. Bird, bird, bird. Birds to all those honking SOBs for not understanding motherly love. They probably beat their children, put them into bed with dirty feet and mossy teeth.

Goodness, where was that pool? I heard a horrible noise and veered into the emergency lane as the cars whizzed by and the people either honked or gave me the "Crazy Lady" head shaking. I leaned over and checked for the pool's whereabouts. There it was banging against the driver's side door and as crumpled as a car wreck. The nearest exit put me in the parking lot of a car dealership where a half-dozen men stood outside smoking while waiting for customers. My pool scraped the ground as I parked next to their fine gleaming Nissans.

I stepped out to make some adjustments, hammering out the dents with my fists and trying to get plastic to regain its shape as I, too, regained a sense of purpose and self. One of the men whistled. That greaseball. You'd think, it being 2010, that even primitive males such as certain car salesmen types, would get a politically correct clue. While I'm not opposed to the well-placed and pleasantly-pitched catcall, I don't want to hear them when under great distress such as right at this moment. The whistling grew more fevered.

I stood and caught a glimpse of myself in the car's windows. *Holy crap! Lord have mercy on my soul!* My right breast had completely fallen out of its Miracle Bra and was dangling pendulously from the scoop of my shirt. I wanted to die. I wanted to cry and crawl under the car. I thought of Aunt Weepie and how she would have turned the moment to her complete advantage.

What would Aunt Weepie do?

Another whistle and some laughter.

"You jerks never seen a D&D bosom before?" Two of them turned purple with heat and embarrassment and a midday hangover. "You know what D&D means? Means Dented and Dated. Get it? Now while I busy myself tucking titties back into position, please get over it and come around and help me with this pool. You might see more if you behave yourselves and get the thing rigged correctly."

They shuffled over to the car as sheepishly as school boys caught smoking around the back of the building. Dutifully, they began fidgeting with the pool, all the while waiting on the next breast to find its way out of Spandex captivity.

"You need to be driving a Nissan," one of them said, mind always on sales, even when bared breasts are in the picture. "Can't very well count on a Honda, can you?"

They all laughed in that way of men in groups who tend to act much naughtier and more irreverent than men alone. It seems when they are in wolf packs, all good taste and decency, all respect for women, go straight down the disposal.

"You look sort of familiar," another one said. This man was lighting a Marlboro with the butt of his spent cigarette as he stood in the sun with his Bee Gee's hair plastered to his oblong head. It was sprayed and lacquered and appeared sticky. He cupped his hand, the one without the cigarette, and boldly blew against his palm to check his breath, more than likely a combination of too many cigarettes, last night's liquor and the Mega Bar at Ryan's.

"We all have a twin," I said, knowing he'd seen me on the news or in the papers during the Murderous Rampage and subsequent trial. People, thank the good Lord, were starting to forget, and their memories were growing dim. And since I had returned to my maiden name and homeland there was even less recognition.

"Could you please help us? If you do, I might consider a Nissan one day. You never know, there's a potential customer in everyone who happens to find themselves in this lot."

The other man, the one who didn't say anything and seemed the most embarrassed about my "flop," so to speak, came over and joined the pack, making the necessary adjustments, never once looking me in the eye. I thanked him, forgiving him of that tanned, stir-fry look he sported and sped out of there so fast I almost ended up in the trunk.

I had just three more miles to go. *Please Lord, I promise I'll return to the fold. I'll find a good church and a decent minister. I realize, oh Father, that most of those called to duty aren't murdering men. Lord, help me get this pool home, and I swear I'll find a place of worship. I just can't go to Mama's church. It's too hardcore with all that screaming and talk of burning in hell. I don't even think You would like it, to be quite frank.*

The pool tottered and wobbled, caught a bit of air, but otherwise remained fixed to the roof. Five minutes later, I saw red in my rearview mirror. A horn bellowed of the deepest and most frightening sounds. The fire truck. Only in Spartanburg would the firemen be so bored they had to get behind a woman with a shaking swimming pool on her roof. The truck followed me the last mile and into my driveway. Embarrassed beyond belief, I got out and thanked them, remembering my proper manners.

"You boys were so sweet to do that."

"Didn't look like that pool was going to stay put," the driver said, and added for professional measure: "You do realize if it had come loose, it could have posed a real danger to fellow motorists and pedestrians."

"Yes, I do. You men are fabulous. Don't run off just yet." I quickly unlocked my door, ran up the steps—grimacing as pain shot through my leg—to the kitchen and dumped some semi-stale brownies in an old Christmas tin, hoping they wouldn't mind Santa in June. They probably wouldn't even notice the container. Most men are so simple, as basic as babies. Feed them and tend to their "diaper areas." No need for all the extras.

I breathlessly trudged up the stairs a second time and saw three messages flashing on the answering machine. One from Aunt Weepie, saying she had a blast at the funeral with me and I missed her best performance at Icy Corn's planting.

"I got us lined up for another one this week," she said. "Plan on dressing nice. The obit listed all sorts of male relatives, so you never know. Oh, and don't worry. Your mama still doesn't know you're cleaning crappers."

The other message was from Amber, my beautiful younger sister, announcing she had painted her grass green because it was dying from a major Georgia drought and didn't look as nice as her neighbor's vibrant spring greens. And besides that, the neighbors had added a new in-ground swimming pool and hot tub and Amber really needed to do something to get back at them.

"I had to put a sign on my grass that read, WET PAINT: DON'T STEP ON GRASS."

She hung up without so much as saying bye.

The final message was from Mama, a non-Proverb bit of zany news. I played it while fixing a glass of water, no ice. Mental note: Maybe the ice is causing the retention and bloating.

**Mama:** *"Prudy, I don't know if I told you this when we talked last night, but you really need to do all you can do to avoid the divorcee's known reputation. They have an unbelievable itch for it. You know what I mean by 'It.' Also, let me know what happened at the funeral. Weepie said it was the best one yet and that she plans* *to train you in the art of artificial mourning, which causes me great concern. I cannot picture my daughter caterwauling and falling all over coffins just for some creamed corn. Call me. I'll cry if you don't. I got big news."*

***

Later, when the kids came home from school and saw the pool wedged in the small side yard of the house, they had a fit of joy, as if Christmas had arrived, which lightened my heart. I considered asking the older couple renting the downstairs portion of the house if they minded, but we never saw them.

The kids squealed as they ran upstairs to put on their swimsuits. They couldn't wait to try out the sad little sliding board with the dent from my disastrous highway excursion. During the entire hour it took to fill the huge contraption with water from the limp and ancient hose, I returned the calls from my crazy kinfolk.

Amber spent my long-distance dollar wanting to talk about herself and her husband, who hasn't desired her since seeing her vagina expand to cave-like proportions during the birth of her twins a few months ago. She said he was flying his plane when her first was born four years ago and never saw the birth, which in her case, was a good thing. She said having the nice green grass made her feel better, and that if her husband wasn't interested in her, then he must have found another woman.

"If your fruits scared the man that badly," I told her, "then he's for sure not going to go barking up that tree again. It would be my clear guess the man prefers his fellow brethren who have units that would never be so bold and adaptable as to completely change forms and functions as can the Great Magic Vag."

"Oh, my God. You are finally getting your sense of humor back. Prudy—'scuse me, Dee—is alive again. I think I'll put up a billboard."

"You do that," I said. "Love you, sis. Wish you and the brood would come visit."

"I will, honey. I promise. Things are just crazy right now. Try breastfeeding twins and see if you don't feel like a friggin' nanny goat. I'm thinking if things don't change, I'll just get another husband. Trade up again like cars, you know."

She laughed, her fragile ego less bruised, considering that new gay option I'd tossed out after concealing my feelings for so long. She was also worked up about whether or not she should spray paint her shrubbery to match the grass, because the freshly painted ground cover made the leaves on her bushes seem rather dingy. "It's kind of like when people apply Crest Strips to their top teeth and completely forget or choose not to fool with the lowers," she said.

As soon as I hung up with her, the phone rang and Mama was on the other line, caffeined up as usual despite more doctors' warnings.

"I've been trying for 30 minutes," she said. "Why haven't you called me back?"

"I was providing my kids some relief from the heat and only now got off the phone with Amber, and then—"

"Never mind, hon. Listen, I got to thinking. Maybe you shouldn't go out with that boy Weepie wants to hook you up with. If he's a grease monkey working for her husband at the garage, that would put you right back to square one, to my own upbringing, and we Southern women have a motto. Never marry down. Even a lateral move isn't good, hon. You need a doctor. Someone who can support you. Here you are living in that rental unit. It's a shame. I can't believe you didn't get two nickels after the divorce. What kind of state gives a killer and his church the marital property? What kind of law is that?"

"It's the law, Mom. Equitable distribution in North Carolina. He gets half. No matter what."

"Left you with half of nothing. One good leg. Forget Weepie's poor little no-pensioned fellow. You know how she is. Anything in trousers is prime rib on a platter. I'll bet he smokes. Or has facial hair. He's probably the type to toot in front of his own children."

"God forbid!"

"Don't say the Lord's name in vain. Mercy, you got me all off track. What was it I was going to say?" I heard her walking around the kitchen, her high heels clicking along the tile floor she and Daddy recently installed during the remodeling and ridding themselves of all things from the seventies. She opened the fridge, and I could hear the crackling of ice cubes, half of them hitting the floor, the others dinging in the glass. "Oh, yeah, I know what it was. All that discussion of sex the other day made me remember that you probably got the itch."

"Excuse me?"

"Carla Tisdale had it bad after her divorce. She went around screwing every man in four counties," Mama said, and I was stunned because she rarely used the term "screwed," especially since she'd been recently "saved" *again* and had rededicated her life to the Lord for the seventh time.

I had this theory about getting saved. First, I could never understand why you had to get saved in the way of tears and wailing and throwing down in a massive altar-side Jesus fit. Could not a person simply feel the presence of God in her heart, and with great composure and elegance, walk to the front of the church and shake the pastor's hand, followed by a sprinkling of water a couple of Sundays later to seal the Christian deal?

That's how the Methodists do it. That's why I converted from Southern Baptist to Methodist until I married Bryce, when I had to switch back to Baptist and his constant threats of Satan riding my tail.

I preferred the Methodist's less dramatic forms of a saving. I just can't figure out why in some churches, after people were saved, they had to keep getting resaved? Did it not take the first time? Was it like getting acrylic nails and every so often a necessity for a fill-in?

I believe the Lord must get rather tired of all the retreads who come dragging up to the confessional. One or two savings is fine, but six to 12? I say if you need that many, then do them in private. Fall to your knees in front of the bed and quit wasting the preacher's time.

I used to tell the Rev. Murder Man that he ought to cut these perpetual sinnings and savings off after a certain point, and he said I was the craziest bitch he'd ever met. Used those very words. Used them many, many times.

"The more they're saved, the more money they give," he said. "A sinner saved is a dollar earned." He thought he was Mr. Wit.

Mama had turned on the stove and was slamming her cabinets as she continued to dispense advice along with the Canola in her pans.

"Carla was always up at the bars, on the hunt. Sugar, I know you've been through a lot and probably haven't given much thought to anything but survival and your new job and the kids' well-being, but now that things are better, I can tell you're feeling frisky." She used the term *frisky* because *horny* was a bad word in her mind. "Once a married woman is used to having it, she can't stop the urges."

She said "urges," as if it were the same type of scourge as E-coli or Ebola. "You just remember that a good reputation is all a woman has. Keep that in mind. A woman's . . . um . . . pretty patch . . . will be there till she dies. But her reputation dies fast if she loosens up even for a second."

"Her what? Pretty patch? What is a pretty patch, Mother?"

"Now, Prudy, you know what it is, and I'm not going to say it, but it rhymes with wussy."

I swear, since my mother went through the change she has gone 100 percent insane. Even the hormones she takes to increase whatever needs boosting are not helping in the oddness department.

A noise from the pool shattered my thoughts of the vagina and its many euphemisms. I could hear the kids splashing in the cold water and fighting over the goggles and inflatable balls, and I was about to end the conversation and go break up the fight when Mama sensed my boredom and changed the subject.

"I want you to take a wild guess what me and your daddy bought today?"

I ducked into the closet on our stairwell and found another pair of goggles, tossing them into the pool for Miranda, temporarily stalling the escalating fit.

"All right, I'm ready," I said, prepared to hear one of my mother's long-winded, screwball tales of utter madness.

"You have to guess. Guess what we've bought?

"A beach house on Hilton Head Island."

"No."

"A Lexus."

"Try again."

More splashing and squawking followed by a loud smacking sound. The sun was scorching, burning a hole in the top of my head as I sat on the top step with the cordless phone, supervising my children. I often wondered why people who wore hairsprays and other chemicals and styling agents didn't up and spontaneously combust. Especially those of us in the bullseye of a South Carolina sun. It would not have surprised me in the least to pick up the paper and read: "Woman's French Twist Explodes While She Gardens."

"Prudy. Where are you? Guess. Be a sport."

"I give up."

"Hon, we bought us a mausoleum. They were on special. Two slips for the price of one. We had to buy toe to toe because we couldn't really afford the side-by-side plan, but it's all right. I won't have to hear your daddy's snoring." She laughed in that high trilling voice that I associate with her beloved bridge biddies, those women who during my childhood would stay up late, ruffle cards, smoke and laugh and tell secrets way past my bedtime. "It's in a chapel with heating and air-conditioning, carpet and a set of bathrooms with all these brass fixtures. Can you believe it? We'll be inside away from all the harsh elements. And your daddy said having them bathrooms would be real convenient, him having prostate problems and all. Y'all can come visit. There's a nice sofa right in front of our little drawer thingamabobs."

"Those bathrooms. *Those*, Mama, not them bathrooms."

"Well all right, *those* but let me say—"

"Please tell me you really got a condo at the beach. Even an RV or a poodle."

"I'm so excited, Prudy. I just need to figure out what I'm going to wear. A friend said a real Southern lady has a dress for the viewing, something elegant but slightly on the flashy side so you'll look your very best while dead. Then you need a separate one that's more formal for the funeral. Something you can meet Jesus in with pride. So I'll need two outfits, I believe. You and Amber will have to see to it that my stiffening body gets changed into the outfits properly."

"I'm sure Dillard's or Belks will come through."

She ignored my sarcasm and pondered other matters.

"The thing is, it's no more expensive to be in a mausoleum than in the ground, and I could have sworn only the snoots got the indoor places, but it's amazingly affordable. We put it all on Visa."

"That's nice."

"It would have been," she said, "but they wouldn't give us any Frequent Flyer miles for it."

She couldn't be serious.

"I plan to place a call to the VISA headquarters about that first thing tomorrow. Good heavens, they give you miles and miles for buying groceries and VCRs. Why not for your burial goods and services?"

"Beats me. Seems rather brave and deserving of flight time." My mind was beginning to lapse into that frightening thought that one day, not long from today, I would become her, an endearing but veritable kook who took herself completely seriously.

"Hon, one last thing. Remember, don't give in to your animalistic urges, okay? We're not too unlike that monkey that flung his you-know-what in my hair. My hair still isn't right. I had Florence Tilly, you know her, the Catholic? I had her minister put some holy water on it even though we aren't Catholics. The thing is, it's not proper to spread yourself and your legs all over town, and I don't want to hear about your horn-dogging, you understand? It's a small town and people talk."

"Mother, I don't even have any prospects, okay? I'm just trying to earn a living and make some female friends."

"That's my good girl. Come on over soon and I will show you our burial drawers. I'm so excited they keep the temperature at 70 all year long, so when we're dead, your father can't chintz out and cut the heat back to save money."

# Chapter Eight

**Morning, Pru-Dee:** *White hair is a crown of glory and is seen most among the Godly.* ***Proverbs16:31***

**Mama's Moral:** *With each white hair plucked, wisdom lands on a shoulder. I've never plucked one. So I may have wisdom waiting to surface. You need to get some extra wisdom. And I don't mean teeth.*

AT THE NURSING home this morning, my second week on the job, my hands were raw from cleaning at the station, and I was exhausted from pacing the floor all night, having received the day before another set of those despicable letters from Bryce. This batch made the first seem like Valentines, and were much bolder, beginning innocently enough, with Bryce telling Jay how much he loved him and how grand life was in prison, that it was just like college and he got to play basketball and work out in the weight room and preach on Sundays to his cellmates and any other prisoners needing a connection to the Heavenly Father.

*"I'm counting on you to be brave,"* he wrote, the letters perfectly typed. *"Be good to your mother. I did a very bad thing and I deserve this punishment. Please, always be a good boy. Love, Daddy."*

That's not the letter that caused me to pace, though I'd have preferred my son and his father never have contact again. My therapist had warned and prepared me that it could, and probably would happen. That the children caught in the middle of domestic violence were as confused as the mothers whose sons had done the unthinkable. You've seen them on TV, moms with wet cheeks and frightened eyes holding up pictures of their sons when they were little boys with scraggly teeth and cow licks. Mamas saying to the Channel 4 News, "My boy would never do a thing like that." Or, "I'll always love him, no matter what they say he's done."

"Jay's loyalty is being tested," the therapist had said after I'd told her about Round One of the letters, the batch to my son. "Give him space. Don't make him feel guilty for wanting a connection to his father."

Well all right, but the next group of letters were too much by anyone's standards. I could never show them to Mama or she'd start up with a shotgun, Bible and trips to the Charlotte prison. Since she went through the change some eight to ten years ago, not even her synthetic hormones could completely level her out. No way I'd tell her about the recent flurry of letters. Her blood pressure would soar and she'd surely blame my bad choice on her vessel explosion. Lately, she never stopped telling me I was one incident away from putting her in her new burial drawer. "Good thing I went ahead and bought it and the two dresses, too," she'd say.

I read the letters in the employee lounge during my lunch break.

*Dear Jay:*
*I sure do miss you. Maybe it won't be too much longer until I'm dismissed. My lawyer says he thinks there's a way for me to get out of here a lot sooner than the judge had said. Wouldn't you like that? We could go to the baseball games and eat hotdogs like old times. I could take you to the go-cart track and wherever you want to go. Nana P. told me you played soccer and T-ball this past year and I hate that I missed it. I think by the time you're ready to hit your first home run, I should be in the stands to see it. Don't show this letter to anyone. Please, son.*

*Love, Daddy.*
*P.S. I think about you 1,000 times a day. P.S.S. Your mother isn't telling you the full truth. There are two sides to every story. Never forget that, son."*

The third letter wasn't really a letter at all. It was a drawing done in chalk and obviously not of Bryce's hand because I'd never known him to have a talent for art. The card was about the size of a 4x6-inch photo. The front had a meticulously drawn man, finely chiseled jaw, streaked blond hair, muscles bulging on his arms as he bent and busted the steel bars of his confinement. The head was out, body halfway there, one leg stepping into freedom, jaw set in a determination to do what was necessary at all costs.

The man wore a pair of blue trousers and a white T-shirt with the name Jeter printed so small, I had to use a magnifying glass to see it. But it was there. All five unmistakable letters like a secret code. The man in the drawing was identical to Bryce, only more exaggerated (but not by much) and super-heroish. I opened the card and found three words printed in charcoal. Square identifiable print.

**SEE YOU SOON.**

"Over my dead body," I said to Kathy Lumpkin, the nurse's assistant who'd been shot in the head, as she entered the break room and came over to see what I was reading. We were waiting on Miss Annie Sue to put on her wig and all her makeup, her good earrings and stockings with the fewest runs and snags. Several years ago Kathy's husband followed her down I-85 toward Greenville, inched his car up next to hers as she veered off at the White Horse Road Exit. She rolled down her window to see what the hell he wanted, riding her bumper for the past 20 miles. Before she could budge, she saw the gun flash against the sunlight, and an explosion ripped near her temple.

The next memory she had was one month later, waking up in a rehab center after weeks in a coma. Just as I had, she had survived what most couldn't. She didn't so much limp as lean, and she forgot things but wanted to work and the residents adored her. They didn't mind if she failed to pack fresh ice in their water pitchers or changed their diapers twice in a row or not at all. She did fine as long as she stayed on the same hall, saw the same faces. If no one steered her down another floor, she could perform her duties and do so quite well.

We had an easy friendship, easier than with some of the victims of abuse I'd met during my long-ago required group therapy visits—those women who'd go back to their partners, or who got better and moved on, no visible wounds and disabilities to glue them to hell. Kathy and I had both been in critical condition, all but dead as we lingered in Intensive Care, both of us too stubborn to die. Both of us mothers of small children so that we couldn't die. Somebody had to pack peanut butter sandwiches and wait in the pickup lines after school. Somebody had to sign newly fatherless children up for Cub Scouts and tap dancing, hold them in the night through fevers and stomach flu and dreams of their daddies coming to kill them or polish off their mommies.

"He's yanking your chain," she said, her one-sighted eye boring into the letters, the other eye blinded by the .32 caliber bullet. "Mine did that at first. I didn't respond and it stopped. He'll stop." She took her paper bag out and unwrapped a tuna sandwich and a bag of Ruffles, three baby carrots and a Kosher dill. I sat with her through her lunch break and drank a Diet Coke and ate a Snickers bar, my stomach too unsettled for real food as I waited on Miss Annie Sue Higgins to get gussied up for her final trip to the Department of Motor Vehicles where she would try once more to get her driver's license renewed.

Tomorrow was her 104th birthday. After that date the license expired. Everyone but me was against her taking the test, especially her driving her Skylark to the DMV four miles down the road, but I thought it was an excellent idea, a way for her to grab a touch of hope from a life that was way past its expectancy. She was in many ways like a car that manages to go 60 more miles on an empty tank of gas.

"I'll take her," I'd said to Theresa. "I'll ride with her."

Her power of attorney, an only son 80 years old and with all warmth either aged out or never within him, signed a paper allowing this to transpire. He didn't think she'd pass the test. He had full confidence that after today, he'd never have to worry about her cranking that Skylark and taking off from the nursing home again. He had tried everything he knew to get her out of that car, but it was what the woman lived for—midnight trips to Wal-Mart when she could swing it, escaping like a 14 year old from her bedroom window. The staff got smart enough to take Annie Sue's keys and give them to her only when they could supervise and restrict her driving to the back lot behind the rest home.

What could be the harm in that as long as she remained in the designated place to practice her parallel parking and 180-degree turns? I believe Annie Sue just loved the feel of the keys as she inserted them into the ignition. She loved hearing the ancient car roar to life. It's not that she needed to drive to Wal-Mart or Piece Goods for swatches of material or yarn. She just wanted to be able to sit in her car, adjust her mirrors and legally drive to the post office to mail a woman who'd been dead 20 years a birthday card.

"You okay?" Kathy asked, finishing her lunch.

"Yeah. It's just the letters. I can't figure out how he got our address and why the prison officials won't stop them. I've called them twice and get nothing but the run-around."

I asked Kathy, more rhetorically than expecting an answer. "How do you think Bryce found us? We have new names, a new location."

"Don't think about it, Dee," Kathy said, tuna on her chin. "He *wants* you to think about it. It's his way of still controlling and abusing you. Most of them do this from prison. I promise if you don't write back, it'll stop. Mine did, like I said. And he's up for parole in two years. Serving five is all the bastard got."

"My God. Shot you and is serving five years. Maybe I'll call my lawyer about the letters."

"Couldn't hurt. But it's a waste of time and money. He'll stop when he discovers it's hopeless."

"Bryce is smart. If he pores over law books in the prison library the way he studied his Bible, he'll find that loophole he's searching for, some way out of serving his time."

Kathy fished around her empty lunch bag, forgetting she'd finished her lunch. Sometimes, she just trailed off, forgot what we were talking about, her short-term memory stolen by that bullet.

It was the routine, the sameness, that kept her sane. Tuna, Ruffles, the east wing of the manor, a schedule that never changed. The occupational therapist had told her to try a few changes, modifications that would stimulate her brain, but she wasn't up for that. We aren't the types who can take all the suggestions therapists throw at us. It's enough to even step into their offices, see all the smiling, bruiseless women on the shiny magazine covers in the waiting lounges, a room palpable with others' problems.

"He ain't going anywhere," she said. "I'm prepared. I got a license to carry a gun, so if mine gets out and tries to pull something. I've got a trigger I plan on pulling."

Annie Sue peered into the break room.

"I'll be right with you, sweetie," I said to the old woman, her wig on sideways, her lipstick smeared to her nose. "Listen, Kathy. I'll be back in a couple of hours to help you with the baths and showers. Don't do too much, okay?"

"No, I won't," she said and stood to leave. "I just want you to know one thing. Not all men are bad. I have a new boyfriend who treats me like a princess. We just picked bad the first go-round. There's hope, honey. Just lay low and take it easy and quit worrying."

"I'm going to take your advice," I said. "I'll forget about those dumb letters."

"What letters?" she asked. "Was that what we were talking about? Oh, heavens. My memory. I pray every night it will quit blinking on and off like a firefly."

"It'll be all right, Kathy. We'll talk later," I said and nodded toward Annie Sue. I gave Kathy no indication the letters was a topic she and I had been discussing just moments ago. She got upset when someone pointed out she'd forgotten the past five minutes of her life.

"I'm all ready and cute as teenager," Annie Sue announced with a head tilt that nearly toppled her wig and a wide-open pop of the mouth, as if she'd been suddenly surprised. "You like these earbobs, or should I wear my red-white'n-blue flags on account of all this here patriotism since the world turned nasty on us?"

I feasted on the sight before me, the tall Annie Sue Higgins, not a bent bone in her upright body, 104 years of fitness and calcium-rich living. She could high-kick like a Rockette and often did, parading down the halls like some ancient majorette. She led the exercise classes three days a week in the activities room, taking the breath of even the staff who were a fraction her age. She'd march and strut down the Top of the Hill's hallways in her polyester pants that yielded enough to allow her sudden and limber movements.

She jogged a turtle-paced mile every morning, those stick legs looking like pencils wrapped in wrinkled tissue paper. They were streaked orange from her repeated massacres with Banana Boat's Deepest Darkest self-tanner. She even wore a jogging bra, though I'm not sure why because, from the looks of things in her nightgowns, whatever she had going had hit the knees half a century earlier.

"I've studied all them signs," she said, opening a stained beige purse at least 50 years old and smelling stale and old-ladyish as she rummaged for her glasses. I was thinking Miranda would adore that purse. "I just hope the good Lord will allow me a speck of vision. You know that's why I failed them other two times. I couldn't see a lick. If Big Foot stepped in that department of cars, I wouldn't have seen him either."

She led me to her Skylark, which was parked in the hot sun, broiling like a foil-wrapped Idaho potato on Bake 450. She entered the old clunker, reached over to unlock my door and then stuck her key in without making the complete rotation to start the ignition.

Annie Sue sat there, windows tighter than a coffin's seal, chatting about the various questions that might be on the test. I sat, patiently at first, but grew woozy from the heat. She checked her makeup and wig position in the rearview mirror. She wiped off a few streaks of Coty coral lipstick that had bled on her nose, which too many years on this earth had caused to sag and sort of fall toward her top lip. She didn't seem to mind or care unless she was in the car, which produced in her a Pavlovian response, signaling her into primp mode.

"You got any rouge?" she asked, twisting her wig around in the other direction, not an improvement, but satisfactory to her just the same.

"Yes, I'm sure I do, Miss Annie."

"Well dig it out, would ya? I look like I died six months ago."

Several minutes of intense, idle heat had built in the car when I gave up and said to her, "I'll hand it over as soon as you crank the engine and run the AC, all right?" I didn't talk to her in the same voice we used for many of the residents, the baby talk that seems to soothe the demented but must be irritating to those who possess their faculties. I talked to Annie Sue as if she were a contemporary. We all did. She wouldn't have it any other way.

She started the engine and it sputtered, the initial misgivings of old cars whose mechanisms coughed and finally caught. Annie Sue yanked the gear into reverse and turned in the tiny space allotted her, a place far removed from the other cars and pedestrian crossings. She pounded and slapped the manual steering as if it were a horse, finally getting it turned around the right way as she aimed the car's broken and hanging hood ornament toward the road, hugging the left lane as she drove. I could hear the car eating bushes and leaves, could feel the tug of the plants she beheaded, deflowered, scalped and shredded.

She did not take notice and proceeded to the end of the parking lot where the area widened until it opened onto the highway. Not until we were in the middle of the road, cars coming in both directions, did she remember the stop sign 10 yards back.

Car horns blared and tires screeched. I was wearing a lap belt, the only kind made back in 1971 when her Skylark came off a Detroit assembly line. The force of the stop hurled me forward into the scorching dashboard, my head thrown like a rag doll's from her slamming on the brakes.

"What's the matter with these drivers?" she shouted. "Ought'n a one of them should have a license. Call the law, Dee. Call 911 on your cell phone, you hear?"

"Settle down, Miss Annie. Come on and inch over here to this side of the road and we should be fine till we get to the light up ahead."

"What light? I don't see no light!"

This must be a death wish, a secret subliminal way to end my life since these letters came from Bryce. This wasn't the right moment to give Bryce a thought in my head, not when I needed to concentrate on keeping Annie from getting us killed before we could get her to the DMV. She made it to the traffic light, but didn't consider applying her brakes. I bit my lip and gripped the aqua vinyl seat that was cracked and sprouting yellowed foam.

She raised her giant size-10 foot in its Reebok cross-trainer, the only evidence of a modern world on her presence, and pounded the brake as we came within half an inch of hitting a Subaru in front of us.

"Shit," I yelled without thinking.

Annie slapped her long skinny thigh, her skirt inching up to reveal a set of beige knee highs she'd worn on top of her pantyhose. "See there, girlie," she hooted, a bit of gold flashing in her otherwise solid, century-old teeth, not a single tooth absent. "I missed it, didn't I? I didn't hit one car, honey pie."

We continued the risky journey, Annie's blinkers going left, then right, though we had no plans to turn for at least a mile and a half. The blinkers ticked louder than a grandfather clock, and she bobbed her head to the beat, as if it were music coming from her radio that hasn't made a sound other than static since 1985. She worked the steering wheel and floorboard pedals like a church organist in the midst of inspiration. She'd start, then stop, our heads wobbling and other cars flipping the poor lady off and cursing from behind tinted windows. After 10 minutes of mobile hell, we turned into the DMV, and Annie squinted from behind her two-inch thick glasses and eased into a parking space, about two feet over one of the white stripes and spilling into the empty space next to her.

After we got out of the car, I inspected the vehicle for damage and began an inventory. It did not look good. The car was scraped and dented, and metal parts sprung out as a result of her evening drives in Top of the Hill's back region. The hedge clipping earlier hadn't helped matters. The rear bumper and trim along the car's side resembled a healthy plant, flowing with vines and blooms, greenery that had been snatched out of the earth this very afternoon as we left the nursing home grounds.

"We need to remove all this before we go in, or when you take the driving test, it's not going to go in your favor," I suggested. "It looks as if you've been driving in a jungle."

"I have no apologies to make," she said, applying a third coat of coral to her lips. "I do the best I can, and that's all a girl can do."

It was still lunchtime for many people in town and the DMV was packed as usual. Annie Sue patted her wig and entered the building, talking loud, on account of her hearing loss and her nature in general. One of her knee-highs had given up and hung loose around her scrawny ankle, and despite her efforts, her wig was slipping, revealing a swath of white silvery hair matted to her skull.

Soon, every dour face in the building had perked up and focused its attention on Miss Annie Sue Higgins, turning 104 tomorrow.

She crinkled her coral nose at the long curving line and shouted to the curious audience: "I ought to have brought my dinner with me. We're having chicken pot pie today at the old folks home, and from the sight of things, I'm gonna be missing out. Where's the buffet line?" A few people snickered, even the sour-pussed DMV officials knew they were in for a treat and began loosening their efficiency-stiffened bodies.

"Looky here," she said to me as I stood next to her like a private-duty nurse or a devoted granddaughter. "If you walk me to where we're supposed to go, I'll just follow your big old large rump." If anyone else had said it, I might have been miffed, but coming from her it fared more tolerably.

The whole place was cracking up or on the verge of hysterics. Annie Sue broke in line, making no apologies whatsoever, and no one dared or even wanted to stop her. They didn't want to miss a thing.

"Here I am, madam of the highways, now let's get on with it," she said to a woman in a uniform and pair of horn-rims, the latest in nerd fashions. "Before we start, I'd like to say a few things for the record." The woman lowered her glasses and waited. "I want you people to take notes. Get out your pad. I want it in my permanent record that I've been driving for near about 90 years and I haven't run over anybody yet nor have I got myself run over, you hear?"

The entire line cracked up and even the people taking their tests couldn't stop themselves.

"I just want you to know that no matter how I do on this vision test, all that I just done told you ought to count for something. Write all that down, hear?"

The DMV woman, non-plussed, told Miss Annie Sue where to stand and where to peer.

"I'll be using these to help out a tad," she said, taking out of her old handbag an enormous magnifying glass, which she held up to her thick glasses that she now pressed against the viewfinder. "I don't see no signs. Where are them signs you want me to talk about?"

"Miss Higgins, if you would relax, the testing will soon begin. Please, when you see one of the signs, take a moment, collect your thoughts and then say aloud the names of the signs you see. Is this understood?"

"I'm ready," she said, turning back to wink at her new fans, then leaning in and studying, rocking back and forth in her cross-trainers, both knee-highs now falling from her pantyhose. She let out a yelp of recognition once her brain clicked into gear. "Lord, I know that sign. That's a deer in the road. I've never hit one of them, if you'd like to go ahead and put that down in my permanent record. Never hit a deer in the road. That oughta count for something, you reckon?"

She continued with the test, stealing precious lunch hour time, though no one seemed to mind in the least.

"Side road, divided highway, two-way traffic, crooked road," she announced. "I'm always coming across crooked roads over 'round Boiling Springs as you near the mountains," she said, adding commentary to her signs test. "It's a nice drive if you—"

"Miss Higgins, continue with the testing, please," the woman with the horn-rims said.

"Speed Limit . . . I've never broken the speed limit, or if I have, I ain't never been caught and have no plans to tell you all about it." She turned again and faced her devoted fans. She let that mouth pop open in a Phyllis Diller sort of way and returned to the signs. "I'm not sure the official name of this sign but I know it means traffic's a'comin' thataway," she said, throwing her long thin arm out to the left and hitting the nearby man waiting on his documents.

"All right, Miss Higgins, if you'll let me know what that last sign is you see in the window, please."

"Lord, God almighty, I haven't the foggiest," she said, more to herself than the tester. "Shoot. I've seen it hundreds of times. Let's see it's the . . . the . . . ain't that the little old cripple person logo?" she asked, and everyone broke into laughter, even the DVM officials.

"What's it called?" the tester asked, giggling, losing all professional pretense. She began fanning herself as Miss Annie struggled with the Handicapped Parking sign.

"Poor little bent-ups," she said. "I ain't never had a problem with my bones and joints. Looky here, I don't know what they call that sign, but I sure as Christmas know that if I saw one of them little crippled up people I'd give them a lift. I'd put 'em in my car and take 'em where they wanted to go. I'd give them a coupla dollars if I had it on me."

"Tell us the name of the sign, please," the woman said, having a fit of laughter, halfway rolling out of her chair.

"Shuuuuuuuut up," Annie Sue said, slapping that thigh, mouth popping open again, wig whirling, crowd going wild. "I just can't accommodate you there. Let's move on to the next one."

"That's all there is, Miss Higgins," the DMV tester said, trying like mad to compose herself.

"How'd I do? Did I pass?"

"More or less," the woman said and the folks lined up at the DMV burst into applause. When it came to the written portion of the testing, Annie Sue wasn't so lucky and continuously pounded her fist in frustration. She knew her eyes were bad, but her short-term memory much worse, as bad as Kathy's. She was licked. It was over. Poor Miss Annie Sue fell into a desperation that was hard to witness.

"You'll need to study up on this some more," the testing administrator said kindly. "Perhaps you could use some new glasses."

"He done gave me the strongest on the market. Look, I know these signs when I see them out yonder on the roads, but when I see them on paper they fly out of my head. Can't you just pass me?"

"You can try again," she said, not realizing Annie Sue's son said this was her last chance.

"I know what I'll do," she said directly to the DMV official. "I'm just not going to let them catch me. I'll wait till after dark then go out and do my business." The crowd hee-hawed. "I know them signs plain as mud, and you people know I know. Go look up my record. I have never in my life hit a cow or a person. I once hit a possum, but it didn't die, and we took it home and nursed it back to good health so something else could run over it later. Surely you people will let that count for something. Put that in my permanent record, too."

As Annie Sue and I left the building, the crowd followed us to the parking lot. They wanted to see first-hand the 104-year-woman who drove herself to the Department of Motor Vehicles. As she ground the gear into reverse, she was growing angrier by the minute and muttering up a storm.

She rolled down her window as she backed out and nearly hit three cars. She beat the brakes, losing her wig once and for all, and offered her wildly excited fans a hearty wave.

They cheered as if watching a parade.

We came to the first traffic light and Annie Sue put the car in park and handed me the keys.

"Take the wheel," she said. "I could use a beer."

"A beer? But you don't drink."

"I do now."

"Why?"

"I made it a rule all my life. Never drink and drive. Now I can't drive. So let's go drink."

I called Theresa Jolly on my cell phone, compliments of my father who said I should never be without one, that I should have had one the day Bryce did his business at BI-LO, not that a phone could have prevented any of it.

"She didn't make it," I said, and I could hear relief right through the blanks in the connection.

"Praise the Lord," Theresa said.

"She wants to go have drinks," I said.

"Drinks? Alcohol? Annie Sue's never touched the stuff."

"Well, she wants to now," I said.

"I'll have to call her next of kin and get back with you. I mean, we believe in making our people happy, but this is slightly unconventional. 'Course Annie Sue's not of the normal variety either."

Theresa rang me right back.

"He says, and I quote, 'Tank her up. As long as she can't drive, I don't care what she does.' Y'all call me if you need a ride home," Theresa said, giggling like a high school girl. "Dee, you are on the clock. I don't know about your drinking habits, but you best abstain in this situation. Not that I think you'd do otherwise."

I drove the Skylark into an Applebee's. Annie Sue gave me an odd look.

"I want to go to a bar," she said. "A real bar with men who have tattoos and ride motorcycles. This is a priss parlor. I can eat Thai chicken or I can drink beer, and I done told you which I was in the mood for."

Oh, Sweet Jesus, help us all. I got back on the highway and drove her straight to Bubba's Hideaway, the roughest place I knew. We entered the dark hole of a tavern, a haven from the blinding oven of a mid afternoon that was cloudless and pure mean. Nothing but a cruel afternoon with no rain in the forecast for days.

Opening the door was like falling into a black gopher hole, but it was cool from the blasting of four or five of those frigid window units. The place smelled like misplaced dreams and early drunks. A song by Sheryl Crow, "All I Wanna Do Is

Have Some Fun," played on the jukebox, and I found myself getting into the spirit of things.

Annie Sue grinned at every redneck and boozer in the joint, moseyed straight up to the bar and ordered a draft.

"Wanna see some I.D.?" she asked, opening that mouth, slapping her license on the counter which showed her to be hours away from her 104th year.

Bubba raised a shot of tequila to toast her as he poured the foam off her beer. She downed it in three or four swallows, then asked for two more before I led her wobbling out the door and back into the stifling heat.

"I'd rather drink than drive any day," she said, falling into the Skylark, wig thrown to the floorboard. I managed to get her partially buckled in, but before we got to Top of the Hill, she was snoring as loud as those old men back at the home.

"We're here," I said as we drove into her parking spot, cutting life from the Skylark, maybe for the last time. Maybe not. I looked at Annie Sue. No, probably not.

It took three of us to get her inside and into bed, her carrying on about a conspiracy against old folks at the DVM and a son who never loved her because she had him out of wedlock during the days when that was a mortal sin worthy of a woman's public stoning. All her secrets were pouring out like the draft from the tap at Bubba's.

"He ought to be more grateful," she slurred. "Where's my chicken pot pie? I need me some dinner, Dee. Hell, I guess that's not as bad as what you need," she said and tilted her skinny face right up at mine, her teeth showing and her breath smelling of wet bread and bars.

"What might that be, Miss Annie Sue?" I said, easing her agile body into bed.

"You need a man, sister. A capital M, capital A, capital N. MAN."

"That's what my Mama says. I say women don't need a thing but self confidence, good friends, family and a pint of happiness."

"You listen to your Mama. Now run get me a gin and tonic and we'll say our goodbyes out on the veranda." Oh, my, she was slipping into a fog of dementia brought on by yeast and hops, heat and Harleys.

She did have a point. With my pitiful wages and lack of prospects, my age inching toward the Uglying Up Decade, what Aunt Weepie calls the "Falling Forties" for a girl, I'd better get busy. All right, tomorrow I'd begin my search, not so much for me but for the children. I'd even date half-wits as long as they were too stupid for violence. My children wouldn't go another year without decent male influence. If I couldn't have the inner city surgeon with Labrador eyes, I'd date anything with health insurance, half his teeth and a fine attitude. I'd do a criminal check and then a body search. Hmmm.

"The way Jay is," Mama would say, "all those brains. Well, his kind can go either way. You need an influence for him, hon. Someone with lots of testosterone. Remember Amber's husband and take note of his lack thereof."

"I need someone without all those rage-inducing male hormones, Mother. Remember?"

"Well don't go bringing an effeminate man into our lives. I mean, I love them and they certainly are good decorators and dance partners, but let's not haul another one in the family. Your sister's 'beloved' hasn't taught her eldest the first thing about baseball or basketball. For all I know they just play with that Pomeranian he brought home and rearrange the furniture every few days." She rattled on about my lack of prospects and I listened, knowing it was useless to argue.

"Prudy, I have waited two years before pushing. Fact is, I thought for a while I was going to be the one to raise Jay and Miranda. Then one day the good Lord listened to my prayers and rose up a half-dead woman for a reason. Now go find him."

"Soon, Mama." I knew she meant well. "I'm really capable of handling things and taking care of myself."

"No, you aren't. That's all I'm going to say because I have a headache and don't want to fight with you."

It's such an effort getting to know a person from scratch. I'd rather have a just-add-water type. A meal-in-a-box.

Maybe I could recycle like the old days. That's an idea. Let's see. Memory lane time. I could go to the library, since I was too chicken to do Match.com at this particular stage in my redevelopment, and do a search on the good old Google engine. I'd pretty much already tested the idea in my head and narrowed it down to six retreads, but the one I really loved like crazy is iffy because he tinkled on our lawn, and my mother may not tolerate giving him another go-round in our lives. There were others she wouldn't tolerate either.

Nobody I've ever brought home was good enough in her eyes.

Oddly, Bryce was.

# *Chapter Nine*

**Hey Dee:** *A murderer's conscience will drive him to hell. Don't stop him.* ***Proverbs 28:17***

**Mama's Moral:** *Allow him to lay in the bed he has made. A bed of hot coals.*

LATELY, I'VE BEEN wondering what caused me to marry Bryce Jeter, as if I'm searching for a flaw in my psyche that led me to a potential murderer.

Most people who knew Bryce would have never thought him capable of what he'd done, but thought him quite the catch, actually. He gave no indication during the "courtship" leading to our marriage, which occurred just two months from the day I got the enormous pear-shaped ring pressed between Psalms in the King James Bible. *Note to self: never again marry a man who offers the pear-shaped diamond. Something about its odd shape could be ominous.*

The wedding was in his church, a small ceremony with my family and his, weirdoes from Virginia who never looked people in the eye, the mother's interest held somewhere in the floor area, the father's fixated on every woman's breasts and buttocks who walked in his line of vision. He had a rectangular head with wedged and hinged features that were a blend of cartoonish and perverted, almost like a ventriloquist's dummy. And he was shifty. He all but swallowed my sister Amber whole, taking her in from her teased blond bangs to red-painted toes, salivating over every attribute and hardly saying two words to me, the bride. He did seem rather appreciative of my 36-Cs, which prior to nursing babies, I kept elevated in good bras.

Dr. Peter Jeter, yes, that's his real name, so everyone was required to call him Pete or Doc Jeter, is an oral surgeon. This made my mother extremely happy. She figured if her daughter couldn't have married a doctor, at least her father-in-law was one. It was a thing with my mama and her friends, all upper-middle-class suburban housewives who'd grown up in mill villages and podunk towns and wanted a higher rung on the social ladder for their own children.

They'd just as soon put ads in the paper in desperate efforts to marry their girls off to doctors. Many were quite successful, their pretty young belles walking down the aisles with some of the ugliest, most boring medical men this planet had ever coughed up.

"Bryce is working on his Ph.D.," I had told Mama during the frenzied four weeks in which we shopped for a wedding dress, mailed out invitations, ordered flowers, a caterer and a harpist for the reception, which to my bourbon-loving daddy's disappointment, included nothing harder than 7-Up and sherbet punch.

I walked down the yellow-gold carpet of Beaver Creek Baptist Church and nodded as I passed each pew, festooned in silk magnolias and loads of white velvet bows. I carried real magnolia blossoms in my bouquet along with daisies and baby's breath. To have spritzed perfume would have been useless and a waste considering the way that Baptist church smelled on my wedding day. Not even the loudest perfume, which in my opinion is a tossup between Beautiful and Red Door, could break through the natural barrier of all the flowers Mama and Aunt Weepie had managed to squeeze into the church.

I felt like a princess in my $1,200 form-fitting dress with a short train, my veil a pearled and netted work of art. Vera Wang couldn't have done better.

Bryce's mother never said a word, only grimaced in my direction and redirected her gaze back toward the floor, which had some sort of hold on the woman. She trembled. She cowered. She was a timid, shaking creature with the palest blond hair and features, almost as if fear had bleached her, or was it regret or the fatigue of giving up on life before its second act? She got her doctor, why wasn't she happy?

My mama, effervescent and more bubbly than a case of champagne, tried her best to engage the woman but never got beyond a semi-paralytic smile, an uh-huh, and once, when the woman didn't think my mama was looking, my new monster-in-law cast an evil eye that would have sheared the wool off a sheep. I saw it but felt no need to mention it.

My mother's the type to keep on talking and charming, filling up a room with her utter vivaciousness. She laughs and heads turn, people wanting to hear her stories, wanting to be near her, all but that Chihuahua of a mother-in-law I was inheriting. Lord, what was her deal?

My mama is one of life's subtle stars, not the kind who has to get noticed and steal all the attention, but the kind who snags it effortlessly. She hugs everyone she meets, finding a genuine compliment to give someone, even if she has to think on it for several days. There was a disfigured man at her church, scalded from a pot of greens when he was a baby, and the burns left him without much of a face. Mama walked up to him one Sunday morning and said, "Wayne Sutton, I've never in my life heard a man sing as beautifully as you. Now why don't you join that choir up there? I imagine the choir members of heaven couldn't sing any prettier." After that he was a different person, wore himself the white and royal blue robes of the Pleasant Hill Missionary Baptist Church Choir, holding his burned head high, smiling as wide as those lips made from nipple and inner thigh would allow.

She has that effect on people. She brings them up and out of whatever depression they're swallowed by, and whatever is ailing them grows distant, like when you look at a pattern of lines or dots for so long you can't even see them after a few minutes. They become a blur, absorbed with the rest of life's patterns and problems. Mama spouts a potion of words and way of saying them and spins them so fast the healing comes much sooner than it would have had the world been left to putter at its own dinky pace.

Daddy is her opposite, a quiet type who likes to knock back a couple of bourbons before dinner on an empty stomach so the glow and buzz will keep until dusk. When he's in that state of Jim Beam grace he tells stories on Mama's funnier stabs at compliments.

"Ask her what she said to the gynecologist," he said, from his green easy chair where he roosts at night and rules the world as he sips from a tall glass of life-easing nectar. "Go on, Lucy, tell them what you said."

"It's Lucinda. You know better than to call me Lucy. Sounds like a woman who wants sex all the time."

"Well, don't you sweet Luuuuuuuuucy?" Ah, the delicious daddy buzz that put a cherry on top of our childhood.

"I'm not going to tell that story to my children."

"Tell them, sweetheart. They're grown women."

She shook her head and pretended to be embarrassed, but we knew she wanted that story told.

Without missing his cue, Daddy kicked back the easy chair to its farthest recline and took another sip of what my sister and I called his sandpaper, on account of how it smoothed life's rough spots for him.

"Your mama was at the gynecologist's last week," he said, holding his face as straight as possible. "After she'd gotten her feet unhooked and her clothes back on, the old fart called her into his office for the report."

Before Daddy could finish his story, Mama jumped right in, not wanting her thunder stolen. "He said, 'Lucinda, I have to tell you that's the cleanest, healthiest vagina I've ever seen on a woman your age. You ought to be right proud of that firm, youthful vagina. Won't have to tack up your bladder or uterus.'" Mama was hee-hawing. Daddy got to laughing his wheezy sick-dog laugh and said, "Your mama walked right over to his desk and hugged him. Can you believe it? She was so happy to get a possum compliment at her age."

"The possum doesn't age, Parker," Mama said. Amber and I were the only children in South Carolina, perhaps the whole world for that matter, whose parents called the female privates a possum.

On the day of my wedding, my mother must have thought for 48 hours straight—from the moment of the rehearsal dinner at the Steak and Ale, due to its special place in our hearts (Bryce and I met there when I was waiting tables)—to the time we all sat around eating buttermints and wishing for real food, trying to muster up a compliment to give Mrs. Pauline Jeter.

In the meantime, Mama kept right on smiling at the woman, scaring her witless as she would suddenly appear with a fresh cup of punch or coffee or a story to tell.

How could Bryce's own mother, a "giblet," according to my mother, who uses this original term for all of the world's wimpy, sad-sack women, not have fallen directly and irretrievably under her spell? Heaven knows Mama was trying her hardest.

I couldn't stop looking at the Jeters—Dr. Peter Jeter with his wooden, unnatural looks, and the giblet mother, squirrel-like in her movements and the way she held her little hands when she ate. She could have been a ballerina in another more confident lifetime.

I saw my reflection in the mirror near the refreshment line, my olive eyes brought up a notch by the stark white dress and my waist indented and of the sort June Cleaver might have had if she sipped an occasional beer or glass of wine. Looking back, I wondered how a normal, way-above-average-looking (at least on my wedding day) woman could agree to marry a man without first having met and road tested the future in-laws.

I remember the quick, one-time introduction on a Sunday as he tried out for a position at one of the churches. I didn't know I'd be marrying the man, so I hardly gave them much thought or attention.

On my wedding day, from all I can recall, I was happy. I can remember basking in my husband's fine physical glow, thinking I was the luckiest woman in the world despite his parents being the way they were. I could look at him for years, watching all 6-foot 3-inches of him and those Bible-toting hands running through his short but thick sandy brown hair that sported random blond streaks. He had the kind of hair that lasts on a man, like good carpeting. My sister's filthy-rich, gay-but-doesn't-know-it husband has two hairs to his name and combs them straight back like a long tongue and greases them down with something from Redken. With all that money inherited from the fried chicken franchise his family owns, I guess if he wanted some plugs and implants, he could most assuredly afford them. For the life of me, I can't figure out why he never had an insurance policy until he met and hooked onto Amber's Blue Cross/ Blue Shield card.

If I had to find flaw with Bryce, physically speaking, it would be the reverend's square chin inherited from Dr. Peter Jeter, which on Bryce came off as a little harsh given the rest of the package. His other facial features were soft, skin like a young boy's, and I believe he could go a day or two without shaving and no one would know the difference. He had a single dimple, only one. His mother timidly said the other disappeared a month after his eighth birthday and never returned. Maybe something had made him sad, maybe his joy had been kidnapped at that young age when boys smell like mud and small animals and scratch about with dirty hands and nails that are either chewed to pink pads or in need of a scrub and a trim.

When I was 16, a junior in high school, my mama took in an unkempt boy in our neighborhood. He was 7, maybe 8, and his mother had died of breast cancer the year before. He'd ride his old bike over and sit in my mama's easy company and beg her to put him over the shampoo bowl and run hot water through his grime-stiffened hair, the curls coarse and unruly. He'd let out a moan of sheer pleasure as all the dirt swirled down the drain and the smell of Twice As Nice shampoo filled his nose, Mama's strong hands working his head into suds and softness.

We'd dry him off and read him a story about the "Little Engine That Could" or "Stuart Little" and show him what a family could be like. He'd come over every day, every single day for two years, relishing in the very services most regular kids fuss about. A bath to him was glory. A supper with different colored foods on the plate, with milk in glasses and buttered biscuits peeping from cloth-covered baskets and the admonishments from my mother when he didn't wash up, were words from heaven.

Mama wanted to adopt him, as she had no boys, but the widowed man and his son moved away after a couple of years, and I don't know whatever happened to them. I think his name was Landon. That was it. Landon, like the father in *Little House on the Prairie.* When Landon grinned he had milk-white teeth and two deep dimples. I wonder if he still has them both.

Only the happiest people I've ever met have dimples, which makes me think my Aunt Weepie's entire face should be dimpled, but it's not, only scritch-scratched in smile lines.

***

It was Bryce's eyes that had drawn me in, caused me to go toward the marriage altar in an almost zombied state, having never been the sort of girl to jump into big decisions up until then. His eyes gave him a fourth dimension that transformed the mere skin and bones of the man and turned him within a blink to the otherworldly, a world I had thought was inhabited only by people like Moses and Abraham; and Jesus, Peter and Paul.

His eyes, during most emotions, were an immobile swirl of blue, like a hot sky with no plans to break. Then they would switch like one of those trick cards, holograms from a bubble gum machine. Tilt the card, tilt his mood, and the image changes and Bryce's eyes would flash to a cold, hard gray.

Something else about Bryce caught me besides the magic eyes. It was that body. He was—and I can say this in all honesty—the only man I'd ever slept with who had a shape like a carved piece of modern art. He could have been a naked statue and it would not have been obscene, but breathtaking.

I've found most men either have handsome faces or nice bodies and very few have both. The best bodies have faces that look as if they've grunted too long under a bench press, those hard I'm-about-to-explode-in-a-minute faces. The best looking men were the softer types, whose physiques, while not neglected, didn't seem to be a priority other than the occasional, better-get-in-a-quick-jog-this-afternoon thought.

My mind was on that body when the wedding harp and piano had begun playing and the hour was upon us. Eleven bells chimed and I linked arms with my daddy and he walked me down the aisle, whispering with a faint scent of bourbon on his breath that he loved me and that I was radiant and deserved the dream chest. He would tell me stories when I was a child, not about lost treasures, vast fortunes under the sea and ground, but of wishes that lay in wait in the dream chests.

Everyone had one, he said. "All you have to do is find it, one dream at a time, like the magician who pulls out one silk scarf after the other from his sleeves." Scarves that never seemed to end.

"I hope," he said. "You've found your first dream. The dream chest is mighty deep. As deep as your desires, sweetheart."

I leaned into him closer and stepped, one-two, one-two to the altar, right up next to my soon-to-be husband in his black tuxedo. Our eyes met and he burned a hole through my veil with his gaze. He didn't look happy; nor did he appear sad. He seemed more matter-of-fact, almost in a hurry to get on with things. I imagined he was anticipating our wedding night, the walk on the beach we'd take once we drove to Kiawah Island, only five hours away from the spot on which we stood. He was probably thinking about my body beneath the outfit I'd chosen for my going-away dress, a flowing sheer swirl of fabric of the sort worn by models pictured outracing the sea in magazine spreads. My long legs, toned and aerobicized, would belong, in the name of God, to him and the passion I felt that made me dizzy and drunk.

I needed to know this man, in the truest Biblical sense. We had kissed a few times during our formal courtship, our "dates" to different churches. He'd surprised me with his heat and his groans and the hardness I felt against my skin. I once tried to take his hand and place it on my breast, but he recoiled, saying, "Don't try doing this to me now, Prudy, my lusty bride-to-be." I could see the erection swelling in his khakis. "We have a lifetime for this." He seemed so pure, so different from the other men who were eager to do it all before we even knew each other's favorite ice cream or middle names. It was refreshing not to have a guy think a seafood dinner bought on MasterCard entitled him to, in the very least, a blow job. I'd rather pay for my own damned fish, I told a boy in college who'd bought me stuffed flounder and then all but shoved my head in his lap while he drove down Main Street, straining in his too-tight Levi's.

Bryce had class. He would never do that. He would be gentle; I just knew it from the way he kissed. He would be the kind of lover every woman wanted, the kind to treat love-making like a meal, starting with a warm-up of kisses that would build within themselves and lead down the body toward the places where women burned. He would find my emptiness and fill it. He would go slow, then faster, always adjusting the speed to the preference of his passenger. And he would take me, I knew it, to a place where women were meant to discover the hottest pleasures. On my wedding night, I thought, I would have all of this.

I held Bryce's hand for a moment, could feel his pulse in the thick veins of his hands, and I listened to the minister hired to unite us, a friend of his from school, as he spoke clearly from his Bible, reading the traditional words and then asking us to repeat after him.

It all went smoothly, followed by the dry kiss and an hour of posing for pictures and then a dull reception of mixed nuts, finger sandwiches and the usual foods people eat when they're teetotallers, people my father has always distrusted.

Bryce never touched the stuff. My family wouldn't have minded an open bar or, in the very least, a speck of wine or even a weak champagne punch to toast the newlyweds into their new lives.

Dr. Peter Jeter slipped Bryce an envelope. His mother gave him a cold hug that could have been delivered by a propped-up corpse. She barely let her stiff arms touch him and quickly moved away, ducking toward the food to collect a napkinful of buttermints. I hated such receptions. The buttermint kind. The icy mother-of-the-groom-sneering-at-the floor-and-bride kind.

I wanted a jazz band and good beer, flowing champagne, hot chicken wings and mini quiches, and scallops wrapped in bacon, spinach-and-cheese-stuffed mushrooms, crab dip and crackers, boiled jumbo shrimp, snow crab legs and raw oysters so the men could get rowdy and feel a hint of control at these estrogen-ruled affairs. This one came across as staid and churchy as a reception ever got. It was a shotgun wedding without the baby. Hurried, inexpensive and thrown together.

Only my dress saved the affair. The dress cost exactly half the entire wedding, but Mama wanted to spare no expense. Bryce was the one putting the controls on her spending, saying he didn't want to appear flashy in the eyes of his congregants. Mama and I decided a cheap dress wouldn't do. Not at all. While a woman could semi-forget her other wedding trimmings and details, she'd never forget the dress.

"We'll go with this," Mama had said to the haughty saleswoman at Once in a Lifetime, a boutique of gowns by up-and-coming designers.

I scanned the church fellowship hall while posing with Bryce for those horrible clichéd wedding pictures where we cut the cake and feed it to each other. Trying to be funny, I put a piece on his head and my daddy howled and the flashbulbs popped and Dr. and Mrs. Jeter gave each other a glance I recognized as the "what-are-we-in-for" kind. They thought Bryce had married beneath himself. Beneath him? I had a college degree. My father had one, too, and Amber had herself a gay, rich man with two private planes and all the chicken a girl could ever eat in a lifetime. My mother had two associate's degrees, and most of my kin, thank you very much, had *inground* pools with cabanas for shade.

We had been abroad, on riverboats through Europe, on Mediterranean dinner cruises, and had taken snorkeling trips in St. Croix and the Yucatan of Mexico. We didn't need the hoity-toity festering mouth surgeon and his skittish wife snooting down at us. We didn't need this giblet woman and her giblet ways. If she'd been a bird, she'd have definitely been a finch, a small, unsteady frailty that falls off its perch and dies with the first taste of misfortune.

My family, we were Pterodactyls, big-nosed and swooping, sturdy creatures, roaming the planet in full force and with life beating through our wide-open wings.

Anyone in her right mind would have looked to the left and then to the right, and seen the finches on one side, the Pterodactyls on the other and, right in the center of all this shotgun fare, a three-tiered wedding cake holding up a trace of hope with eggs, Crisco and sugar.

The cake soon became the focus after the photographer had done his appropriate hackneyed shots. Before anyone had time to notice, Aunt Weepie had removed the bride and groom and replaced them with a naked couple—a plastic hooker bride with giant boobs, plastic groom with a huge and very erect penis sporting everything but the pubic hair.

My daddy laughed so hard he had to leave the room. Weepie was falling over in fits, tinkling in her Control tops. Mama said it was on the naughty side and behind her hidden smile she helped poor Mrs. Jittery Jeter replace it with the original. But not before my photographer friend returned for a couple of wonderful close ups.

I was so happy that day, I wanted to cry but didn't. A woman 30 marrying someone as handsome and moral as Bryce Jeter did not count her misfortunes. She counted her blessings. She imagined how wonderful such a person would be as a father and husband. How he would never raise his voice or be the type to cheat or break any commandments. A minister was far preferential to a doctor. He wouldn't have to go out in the night and deliver babies, stare at other women's possums, feel their supple breasts for lumps. He would work a calm job and smile at old ladies with inheritances and delicious offerings, both for the silver collection plate and casseroles weighing down their dining room tables.

We would live in that lovely white Cape Cod, provided by this very church, these very people who didn't really know us but certainly bestowed as many blessings as a plastered grin could hold.

Toward the end of the reception, Mama approached me again.

"You have some good, clean, Christian fun tonight," she said and gave me a big lipsticked kiss on the cheek, which later showed up in three of the wedding pictures. "You've remained a virgin for this long. Time to give the old preacher his big reward. He's given you his."

"What's that?' I asked, trying to keep people from listening in on this conversation.

"His name. What else, Prudy? I've told you and Amber since you were old enough to know what a possum is, that if a girl holds it pure and untouched, it's the best gift she could give her husband on the wedding night."

Great. I'm going to give Bryce Jeter the old possum-roo tonight. That sounded so romantic.

"I'm sure he's so excited he'll bust," I said, and she shook her finger in a shame-shame and swished away in search of her husband who was sneaking bourbon from his flask and dumping it into the punch bowl.

I wanted to tell her she was crazy. She knew I wasn't a virgin. She knew I'd lived with two men on a part-time basis before I'd hooked up with the preacher. What did she think I did in those houses with those men? Vacuum? Fold their clothes? But some part of me felt all the sins I held in my private closet could be finally cleansed and righted upon wedding a man with a direct line to the Lord. Believe me, Southern women who grow up Baptist hold onto guilt the way some men hold onto money.

I mingled with the guests for about half an hour, then noticed my mother standing in a daze by the punch bowl, staring into her cup.

"You all right?"

"Some days I don't know who I am," Mama said absent-mindedly as the pianist played and one or two bold couples tried to find enough merriment and courage to dance in a Baptist church basement. "It's the change. One minute you're certain of your convictions and beliefs and so calm with life, and then all of a sudden you want to hop on a plane and say, 'One way, please.'"

"Really?" This was new to me. Who was this woman? Half an hour ago she was my mother. I laughed suddenly. Daddy had given her a full cup of his doctored-up punch, and she had no idea it was loaded with truths in the form of Jim Beam. Normally, she never drank anything stronger than a glass of wine or a weak bloody Mary. "Oh, I need a proverb," she said. "Where's my Bible when I'm craving a proverb?" She sipped her punch lustily. "Parker!" she hollered after my dad. "Go out to the car and get me a proverb, hon."

He didn't budge. But he would. He had to hear a request three to six times like most men.

"I love you despite all your proverbs," I said to Mama, and we cried, mother and daughter, while the Jeters stood off to the side and ate their crustless cucumber sandwiches, neither speaking to the other. That brief time I'd met them before the wedding, I found it odd how Pauline cowered when the good doctor came near. How she jumped up like a frightened child, scooting around the room as if she were the maid, pouring tea and coffee and tending to him like he was some sort of visiting dignitary and not her husband of 35 years.

At 1:10 p.m. the event was finally over. I shed my corseted body of the spectacular wedding dress, Mama promising to send it off to be sealed and cleaned and preserved for my own daughter I was certain I'd have one day. "That is, hon, unless you wait too long and then you'll have yourself a Downs baby. Don't get me wrong, they are precious but don't grow up tall or thin enough to wear size-8 designer gowns. I'm not sure they can legally marry. Parker, can a Downs child—"

"Mama!"

As soon as I'd thrown the bouquet and stepped into the plain and undecorated car with no exclamations of "Just Married!" or rattling cans and streamers, we were on our way to a honeymoon, five days on Kiawah Island, an upper-middle-class inlet of ocean, 30 minutes outside of Charleston, a tiny playground for those with money. A church member had loaned Bryce her vacation home free of charge, all in the name of the Lord and getting to Heaven.

As soon as he hit the accelerator and turned out of the church parking lot, his eyes flashed and changed, those trick-card eyes. He grabbed my hand with urgency as we entered the second hour of our marriage.

"Things will be fine," he said. "You just follow my lead. Like the Bible says, and we'll be okay."

I scooted next to him as he drove, both hands gripping the wheel of his Mercury, official car of the middle class GOP. I tried to kiss his strong perfect hand and he flinched. I saw it, felt it. There was a slight jerk of his muscles, as if I were Sin in Disguise, which is what he'd come to call me over the next six years. Sin in Disguise.

Still, I sat there closely, not leaning my Eve-in-the-garden head on his, for that would seem too bold, too risky, but at least sitting close enough that I could smell him, that clean mix of Dove soap and Calvin Klein cologne. I wanted to touch him so much I hurt. I wanted to feel his thighs, inch down in the spotless Mercury, way down, and give him the first real taste of the kind of preacher's wife I aimed to be. I didn't even need a seafood dinner to do what I had planned for our honeymoon drive. Submit. I'd show him some Southern submission, all right.

Just wait until he saw what I was wearing—and not wearing—under my going-away dress. Just wait until he saw my 130-pound, thinnest-since-college body, bronzed from the ten sessions at Malibu Express. Just wait. He would praise Jesus like he never had in his life.

This is what I thought would happen, even as we got out of our car and walked up the stairs to the adorable gray, cedar villa, overlooking a calm bend in the Atlantic Ocean, sun beginning to fatten with first indications of setting, a golden warmth made bearable by a breeze delivered with generous enthusiasm. The air smelled like salt and sea and whispers of ocean life.

This is not, however, what happened. I've never told a soul what really happened on what is probably the worst honeymoon on record. Not Mama, not Aunt Weepie, not Amber. No one. It was too awful.

Once, in the courtroom, woozy from pain medication and thinking doctors may have to amputate my lower leg, I almost blurted it out. But I didn't. The state had its case. I didn't need to air one more set of dirty undies on my heavy line.

***

I'm not sure what bit of nerve wove itself into my brain, but later that night I turned on the computer, and, instead of checking the weather and other mundane news, I Google-searched people. I needed to find my old boyfriend. I poured a glass of Chardonnay, compliments of Aunt Weepie because she said my future funeral antics were certain to make her proud and were guaranteed to be good for business. I took a long sip from a plastic cup, wishing I had a set of glamorous wine glasses. It tasted of oak and bitter, rotten fruit, but I drank anyway—for courage, for a bit of peace of mind. Maybe I was drinking to remember or maybe to forget.

Maybe I drank because Bryce never let me.

The search proved easier than I could have ever dreamed. I typed in "Croc Godfrey," the most luscious, talented, kindest boyfriend I ever had, but the one who peed on Daddy's lawn one night when he and a bunch of other boys got rowdy on Miller Lites and sang off-color "Christmas" carols, changing the words and throwing in a few profanities. This is what ended our relationship.

"You ever see that boy again and you're out of this house for good," Daddy yelled the next morning, climbing into his old Mustang and driving to Croc's house at six a.m. to tattle on him and wring his neck. "Any boy into rock'n'roll and naming his band 'Snatch' is a no-good hoodlum you aren't going to be seeing again. I'll make sure of that." The engine roared, rubber burned on our white cement drive and off Daddy went. No more Croc Godfrey. He was as much afraid of seeing me then as I was of my father.

Time passing is both a beautiful and heartbreaking reality. The years gone by soften things, blur them in the mind and distort facts enough they can often be reabsorbed into other memories. I am pushing 39 and what have I got to lose? What? Is Dad going to come after us both with an ax handle if we end up meeting over a hamburger or cold glass of beer? Croc was probably married and a father of five. He was most likely the Labrador doctor I'd invented who treated his wife with the utmost respect and brought her flowers twice a week.

Only one way to find out. Soon after typing in his God-given name, a list of stories came up. I read the top three and my heart nearly stopped. Oh, my God. No, no, no. Jesus Christ, bless his poor soul.

Surely, all of this couldn't have happened to the Croc I knew. It had to be another Croc, as if there are millions of people with such a name.

Tears pooled, and I turned off the computer. Maybe, just maybe, I'd call him tomorrow. What in the world would I say after reading all of that?

# *Chapter Ten*

**Wake up, Pru – Dang it, I mean Dee:** *Wine gives false courage; hard liquor leads to brawls.* **Proverbs 20:1**

**Mama's Moral**: *If you drink too much, the man you bring into your home won't have a lick of sense. Neither will you. Plus, you'll have bad breath and eye bags.*

**P.S.** *I don't think it's a good idea to take 104-year-old women out drinking! Shame on you, Prudy.*

REGULAR SCHOOL HAD been out for a month and all of Spartanburg had collapsed under this oppressive tin roof of heat. People without ten cents to rub together were calling pool companies and having their back yards dug to uncharted depths for that cement relief. Even those living in single and double-wides were putting above-grounders on their credit cards. Well, at least we had our dented Kmart plastic pool.

Riding down the street, one saw kids playing beneath sprinklers, metal manifolds in plastic framework spinning and spewing overtime to water what hadn't turned brown or given up during the month-long drought.

At night, as I lay in my bed, the high ceiling above me having kidnapped the sun's soul and trapped the apartment with a suffocating wet heat, I started missing the mountains in Asheville.

It is truly a place surrounded in beauty, the blue and purple mountains like layers of protection as they rise up and encircle the city. I had loved it there, the odd mix of people, the deep pockets of mountain folks who lived back in the hills and rural hollers and coves, the city people, artists, many who were brilliant transplants from bigger cities and who'd heard about the freedom in Asheville, the open-mindedness of a region enclosed by mountains.

I missed the rivers and the Parkway, the smell of summers there, an earthy blend of indigenous plants and trees mingled with the faintest trace of mountain flowers, the kind that bloomed beautifully but didn't overpower like the magnolias, gardenias and oleanders of the flatlands. Infused in that cool mountain air were the sharp smells of woodstoves burning in the log cabins and fires roaring in stone hearths as late as early June.

I missed my friends, especially Jenny whom I hadn't seen in more than a year. Bryce had gradually cut me off from most friends while we were married, those he didn't approve of.

"You're a preacher's wife. You'll befriend my congregants."

One by one, the force of his anger behind me, the loss of self in front of me, I eliminated my associations. He had me under his spell, those trick eyes, that way about him that seemed as if I were following a cult leader. Back in my old hometown, I wondered who was still around, who hadn't moved on to bigger cities and better outcomes. I wanted friends. It had been so long. The church women had been nice and a few a lot of fun, but I always held back, and so had they, because I was the preacher's wife.

My thoughts of Asheville shattered at the sound of the old doorbell, no doubt my mother coming to inspect my living conditions, to see if they'd improved post-employment, though she still didn't know I was the local cleaning lady at WUSC radio.

"It feels like hell uprooted out there," Mama said, lugging huge bags of luxuries from Bed Bath and Beyond into my apartment, which over the past month had taken on a more optimistic light. She'd adopted the place as her orphan, and had received lots of pleasure buying seafoam-green towels and a real cloth shower curtain to go around the clawfoot tub, which she scrubbed with bleach, managing to rub all the brown stains out. She'd been watching Trading Spaces on TV late at night and decided to tackle my apartment as her project. We were now the inhabitants of a soothing haven, with thick comforters, lovely candles and end tables, a birch futon with fabrics she selected from a swatch book of fifty choices.

The owners of the old house thought she was insane, but gave her the go-ahead when she decided to hire a painter and turn the exterior of the wooden, faded-to-gray white two-story into a gorgeous shell pink that made me happy every time I drove down the street and saw it, that glorious salmon shade emerging from the pines and magnolias. It's hard to be depressed when you live in a pink house. Mama also painted all the nicked white walls with warm taupe hues, framing them with pretty borders she found at Home Depot and accessories from Pier 1 Imports, where she also chose long, wide rugs of the richest colors for the hardwood floors.

"This is too much, Mama. Really you shouldn't be spending all the money on—"

"I get Social Security checks earlier on account of your Daddy's doings, and I'll spend them on what I want to, thank you very much. These kids need a decent home."

"Well, thank you. Anyway, I've got some news," I said, fanning myself with a rustling bag as she unfurled the new linen placemats and napkins on my kitchen table. She looked at her handiwork and seemed pleased, paying me no attention as she lit a blue and maroon marble candle in the center of the table, a candle that cost as much as my Goodwill chest of drawers.

"I've got a date," I said, piling my long hair up with a clip, finding relief in the smallest ways from this soaking humidity.

"You know, Prudy, Dee, whoever you are, I think I can go back and get that brass corner unit and you could display those pretty new Mikasa plates Amber gave you for your wedding, only dang thing Bryce's people didn't grab. Those would look great and offset all the blue in here. A touch of green and more maroon would blend the look together."

"You sound like the Home Decorating Channel." She was completely ignoring my earlier comments about having a date, a tactic she used when she didn't want to face reality or confrontation.

"Umm. I guess I do. How's work, hon?" she asked, not looking at me, as if she didn't expect or even care to hear an answer. She had come to accept my new down-sized lifestyle, the job at Top of the Hill, which thankfully had grown to five days a week so that now I could pay the rent and bills. Chuck had been promising lately if I kept up the good work with Tilex and a scrub brush, he had a special job for me—my own show about parenting.

"We want you to be funny and informative at the same time," he said. "This is a call-in show and we have three psychologists on stand-by to help with the questions. You'll pick a topic, say the family bed or breastfeeding till a kid is 3, and then we expect some humor. You dig?"

"I can do it. You know how funny I used to be in high school."

"Well, I hope you're still funny after all you've been through. Training starts in two days, and we'll have you on the air by next week if all works out."

I couldn't believe it. I was thrilled. "It pays an extra $100 a week and you'd still be cleaning johns until we see if you work out. Deal?"

"Deal." Now I'd have money for extras, like new shoes for the kids, maybe some nice eye cream for myself.

"Prudy? I ask how was work going?" Mama said, arranging all her new goods around the apartment.

"Good. Top of the Hill is great, and they're training me for a nursing certificate right on the premises." It was true. Lately, everything had been running fairly smoothly. No more dreams. No more letters. It had been weeks since the last batch Jay handed me from beneath his mattress, and, since getting him into therapy, he had settled down and the nightmares stopped.

"He's progressing and beginning to act like a regular little boy," the therapist had said. I still don't know how the letters got to this address but don't care as long as they aren't coming back.

Kathy was right. Bryce was pulling my chain, trying to exert that sick control in a world where his is stripped bare.

"Have you thought any more about applying for real nursing school, not just that dinky nurse's aid business?" Mama asked, lighting the gas stove, putting on a kettle for iced tea. Lord, was nothing I ever did good enough for that woman?

"Not really. And it's an LPN degree, then later, the RN training. Did you hear me while ago? I said I have a date."

"You have a what? A date? I hope he's not a drunk. Is he effeminate? Where does he work? Has he got an education?"

"Hold on a minute, Mama."

She sat down and I observed her face. These past two years had taken a toll. Frown lines gave her a scowlish appearance, and it didn't help that she was losing weight, most of it in her face and chest. My theory is a woman needs a few pounds after a certain age. I love the quote from Marilyn Monroe, "Five pounds is a wrinkle's best friend," or something along those lines. Every time I want dessert, I think of Marilyn and indulge. That's why my fanny could double as a dinette set and seat a family of four. *Mental note. Go on slight diet.*

"Who's this man, Prudy? You know you've never had good judgment when it comes to men. You remember that thing you drug in the house, who stopped up my toilet after that big spaghetti dinner?"

"I'm trying to forget him," I said. "And I'm not bad with picking men. I made one mistake and you're acting like all I do is troll for killers and losers. You're the one who thought Bryce was Jesus himself." I didn't dare tell her I chose Bryce thinking he could help absolve me.

"Don't you talk to me like that. It's blasphemy."

"Look," I said, "you know this one; you tolerated him up to a point as I recall." I walked out of the room, trying to help Miranda find her old ballerina costume, calming down her wails when the taffeta tore and the pink slippers were too small for her feet. I wiped her tears and shoved her on my back for a pony ride, the only soothing she'd have when self-placating was out of the question. She and I have spent a lot of time since the Murderous Rampage in this position. Wasn't exactly helping my leg, but I could take the pain if it would ease hers.

Jay was away at summer enrichment camp, taking courses in all kinds of fascinating subjects like Supermarket science, in which he has big plans to concoct experiments in a lab from Borax and vinegar, soda and macaroni. He was also participating in a class called "Inside Egypt" where they would "mummify" a chicken. "It's not a live chicken," the teacher assured me. "We buy them at the grocery store . . . in a pack."

I also signed him up for the Basics of Basketball, so he won't end up an introvert with a pencil pouch and too much computer interest. He's a good kid, not freaky like some of those Junior Einsteins, and I'm hoping his intelligence will taper off a bit, not morph into one of those off-the-chart geniuses like the Unabomber who act bizarre and never satisfied or mentally balanced. I try not to think of Ted Kaczynski, Ted Bundy, or any of an assortment of psycho geniuses named Ted.

As it stands, Jay's learning rate had slowed some, especially after the accident when he'd miss school and throw up every morning and want nothing but to be at the hospital with me. For eight straight days, he slept by my side, next to the tubes and wires, the monitors that sang to him like lullabies.

I walked back into the kitchen to find Mama exactly where I'd left her, same expression. "What do you mean I've met him?" she squawked. "Who is this man I've already met?"

I was still thinking about the kids, how they were adjusting to everything they'd been through. How true it was, that saying about the resilience of a child, and wondering why this miracle of resilience couldn't apply to adults as readily.

Miranda was twisting around on my back, my skin pinching from her movements, and I found a chair and released her, despite a mild protest on her part.

"I'll tell you right now Prudy, that there's not a single boy from your old buzzard fleet I'd have in my house again."

"My house," I corrected.

"I decorated it," she said. "Who is he? Tell me so I can run to Eckerd's and check my blood pressure to see what this latest news is doing to my heart. Between you and the reverend and Amber and her troubles . . . did you know she called me and said the Chicken Man (that's what we call her Fowl Franchised husband) hasn't touched her in months? Listen to me, I should not be telling her business. There's a verse in Proverbs that says—"

"She already told me. I know all about the births scaring him. I've got her beat by nearly two years," I said, thinking about the lack of sexual relations, even a warm hug and soft kiss from the opposite sex.

"But she's married," Mama said, urging Miranda into another room. "Married women have certain rights." Mama stood to take the boiling kettle off the stove, probably so she wouldn't have to face me while talking about sex. She continued with the sex talk and tea preparations, her scrawny behind wasting to bone and skin in her black jeans. A thin woman, take note, should not wear black. It will make her appear withered, as if she's been roasting on a gas grill for two days.

"Rights? What rights?"

"Prudy, you know what I'm talking about; you just want to challenge me."

"Don't you think I have rights?" I was almost at the point, lust-wise, of putting a personal ad in the paper. "Wanted, DFHMWMOT (Disease Free Heterosexual Man With Majority Of Teeth) for three to four nights of fun. No attachments. No commitments." But I would never do something like that. Not me. Not Prudence the Pure. I would dream about it and avoid thoughts of lust like the Baptists warned against, like my mother feared worst than the Devil, using as an example that divorced friend Carla Tisdale with the uncontrollable urges.

"She hits the singles bars every night," Mama said for the umpteenth time, cutting off the gas stove. "Drinking her tequila like it was water and then taking men home and doing Lord knows what to their male parts."

"I'm not Carla, Mother." She poured the hot tea in a ceramic pitcher to cool. "Don't you think women have needs in the same way as a man?"

She paused and her body tensed. "No," she said. "I do not. A woman receives rights when she marries. Only then can she engage in the Biblical duties. Only after participating in these rights does she begin to feel the stirrings of needs. Watch the nature shows, pornographic as they are, and, by the way, since you got cable I'm insisting you block that nature channel from those innocent children. They certainly don't need to see all that howling and humping. The monkey nightmare at the zoo was enough."

I couldn't stop laughing at that memory, and Mama swatted me with a bag from Pier 1. "Why do you think all the female tigers and deers, the elephants, whatever animal they show . . . haven't you noticed it's the girl that's always running away from the frisky male? She doesn't want to participate in the whole mess. We only do it because of our duties."

"Duties?"

"Enough, Prudy."

"DEE! It's Dee and you always forget to call me that. Listen, Mama," I said as gently as possible. "I'm almost 39. Amber's 36. We've had lots and lots and lots of sex. You can give up the Virginity Preservation Campaign."

She turned on me and her chin zoomed into a full angular jut. It couldn't have been pushed farther from her face.

"Sex is something the man enjoys."

"You don't like it?"

"Heaven forbid, um, Dee. I do my duty. I'm going to leave if you can't get your mind off these vulgarities. Who are you going out with? Go ahead and sock it to me. Then I'm out of here. I'm craving the coconut shrimp at Red Lobster."

I was, quite frankly, afraid to tell her. Then again, I should go for it. I'm a grown woman. What could she do? Make me stand in a corner? Write sentences, *"I will not date old boyfriends who piss on lawns and cuss at Christmas?"*

"Croc Godfrey."

The chin unhinged itself from the jut position and fell completely to her protruding collarbones. One of her eyes twitched and spasmed. I hoped to God she wasn't having that stroke she kept promising was her rightful and likely due. *Please, God, let this settle in without stopping her heart or bursting an artery.*

"Croc Godfrey," she seethed. "Now there's a catch." She had enough ax-sharp sarcasm in her voice to split wood. She snatched up her purse, her empty bags and marched out of the house, clomping as loud as she possibly could in her Bass loafers, having herself a 60-year-old hissy fit and not even ducking into Miranda's room to tell her goodbye. "Well, I never," she said. "I never."

She stopped at the stairs that would lead her outdoors and away from what she considered my Falling Down Life. "Is he going to come by and tinkle on your grass like he did mine? Where'd you dig him up? The local pool hall?"

"Google. Google.com." Took less than an hour to track him down, found him all the way in Nashville, Tennessee, and I rehooked him on my line as if more than 20 years passing by were nothing but a week or two. A tiny hole to darn in time. The homecoming King and Queen. Edward "Croc" Godfrey. Prudence Faith Millings.

Wasn't a thing much wrong with Croc Godfrey, and best I recall he was the most romantic man, well, boy back then, I'd ever dated. The only thing that booted him from favor was that whiz on Daddy's fescue.

"He's had a very tragic time, Mama. He buried his poor wife after she died in a car accident." I didn't tell her Croc was driving or any of the other details.

"Was he tanked up on the joy juice?" Mama asked, hands on her hips. This was one woman who didn't miss a beat.

"That is an un-Christian comment. An oil rig hit them and he was hurt, too, but not so bad. He was all torn up on the phone and his tragedy was twice as long ago as mine."

"That's a shame, and a sad story, but doesn't redeem him and give you rights to put us through that romance again," she said. "My heart is not going to beat much longer if you and Amber don't straighten out. I thought when I had kids that after they turned 18, I was in for a free ride and some peace and quiet. Y'all are giving me more fits now than when you were youngsters."

It's my belief we all bear scars if we live long enough. His were inside; mine were inside, outside and up and down, striping me like exclamation marks of horror. Seems he'd be good for me and likewise, me for him. He had a son, about a year or two older than Jay.

"My son likes motorcycles and guitars," he said, after I'd given him my number and he called, that pure voice not tinged by time. "I can't believe you found me. I've thought of you so many times. You have no idea. Tell me about your kids."

I lied and told him Miranda was a typical girl, leaving out the fact she has gone from simply carrying grandma purses to wanting to wear that style of clothing, and that Jay liked to play basketball and was all the time outdoors getting into something. I didn't say that in order to lure Jay from his room or the computer, I had to bribe him with science books and promises of dissections. Croc and I enjoyed a nice conversation, an hour long almost.

"I'd really love to see you again, Prudy," were the magic words that have set off something that could lead to . . . well . . . anything. "I kept up with you. I know all about what you've been through and am so sorry, sweet girl. Do you want to talk about it? I'm a good listener. Better than back in high school." He laughed and it was good to know mirth could still exist where tragedy tried to inhabit.

"Maybe one day. Oh, I'm going by Dee now, but I'll let you call me Prudy. Just nobody else. Anyway, I don't remember a lot of the incident. I mean, all the doctors and nut specialists say that until I can accept and remember the full brunt of it, I'm going to go insane or explode or something one day. I'm hoping otherwise . . . you know . . . that if I just keep forgetting it, maybe it will melt into a little black puddle like the witch in *The Wizard of Oz.*"

I told my mother none of this conversation but allowed her to remain stuck in time like a broken record, focusing way too hard on a poor teenage boy's misstepping youth.

"Croc Godfrey," my mother repeated, hissed out as if naming the return of some vile bug or spreading pestilence. "I'll bet he hasn't amounted to much."

"What's much, Mother? Is it becoming a doctor, like Peter Jeter, and doing whatever he's done to turn his giblet wife into a jumpy squirrel? Is it being a preacher, then going mad in the church passenger van and nearly killing his wife?"

She didn't blink an eye, standing on my sidewalk as if dazed and zapped by a stun gun.

"Why does a career have to define a person, and if it did, then what am I? A barely-above-minimum-wage butt wiper and hand holder? A non-pensioned woman with a B.S. in psychology and no real job or future? Did you know I can barely pay my rent next month? It's due in a week, and I had to feed the kids and buy them summer clothes and lay down camp tuitions. I guess I'll offer my body up to one of the richer toothless men at the nursing home for cold hard cash." The words came out mean, and as soon as I said them, I felt pains of regret. My mother was only trying to help, in her own way.

Suddenly she sprang to life—from her wilted state after the Croc news. "That's enough from you. We helped pay for those camps, Miss Priss. All I get is total disrespect after all I've done for you. I'm leaving. When you can be a decent Christian, call me. Otherwise, find another mother."

I watched her get into the car and leave and felt a twinge of guilt. In a sense, though, it's long overdue she let me try to make it on my own without her acting as if she were a set of crutches from a medical supply closet.

"We're not making that rent payment for you," she yelled. "You can just take yourself to a women's homeless shelter and leave the kids with us. You've had plenty of time to find more work."

***

At night I always climbed into bed with each of my children, no matter how tired I was or how late the hour, first brushing my teeth, washing my face with Dove and slathering on Oil of Olay, wiping the smells of Top of the Hill from my skin.

With Miranda, we'd read a story from her favorite fairytale book, then make one up, silly tales that gave her giggle fits. With Jay, I lay in bed with him closely, our feet entwined as if we shared something that required touch to process. I felt his soft skin beginning to roughen at the elbows and knees, his feet hard from wearing sandals and going barefoot, his skin warm, almost hot and dry. I'd help him read the big words in Harry Potter books, answer the questions about his father that were never directly asked but spoken in the way he still clung to me, even at 7, even with his advanced brain.

One might qualify as the smartest kid on earth, but the need for a father's love is as basic and natural as that for food. I knew he ached; I knew there was constant wind blowing cold in his heart where the hole from loss never closed.

Maybe Croc also slipped under his child's Star Wars or Spiderman sheets, felt the stumped toes and sharp toenails and read his son stories or smelled the sun-dried sweetness of childhood as it gave way, almost overnight, to the saddle smell and musk of older boys who played hard and ran faster, as fast as they could on legs that try to chase away demons.

His son was only five or six when he lost his mother. So maybe he was okay.

As I pondered these things, I heard a loud car engine and turned to see Mama had come back from the end of my road and was heading straight for my house. She screeched to a halt.

"I am simply not through with this conversation, Prudy," she said, exiting her Town Car, one long leg at a time. "There are plenty of fish in the sea and many of them have a full set of scales."

"You should be happy with his last name," I yelled as she slammed the car door and marched toward me. "Godfrey. It's got the word 'God' right there in the first part of it. That ought to count for something." She was stepping into the shady side of my yard, bumping her leg on the rim of the blue plastic swimming pool filled with leaves and dead bugs and uttering, "Drat" and "Dad-burnit" and all sorts of 60s sitcom "cuss" words.

"At least he's not in prison," I hollered. I hated it when we fought, especially after she'd just spent hundreds of dollars on the betterment of what she calls my "poor little rental unit." One step above a trailer, she often said.

"This is a mistake," she said. "You're a stubborn woman. The only good thing about you being stubborn is it's the very reason in the medical world you didn't up and die. You're the only woman who could have lived through getting run over and stabbed to death."

"Mama, stop!" I hated hearing about the incident at BI-LO and she knew it. "I'm not dead."

She turned around and shook her ass in a deliberate, "kiss-my-butt" motion, opened her car door, and all but jumped into the driver's seat, cranking the engine. Only one part of her was visible, a single finger, the middle one, rising up in a streak of sunlight that had shot through the leaves of the maples that line our street. That one finger soared proudly with its French-manicured nail. This was a new sign. A very bad sign of what she thought of me and the recycling of Mr. Croc Godfrey.

"Decent Baptists don't shoot birds," I yelled, but by then, all I saw were taillights at the stop sign.

# Chapter Eleven

**Wake up, Miss Dee:** *A wise child accepts a parent's discipline; a young mocker refuses to listen.* **Proverbs 13:1**

**Mama's Moral:** *I heard about you becoming a maid. Aunt Weepie told me. Now, there's nothing wrong with that except I cannot tell my bridge biddies my college-educated daughter is cleaning other people's poop all over town. First at Top of the Hill and now at the radio station. Couldn't you have found something else? Oh, well. Bye.*

ON MONDAY, I took a personal day off at Top of the Hill to record some shows at the station, even though Theresa told me Annie Sue was crying and having fits because I wasn't going to be there to do her hair in Bo Derek braids.

"She's watched that movie '10' a hundred times and is purely having a conniption to look like her. Even told me, 'I got Bo's body, now all I need's her hair,'" Theresa hee-hawed.

"Tell her she'll look just like Bo on Tuesday," I said, settling the matter before my debut recording session. I could do this.

I had to do this. Be funny. Be smart. Tell every mother it's okay if her kid wants to eat nothing but Lunchables, as long as she puts a few raw carrots on the plate.

Chuck was ready to go when I arrived at the station, a sheaf of notes in my hand and my nerves calmed with green tea and dark chocolates, drugs of choice when beer or wine aren't on the menu.

After recording four shows in a matter of two hours, it was over. I felt as if I were a day-old balloon in need of inflation, but that I'd done well and this show just might work.

"You did good, kid," he said. "We'll start early in the mornings, before you go to your other job. Your show name is 'Dr. Dee, minus the Ph.D.' Shouldn't take but a half hour since the show's only fifteen minutes each morning during the 8:05 a.m. time slot. Prime driving time. I'm expecting it to be a hit because our research shows moms are our early morning audience." He stood to lead me out the door and I shook his dry hand, smelling the cigarettes and Old Spice permeating his body.

"Thank you. I appreciate this chance."

"Don't blow it."

"No way. You'll see."

***

This evening I was to meet Croc, after having not seen him since high school graduation in 1988. He'd left town, so had I, pursuing different colleges and different dreams. I stopped by Mom's to pick up Miranda, and then had errands to run to prepare for my big date. I turned on the radio in my car, popped in Gloria Gaynor's "I Will Survive" CD, and Miranda and I sang at the top of our lungs, all the way out of Mama's driveway as she squawked and told me if I went out with Croc not to EVER call her again.

"You're being cheap," she said. "Carla Tisdale cheap!"

"I'm just having a steak dinner," I said. "Maybe a baked potato, even though you won't let up about the size of my ass."

"It's fanny, Prudy. We don't say 'ass' in our family. My point is, this Croc reject knows your needs."

"I don't even know them."

"Wait, Prudy, turn down that music. Let me get you the proverbs I found—"

"No thanks, and it's Dee for the last time." I waved and sang and listened as Gloria told me I was back, back on my feet, no longer petrified or terrified. Just back. And ready to go someplace.

"Listen, Miranda," I said. "We've got to get Jay in an hour. I need to shop for a special outfit, so if you're good and don't run off or hide under the racks and dressing rooms, Mommy will buy you a pack of gum."

"I want a Barbie," she said. "I already had gum at Mama Millings'."

"I don't have money for a Barbie."

"I do." She reached in her pocket and handed me 28 cents.

"Thanks, honey. We'll see what we can do."

I looked at her in the rearview mirror. She was the prettiest child, and I'm not saying that because she's my own. She didn't inherit all the pointy and angular features like the Millings side of the family. Where we had high prominent cheekbones and beakish noses, thin heads and faces, Miranda had a gorgeous full-moon pie face. It wasn't fat; it was round and perfect, Asian-like, her chocolate-drop eyes set in perfect proportion and dancing with sparkle and life. A lot of people with dark brown eyes don't have the twinkle, their eyes lying flat in all that color, sort of overpowered by it. Miranda's exploded with wonder and spunk. They reflected light and always took me by surprise in that they would change, like Bryce's, but not from good to evil, as his had done.

Miranda's eyes would flip from dark to golden, a reflection of the purity one knows lies in her heart. Her hair, since the jet-black days of her birth, was now sandy brown, streaked liked Jay's from the fingers of a sun that just had to touch the children, the way I did.

At the stop sign I applied some lipstick and checked the balance in my account: $56.12. I had never been this poor except in college. While all right to be poor in school, it was not particularly respectable to endure this sort of financial imbalance when two children were involved, as well as rent, bills, food and the every day costs of sucking down this pre-breathed South Carolina air.

Inhalations in this state felt like gulping the exhalations of mouth-to-mouth resuscitation, Aunt Weepie always said.

"Where we going, Mommy?" Miranda asked. I had her buckled in her car seat as tight as possible in the center of the backseat, not taking any chances on some quack hitting my car.

"We're running on over to the Junior League thrift store."

"Do they have Barbies?"

"They have everything the rich ladies and their over-indulged children have gotten tired of." I really didn't want to shop at "A League of Their Own," the second-hand clothing store operated by the doctors' and lawyers' wives of Spartanburg. I probably attended high school with half of them, and for those women to see me limping in and poking through their old discards, well, it was too humbling for words.

Only this upcoming date with Croc Godfrey unraveled my pride and pushed me right through the doors of the Junior League's world. A recycled date. Might as well wear a recycled outfit.

I needed to look good. I needed, in essence, to look sensational, which meant a sheer miracle due to my ever-expanding rear end. I should have gone on a diet three weeks ago. Oh, why had I forgotten? Why had I let Marilyn Monroe's wrinkle theory wreck my rearview and the three funerals attended so far with Weepie turn me into a glutton? I was known in high school as the cheerleader with the nicest butt. Goodbye nice ass.

Panic set in. Croc had not seen me in nearly 20 years. He'd be expecting little Miss Perky Firm, not big Ms. Dented and Dated. Then again, he sounded mature on the phone and didn't indicate that youth and washboard abs were a priority. I'm certain having suffered a terrible loss, such as that of a wife, has given him depth. He sure had more than most high school boys, and as an extra bonus, an electric guitar slung across his shoulders and the best voice I'd ever heard. He was my own Jon Bon Jovi, my personal Steve Tyler.

When a man's in the spotlight, he can do no wrong in some women's eyes. Stage, auditorium, TV camera . . . pulpit.

Why couldn't I be attracted to the calmer, more secure men who didn't mind, even preferred, living in life's shadows? Didn't Mama send a proverb once about loving the meek?

We got to the shop and immediately I spotted the dress I had to own. It was a Maggie London, cotton and casual, high enough on the neck to cover my scars and long enough to hide my bad leg. I held up the pale pink fabric, a smooth lightweight material that reminded me of comfort taken in my grandmother's lap. This was my color.

Once, I'd had my colors done, and the woman said I shouldn't wear gray because it made my teeth look yellow. After that, when she tried to say pink "washed" me right out, I thanked her for her time and ended the Color Me Fabulous session right then and there. No one would desecrate pink, the happiest shade in the world. Not even the professional Color Woman.

I glanced at the price on the dress, $35. How in the world could these rich women get away with charging this much at a consignment shop? I may as well go to Belks or Dillard's. Dresses at the Goodwill, my usual haunt, were about $5.

"Is there something I can help you with?" The voice came out of nowhere. I looked up and caught my breath. There before me, in blonde glory, Botoxed immobility, and an Angelina Jolie upper lip, thanks to a few jugs of collagen, stood Kippie Murray.

*Please, God, don't let her recognize me. I'm fat. I'm not made up properly. My daughter has stains on her clothes, which she chose and don't match. If you never answer another prayer, Lord, allow me mental exit from this woman's memory. If you do, God, I'll obey my mother more often, even though she's an odd one. I'll even press*

*Play on the answering machine twice and hear her proverbs a second time each morning.*

Kippie scanned me and my daughter who was fondling all the dresses with her dirty fingers. She tried to frown, in concentration, but nothing on her face moved but those enormous lips.

After a few moments, it registered. "I don't believe it!" Kippie shouted. "It's you. It's Prudy Millings! Oh, my Gawd. Oh, hi-i-i-i. How are you-u-u-u?"

*Thanks, Lord. I owe you.*

"I'm doing fine, Kippie. What's up with you?"

"I'm doing my League work, running this shop, trying to give the poor a price break on haute couture." She giggled. She had the exact same figure she did senior year in high school when she performed a vocal solo on the football field, her rendition of "The Star-Spangled Banner," then ran offstage to whip off her graduation cap and gown, underneath which sparkled a high-cut leotard in red, white and blue. The principal of the school lit both ends of her fire batons and she tore down the football field like an exploding set of firecrackers, twirling and skedaddling across the field, flames and cheers rising around her in a most adoring fashion.

"So what's this I hear about you getting all beat up?"

My daughter poked her face from the rack of clothing and stared at Kippie. I didn't know what to say. I felt for a moment my very body being transported by the Spartanburg High memories and the catty likes of Kippie Murray. She used to burn me up, and here she smirked, same kind of girl, stuck in time, only with more money and the exact tiny mind and gerbil brain.

"Mama didn't get beat up," Miranda said, tugging a silk dress. "She got runned over."

"Oh, how cute, 'runned over,'" Kippie said. "Don't you just love it? Bad grammar starts early in certain Southern families, I guess. How precious is that?"

"You haven't changed a bit," I said, deciding the dress wasn't going to work, that $35 would buy nice groceries for my babies, new books or the sandals Jay's been wanting.

"Guess not," Kippie cooed. "What with all the running, you know I do marathons, and Lem—I married him and now he's a psychiatrist at the children's center—he keeps me so busy in his office, all those kids needing therapy and medications at such a young age. It's pitiful. Ooops. I'm sorry. Listen at me, putting my foot in my mouth, yours might have gone too."

"My kids didn't need to go," I lied. "I chose not to screw them up worse, no offense, of course. Here." I handed her the dress. "I was going to get this for a homeless woman I know, but it's not good enough for her. The odor . . . I can't place it." I let loose my fakest smile. "You have yourself a good day."

We opened the door, leaving Kippie Murray standing in a pool of light flaunting that sorority girl expression of "Well, I never!" that she could have patented herself. Even so, she did the Southern-girl thing and shouted, "Call me sometime. Maybe we can do lunch at that new French place and catch up."

"Sure. That'd be grand."

"Oh, gosh. It's expensive. I forgot about the prices for French food. I know if you're shopping here your finances must be—"

The bell on the door jingled as I left, saying no more and thinking I'd just wear some jeans and my lavender tunic. It would cover my butt, and accentuate my still-slender legs, and maybe, just maybe, I could take two Advil and get away with higher heels. I don't think I'd feel very sexy in a pair of the old air cushions the doctors kept pushing my way. Lesbian shoes, my mother calls them.

When I got home, I took a nice hot bath in my clawfoot tub, pouring in scented oils, lighting candles and letting the water cook me to medium-well, my face as pink as the tile in the floor. The candles bathed the room in a glow I certainly wasn't getting from within. Not after today's run-in with Kippie Murray.

Miranda sang in her room and Jay played video games, which made me happy because his nose was usually planted in a book.

Aunt Weepie had promised to babysit because Mama had refused, saying, "I'll be no part of excavating the old and festering grave of that eyesore Croc Godfrey. You need to start fresh, not straight back to the very beginning. Be sure and bring him a Pamper in case he has to pee somewhere on your date. Wouldn't want to see your name in the paper associated with his lewd acts on lawns."

# *Chapter Twelve*

**Hi there, Prudy. By the way, I've decided to refuse calling you Dee. I realize it's not 7 in the morning but closer to 7 at night but you just HAVE to hear this proverb I just now read:** *As a dog returns to his vomit, so a fool repeats his folly.* ***Proverbs 26:11***

**Mama's Moral:** *Do not repeat the mistakes of your past. You have vomited enough. Move forward, not backward.*

Aunt Weepie stood in my room and watched as I continued to apply final touches for the tenth time for my date with Croc. I felt nervous, had to go to the bathroom every five minutes, my bladder in a state of freakish elimination, my mouth dry and hands a mess. I took a long look at the erratic shape of my nails, which reflected various stages of nervous gnawing. Might as well bite the rest of them off.

I spit the remnants at the mirror, aiming for the image reflecting my carved-out chest. I had wanted to hide the marks but Aunt Weepie said it was too hot outside for turtlenecks and that if I was planning on some "action," I'd better let a few of the scars show now, "so as not to send him in 'Total Recoil' when all the clothes come off." She was proud she'd coined the phrase "Total Recoil" and all the time threw it around.

"He's going to have enough to absorb as it is," she said, not mincing words.

"Who says I'm going to sleep with him?" I asked, my heart thumping irregularly, skipping beats altogether, a condition the doctor detected after the Murderous Rampage, calling the erratic beats PVCs—benign premature ventricular contractions brought on by stress.

For a while I sat in front of the mirror, turning my head this way and that, hoping for forgiving light, angles that reflected the youth that had once been mine. Kippie Murray couldn't stand it when I was voted homecoming queen and "Most Likeable Senior," and she was cast aside and merely a member of my court. She also was miffed that her superlative wasn't "Most Beautiful," and instead the letters beneath her senior yearbook portrait read: "Most Likely to Succeed at All Costs."

I pinched my cheeks and wondered where all that firm skin I took for granted in 1988 had gone. I was sliding each year into the "attractive" category, to be followed by the "handsome woman" category, to be followed by "cute old lady" category. Aunt Weepie and I are of the utmost and solid opinion that the older you get, the crazier you must act in order to offset all the wrinkles and aging factors.

Everyone, she said, loves a wacky old woman. Annie Sue, case in point. My mother, on the other hand, said she would grow old with class and dignity. In other words, Mama would be a wrinkled old bore if she didn't change her tune, and no one would want to sit next to her during senior Bingo nights.

The mirror, scratched and dimmed by the years, showed my dull-green eyes with the flat stare of a dead woman. Olive-green, lifeless-woman eyes. Maybe blush would help. More lipstick. God, if he didn't hurry up, I was going to drown in layers of Clinique, leftover from my other life, and Cover Girl, the only brand I could afford in my new life.

Croc used to call me "Purdy." He transposed the letters U and R and gave me a whole new feeling about myself. In his skewed and hormone-induced view, I was pretty, not prudy—the hot little cheerleader with the long tanned legs, the slightly bucked teeth and a fanny that back then was the perfect size, firm beneath my short blue and gold cheering outfits.

"Come on, Purdy," he'd say. "Let's go take the boat out. Purdy, I love you. Purdy, you're the best thing that's ever happened to me. Purdy, don't run from me. Purdy, will you marry me? Oh, Purdy, why can't we always be like this?"

I had loved this man with everything I had. Hot teen love. To commemorate my eighteenth birthday, we decided to park his VW Rabbit close to the eighteenth hole at the Hillbrook Country Club for what had become a nightly routine of progressive exploration, lustful discoveries that before I would apply the brakes, took us right to the precipice of lost virginity. On that night of my celebrating, after one too many beers and Peter Frampton's "Baby I Love Your Way" luring me into directions my mother feared, I yielded to the yearnings of body and heart, despite a brain telling me to wait.

I lost my virginity on the eighteenth hole, half my body on the fringe of the green, the other half in the cold silk of moon and sand. It had hurt, a burning tearing pain, and I'd cried for two hours afterward—partly because I loved him so much, but mostly because I'd just lost a huge piece of myself and didn't even have a teensy diamond to at least assuage the guilt.

"You're beautiful," Croc had said, stroking my hair and brushing away the tears with the tail of his shirt. "I love you more tonight than ever, sweet girl."

I went to church that Sunday morning and promised the good Lord I was sorry as I could be and would never do it again until I was married. I told Croc, "We just can't be doing this anymore until we're at least engaged."

The next night we were on hole five and before the summer ended and we were to go off to separate colleges, we managed to par every single immaculately manicured hole of the Hillbrook Country Club with our love.

All this reminiscing screeched to a halt when I heard a few weak knocks on the door. In the old days when Croc came to our house, he'd pound out a rock tune on the windowpanes, driving Mama nuts. Tonight, his knock was unsure and timid. I touched my face, and it was as hot as if I'd had the flu. The room spun. My heart skittered, stopped, paused, then tried to beat its way out of my skin.

"Aunt Weepie, I'm going to pass out."

"Before you do, I need to let your past in the door. I can tell by his knock that if I don't hurry he'll go on home. If I remember correctly, he ran quite a few times from your mama and daddy when y'all was in high school."

Her footsteps flew down the stairs, and I heard the door open with the groan of ancient wood. I wondered how many people before me had let old boyfriends through that once-white door now the prettiest shade of pink a girl could ever lay eyes on.

I gave myself another critique in the mirror. Opening the drawer of the antique vanity, I took out a bottle of Lauren in the square, dark red bottle. The scent of the early '80s. The smell of my neck under Croc's nose. He would remember the perfume. It would transport him in time to the me he first held, even if my face and figure showed another woman entirely.

The voice came closer, up the steps, the loud wooden steps. I listened to the voices, a man's, deeper than I remembered from the phone, and Aunt Weepie's drawling, high-pitched tones. They moved into the kitchen. The refrigerator door opened and Aunt Weepie was saying, "I can't believe I'm seeing you after so long, Croc. You look just . . . well . . . you sure haven't gained any weight, which is more than so many can say these days." She was doing the nervous woman thing of spilling too much information. "Can I get you something to drink? How about a beer?" I crept to the door, opening it a few inches to hear what they were saying.

"No, thank you. I had to give the stuff up awhile back. Didn't agree with me."

Great, I thought. Croc's an alkie. He'll drag me to Al-anon, and I'll become a smoker and a Big Book thumper, which is all well and good and has saved many lives, but I didn't care for another super-sized serving of Self Analysis—Anal-Asses, I liked to call it. I'd had quite enough the past couple of years.

I sat frozen at the vanity unable to move. "Looky here," I heard Aunt Weepie say, "this is Jay, he's 7, and the one hiding under the table in the Ariel mermaid costume is his little sister, Miranda. Jay is the brain of the family. We have no idea where he gets it, me probably, and Miranda under there is the charmer. She's also an old soul, the nun of the family who'll count exactly how many beers you drink and tell you to pick up your trash and put it in the correct bin. I've never seen such a churchy-type little girl. They are wonderful children who just need some guidance and direction, if you get where I'm coming from. Poor Prudy does all she can, trying to make ends meet, not wanting to bum off her kin, and she is the best mama you ever did want to see and a good little cook, too."

Why is Aunt Weepie doing this, giving him the rundown as if he's coming to apply for the job of husband? Come on, Aunt Weepie, this is more my mother's style. You, Aunt Weepie, should have your arm around him by now, giving him a rousing pre-show before I come onstage.

"You sit tight and I'll go see which gear Prudy's stuck in." There was low talking, mumbling and laughter, and I heard Croc say, "Sounds just like Prudy," and my aunt's answer, "You know it, mister."

I pictured my kids, especially Jay, miserable with the small talk and introductions. I imagined his face sour and bunched in a frown, his arms folded, his mind ticking. Another man. Another set of problems. Another van. Another screwdriver. Another nearly dead mommy.

"Let me run and see what's taking her so long," Aunt Weepie said loudly, giving me a cue that the hour was nigh.

"There is Coke and Sprite in there, but Lord knows how long Prudy's had it. She'll swig out of the jug, too, so watch out for wet potato chip crumbs if you dare have a glass." Oh, Aunt Weepie, stop. I heard the patter of children fleeing, running from Croc Godfrey as soon as Aunt Weepie had left the room. Who could blame them?

"Pruuuu," my aunt cooed, opening my door without knocking. I could see half of Croc's body from where I was sitting. He wasn't big as an exclamation point. He had a hump on his back, a neck that seemed to lack support. I sure hoped the second half of him was an improvement, but I couldn't see that being possible. A person typically has two fairly equal sides.

"I'm not going out there, Aunt Weepie." She scooted a chair next to mine, and I laid my head on her shoulder. "I'm not ready. I can't do this. He looks like Gandhi."

"He's taller than Gandhi, sugar. You know, when you fall off a horse you gotta get back on," she said, stroking my hair.

"I didn't fall off the horse. I fell off the Empire State Building."

"Well get back in the elevator and punch the top floor." We both laughed and then Aunt Weepie handed me something curled up in her fist.

"Here," she said, giving me a silver heart etched in gold. "This has never brought me anything but love. Tony gave it to me when we first met. He's been the best of my four husbands. The very best. Now, give it a kiss for luck and put it somewhere safe in your purse."

"Thanks, Aunt Weepie. You aren't nearly as mean as Mama says you are."

"And she's not nearly as innocent as she tells you and Amber she is. Trust me."

"Hard to imagine."

"Then we won't." And she cupped my face in her soft hands that held the overpowering scent of gardenias. "You look prettier than I've seen you look in years."

"I'm huge. Thank God for this set of bad nerves, otherwise I wouldn't have tinkled in two days. You know how I retain."

"You're beautiful. Go on out there. Truth be told, it ain't going to take much to impress him. He can't weigh 90 pounds. Most of it is in his nose." I shook my head and shot Aunt Weepie a naughty expression. I stood up and my jeans clamped tighter, hugging every inch of me, making me feel like a swamp sow. I managed a couple of deep knee bends, trying to stretch the material from the dryer's frying an entire size out of them. What could I expect from a dryer bought third-hand?

Finally, ten yoga breaths later, I walked into the kitchen, saw that Aunt Weepie had lit every candle I owned, bringing the extras in from the bathroom to scatter around the kitchen and living room. She knew exactly what a girl past 35 needed to soften her edges and give her a warm glow.

I saw him, too, Croc Godfrey, and my breathing ceased. What in the world had happened to the man? I know his wife died, but he looked as if a parasite was eating him alive. Instead of appearing 38, he looked 10 years older even in the candlelight. When he smiled, his teeth were dingy, and I bet he hadn't seen a dentist in years. Part of his front tooth was chipped, and it gave him an unsettling look I hadn't expected. I'm not sure why I thought he would step right off time's pages, torn right out of the '80s, head bobbing and body jiving to the Doobie Brothers and Electric Light Orchestra, Eddie Money, BTO, Ambrosia and all those rock groups his own band copied at dances in school gyms and roadside dives.

I expected him to look like Jon Bon Jovi, who in my opinion, aged as beautifully as any rock star could humanly do. Instead, Croc was only a speck of his old self, a flash of recognition in the eyes and the coloring, the height and the voice. The voice, beautiful and perfectly pitched, was exactly as it had been nineteen years ago, not deeper as I'd thought earlier.

"Prudy," he said, gulping. I could see his Adam's apple bobbing up and down with nerves. He held out a hand for me to shake, as if we'd never had relations on a golf course in our lives.

I took his hand and it trembled against my palm. I did what Amber does when she's pretending to be a gracious society hostess for her gay chicken man husband's crowd. I cupped his shaking hand with my other, protecting it, letting it know I was there for it, for him.

"You look the same as ever, as pretty as you've ever been."

"That's a stretch," I said, trying to infuse humor into this funeral parlor-toned date. "But thanks. A girl never tires of that remark, I assure you. How was the drive from Nashville? That's an awful long way."

"I worked a gig in Knoxville last night and stayed at the Ramada. I'm doing fine, sweet girl. It wasn't a bad drive at all. Just a few short hours."

Aunt Weepie bustled in, waving around and putting on her mother-of-the-bride act, stepping in for my own mother who refused to show up "over my dead body."

"Go on out with him and you might as well put me in my mausoleum," she had said. "Toe-to-toe. Don't forget. We couldn't afford the side-by-side plan. By the way, I got my Frequent Flyer miles so after this Croc business finishes me off, take yourself a fine trip around the world on my dead dime."

"You two don't worry about a thing," Aunt Weepie was saying. "I've got the kids covered. Movie. Popcorn. Bedtime at 9:30 or 10."

I checked my watch. It was 7. I hoped I'd be home long before 10. Why did I possibly think I could resurrect nineteen years by typing his name in Google? I wondered how many reconnections the Internet had sparked. Plug into the worldwide web and cast a net for all the exes out there waiting to be reeled in once more.

I kissed Miranda bye and tried to hug Jay, but he wouldn't even look at me. "I love you," I told him. "I love you forever and always like in that book we read."

"That's a baby book," he said, briefly making enough eye contact so that I didn't feel like jumping off a bridge into cold, deadly water. At least now he occasionally looked at people's faces, thanks to the therapy sessions. Children seem to know just how far they can push it without polishing you off.

Croc walked me outside into the stale air that had refused to cool. It must have remained in the high 80s, and with the humidity it felt like breathing the steam from a bowl of just-cooked pasta.

"Got any place in mind?" I asked, wondering how to have a conversation with the man you lost your virginity to so long ago it may as well have been a clean slate. Born-again virgins they call us. I can see why. If you don't keep at it, keep those sexual wheels in motion and in gear, they lock up, freeze, rust, forget what they are meant to do.

He opened the car door for me, which he'd always done in high school, even when the other boys didn't. His good manners, the fact he'd bring my mother flowers from his folk's garden or home-grown tomatoes, were lost on her after his boozed-up Christmas caroling. The car was new and smelled like the factory, an aroma of leather and paint, carpet that hadn't held a thousand spills or lost French fries. It was some sort of huge beastly four-wheel-drive, an Expedition or a Honda Pilot, I couldn't tell, but I wondered why one man and one child would need such a behemoth.

Suddenly, I remembered he was in a compact, maybe a Corolla, when the oil rig hit, so he probably feels protected in his gas guzzler.

"You still like steak?" he asked. I nodded, sizing us up as we sat in the car, two stiff figures, one thin as a drinking straw, the other with a metal leg bone and scars through her neck and hands, along with a pair of jeans that pinched a stomach protruding over her pant's zipper.

I patted his arm, which I suddenly realized is what I did to the old folks at Top of the Hill. "Anything's all right with me. I'm starved. How about you?"

He didn't say either way, but I'd be surprised if he ever felt the pangs of hunger. Some skinny people look hungry. His starvation was different—a more internal kind of hunger.

Whatever he was wanting, from me, from life, food had nothing to do with it.

"You know, Prudy, I was really surprised when you found me," he said, turning on the CD player.

I was expecting to hear Foreigner or the Eagles, Peter Frampton or music from our days and passion, when his big thing was playing '70s hits, skipping most of the '80s all together. Instead, he slipped in an Allison Krauss CD, her exquisite voice always bringing me to tears, and his choice taking me by surprise.

She was one of my new favorites, besides my standby Dixie Chicks, but Croc had always hated country and bluegrass. He despised it in high school. I love Allison, her sweet tiny voice as beautiful as any I'd heard, the kind of voice all the princesses in Disney movies should emulate in order to lure to their sides flocks of birds and animals. Disney should consider paying Allison to sing when they draw up a new set of princesses.

I leaned into the stiff leather seat and let the music take me where the conversation wasn't.

Finally, he spoke. "What made you do that? Look me up on the computer?"

"Oh, right." I thought for a moment and considered lying. I'm not sure why, but I told the truth stripped of games or pretenses, just as the evening was whittled of every expectation I had carried for days about a scorching reunion—a romance-novel pairing, heaving-breasts reunion, with promises and urgent kissing.

I pushed a tear away before it fell and swallowed a huge lump in my throat. "I wanted to be *her* again."

He was quiet. He was a smart man. "I understand. She was something else, I'll tell you. And you know what? I'll bet she still is."

We rode through what seemed half of Spartanburg's dozens of traffic lights, and Croc would slow down and come to a near stop even if the light was green. He'd reach for my hand and hold tightly, as if trying to keep me anchored to this seat, or maybe his heart.

For a town this size, Spartanburg had a lot of traffic lights, or maybe it only seemed that way because I was nervous and Croc was driving like a little old man. I'd almost rather join Annie Sue behind the wheel.

We passed all the usual sites – a couple of prestigious private colleges, a university branch, malls and outlets and huge superstores that popped up overnight, places like Old Navy and Toys R Us, Target, Super Wal-Marts and Kmarts, all signs the world thought it needed to grow bigger to feel better.

The downtown was what I liked, old stores like the Leader, and Bon Marchè, the Belk's building now a law firm and accountants' offices. Each time I pass I remember shopping for Easter dresses with Mama, the smell of new clothes against my face, blinding white gloves, as I held them with excitement. Most of our life's milestones were marked with trips to Belk: training bras, first pair of tap shoes and back-to-school clothes, even prom dresses. Whatever life dished up, Belk was ready to serve its purpose.

Lots of character remained downtown, and I was thankful the Floridian-conforming developers hadn't come in and stucco'd it like they had all the aluminum-sided strip malls. If I never saw another pale yellow stucco strip mall or gray-sided spec house trimmed in white, I'd be one happy woman. A town needed to keep its originality, didn't need to lift its face except for a bit of paint and simple upkeep. Let the character shine through.

That's the one thing lacking along the perimeters of most cities with more than 40,000 people nowadays. They all look the same. Throw a person along the outskirts of any town in any state and the scenery wouldn't change. Burger King, Taco Bell, Cracker Barrel and the gas stations with the restaurants unappetizingly attached. There is something quite depressing about walking into a Subway that has a Shell station sticking out front.

I glanced at Croc and thought he could sure use a few burgers. It wouldn't hurt him a bit to gain a good 30 or 40 pounds. I didn't remember him this thin in high school or the first year of college when we dated weekends, before drifting apart, victims of distance and disinterest and my parents.

He kept his eyes on the road, focused and intense, head nearly in the dashboard as he drove, eyes darting right to left as if trying to avoid enemy fire and didn't know from which direction it might arrive.

He didn't ask me where I wanted to go, but kept driving, all the way down Pine Street until it crossed I-85 and he came to the Herron Traffic Circle where he pulled into Steak and Ale.

I froze. I couldn't breathe. My head filled up with too much hot blood. I had been listening to the silence filled with Allison Krauss, and before I knew it, this is where we were. Oh my God in heaven.

"I hope this is good."

I said nothing. I tried, but couldn't talk.

"What's the matter, Prudy?"

I shrugged and hugged my body as if it were 20 degrees outside.

"I'm sorry but I don't guess I'm hungry," I said. This is where Bryce used to take me.

"I guess I'm not either."

He turned around and pointed his wheels toward Asheville, got on I-26 for a few miles and veered off at the exit that would lead us to Lake Bowen where we'd spent much of our time getting to know each other at the edge of the water, deep in the woods, on decks, piers, houseboats. He searched for a place we used to go. After 19 years, it was still there—empty, dark . . . waiting for us.

He parked in a clearing, opened his trunk and removed a wool blanket, a cooler and a bouquet of pink and orange Gerber daisies, my favorite. No fancy picnic basket. No Brie and crusty breads. No wine or champagne. Just a cooler filled with two beers, "in case you want one," and two Cokes for himself. He also had a quart of chocolate chip ice cream and one big spoon, a couple of flashlights and some insect repellent. Practical, a side to him I'd never known.

He opened a beer and handed it to me. The cold glass of the bottle sent a shiver up my spine, in contrast with the airless, muggy night. "It's a Miller Lite," he said smiling, moonlight catching his chipped tooth, the beams over water actually making him a whole lot more attractive. "I remember that's what you and Claire drank. Whatever happened to her?"

"I've tried calling a couple of times and just gave up." I didn't tell him I was too chicken to leave a message.

He popped the tab of a Coke for himself. "Cheers," he said. "To the present and the future." It is odd that he didn't say "the past" for wasn't that why we were here, to fall back into those years that had been so good to us?

I wanted that past. I wanted it so bad it hurt until I thought of Jay and Miranda and how that past didn't include them.

We walked farther into the woods, listening to the crickets and katydids, a dog howling in the distance, everything illuminated by this energetic half-moon and the faint yellow light from lakehouses pushing through the fully dressed summer trees.

"You're shivering. You scared?" he asked, slipping an arm around me as I sipped the beer, tasting my youth, my virginity, the woman I used to be before I'd come to the crucial fork in the road and married the man I thought could make me better, whole again. But if I hadn't taken that wrong turn, I wouldn't have my babies. I'd have other kids or no kids. How could I get as mad as Mama, as mad as the therapist demanded, when I had those babies' faces to hold against my heart every single night? How could I hate the man who gave them to me, who made it possible for me to be their mommy?

I tried to hate, but I couldn't. I felt a lot of things toward Bryce. Anger, pity, depression, shock and denial. I did not like him. I would have kicked or spat on him if I saw him. But my days were not filled with despising Bryce Jeter. I hated the event, the aftermath, the letters I'm still too afraid to show my parents, but I didn't hate the man, which totally confused my therapist and made her want to toss me out a window or reach for her big teeth.

Croc spread the blanket on the tall grass, moving the rocks from beneath it so we had a comfortable view of the stars, all of them spraying the sky like a quilt with peepholes to heaven. We played the ridiculous game of trying to count and name constellations, which is nothing but a ruse, a preamble to the real reason for being on a blanket in the dark of night, deep in the woods.

He reached over and stroked my cheek, and I trembled, not so much from desire but from the feel of a man's hands being tender for the first time in many, many years. He let his hand trail farther down, to the ridge of my collarbone, my neck, to the indentations where his fingers rested. I didn't stop him. I let him move from scar to scar, the valleys of near-death, lightly tracing around them, fingers dipping and bumping before finding smooth turf again.

"Prudy," he said, his voice cracking. "Purdy, Prudy." He did not try to kiss me but continued his inventory, unbuttoning my shirt as I lay there and felt the tears, cool compared to the heat in my skin, fall from my face and onto my neck. He traced the outline of my white bra, a Victoria's Secret indulgence with laced and patterned straps. Aunt Weepie had bought it, thinking it vastly important I have pretty underthings. More so now than ever. "They'll go a long way to helping you forget the scars."

He touched the straps, the edges of my curves, and then his long gentle fingers swept soft tickly patterns across my chest, finding every one of the stab wounds my husband carved in his rage. My skin beneath the tight jeans and 85-degree night rose with goose bumps.

"How many are there?" I asked, knowing but not remembering. Not recalling any pain or Bryce's busy hands as he did this. "I found 12," he said, and began rebuttoning my shirt, disappointment washing over me.

"Try 15."

He scooted his thin body close to mine, as if it were wintertime and we had to share our heat to keep from freezing. We held hands as I sipped my beer and he drank his Coke, neither of us saying much. We clung to each other the way people do who are falling, not who've already fallen. It was a tight hold, a non-sexual grasping of each other's bodies, and while I never openly sobbed, the tears pooled like silent dew and he kissed them away, his full lips soft.

We must have fallen asleep. I awakened covered with the other half of the quilt he'd vacated and noticed the frame of flower blossoms he'd placed all around me, every color, every variety. I scanned the lake's bank and saw Croc sitting near its edge, the half-moon hanging off-kilter over the water. Quietly, I approached. His shoulders rocked with an anguish I'd never witnessed in a man.

"Croc," I said, placing a hand on his head.

"Sit, Prudy. Watch how the water always changes. Light will change it. A rock will change it. It's never the same." His wet face revealed regret and grief.

"You miss her." Why had I said this?

He sighed deeply and threw gravel in the lake, rippling the surface and shooting plipping sounds across the water.

"I killed her." He stood to leave.

"How can you say that? You loved her. You were married 10 years. You had a—"

"I was drinking. We'd gone to a party at my company. I had a music recording business in Nashville and we were working with some really big groups. Huge potential. We had a party and were celebrating the finish of one of the CDs. I drank too much, three, maybe four drinks. I told her I was fine to drive and she trusted me. She believed I was okay and I guess I believed it, too." He grabbed more gravel and threw it into the water, one rock at a time as he spoke. "We were almost home when the truck, an oil rig type of thing, came flying from some dark side road and hit directly on her side of the car. I've never heard a louder noise, like an explosion."

I reached for his hand, squeezing it and the remaining rocks, shaking them out and putting both our hands to my lips.

"All I got from it was a stiff neck, a few cuts on my knees from hitting the steering column, this chipped tooth I feel too guilty to fix. She died in 10, maybe 15 seconds." He released his hand from mine and sucked in a breath of inky, night air. "She turned to me, her neck twisted and all wrong and she smiled. She mouthed a little kiss to me and then closed her eyes and died. Her lips stayed puckered like that, too."

I led Croc back to the blanket as he broke down and wept, four years of keeping the demons at bay now rushing out over Lake Bowen and my cotton blouse. I rocked him as I'd done Jay, as I rocked my own body when no one was there to do it for me.

"I blew a .07. Almost drunk. Got probation for involuntary manslaughter."

"That wasn't why she died and you know it. The truck didn't stop like it was supposed to. The driver ran the sign." I had read the reports on the Internet. "Nothing you could have done would have prevented this."

"I could have left the party earlier."

"True. You also could have skipped the party or not married Shannon or not done a million other things that over time lead us to these moments we can't stop or predict. I could have left Bryce the first time he sent me into domestic orbit. I never even told Mama."

"Did he hit you?" Croc asked, and my first reaction was to become defensive. People always ask that; they assume you've done something bad enough to elicit a beating.

"It had been building. Years. He thought because I enjoyed sex I was immoral. Eaten alive with sin. He used to say no woman should pursue a man for sex, that I was marked. He used to say after sex I was the Devil's Whore. He sure played up to it before it was all over with."

"Sick," he said. "How many times did he hit you before he tried to kill you?" Croc and I lay back on the blanket, staring again at the full-leafed summer canopy throwing patterns on a half-lighted sky.

"Once, but he swears it was an accident and that he was thrown off balance and fell into me. I gave him one more chance."

After a few minutes, Croc rolled over onto his back and pulled me into him. "You were a little wild woman," he said, changing the subject to the past, smiling and brushing the hair from my eyes. "I remember those nights on the golf course. You don't hear me complaining. Sounds your ex was one big nut job."

"It got worse every year. The paranoia. The imagining I was having an affair. I was thinking about it in the hospital and figured it started after Jay was born. I devoted all my attention to that little baby. I neglected Bryce. I had what I needed all along right in my arms. And it wouldn't call me the Devil's Whore. I'd never felt any kind of love from him after I had Jay. I guess that's selfish, but it's how things were, and it only got worse when I had Miranda."

"It's odd how children can affect a marriage," Croc said. "It can go either way. With Shannon, our son brought us closer than ever. We couldn't believe what we had. We'd tried for so long . . . never had any more after Sam. He's great."

"I can't wait to meet him."

"You will," Croc said, and he took my hand and kissed the fingers, making me wish I'd at least not chewed my nails to shreds. He sat up and wiped the sweat and dew that had wet his back, then he rolled a few times off the blanket toward the trunk of an oak. There was nothing beneath him but earth and weeds, grass that grew wild without any tending. We stayed in those woods by the lake until after midnight, then drove home, holding hands the entire way and saying nothing.

The kids were asleep. So was Aunt Weepie, in the middle of their room on a Power Puff girl sleeping bag on the floor. I loved that woman. I woke her up and Croc offered to drive her home. He thought she was too sleepy to drive herself and he insisted. He promised he'd get Aunt Weepie's car to her first thing in the morning.

"No problem, darling," she said through the fog of sleep. "Morning to me starts up around lunchtime or shortly thereafter. Nighty-night, Prudy. I'll call you tomorrow. I got a funeral at 3, wish you could be at this one, honey. Then I'll be home." She paused in the living room, giving Croc a chance to tell me goodbye in semi-privacy.

"I know it wasn't like you thought it would be," he said, reading my mind concerning our reunion date.

I shook my head. "No. But it was what had to come out first. For both of us." We hugged, had a hard time parting. He promised to call and I believed him. I had no reason to doubt him.

The next morning my son woke up early, came into my room hyperventilating and hysterical. He had two letters in his hands. Both addressed to me and unopened. He had been so brave to hold them, so good not to open the envelope and set evil free. The return address was from an unknown law office, the postmark Charlotte.

"It's all right," I told Jay, taking the letters. "Don't worry because Mama will take care of everything." How many times had I said that? How much longer could I really pull it off?

"He'll rot, Mommy," my boy said. "He'll rot in prison."

"Who told you such a thing?"

"Mama Millings is always saying it to Grampy. 'Let him rot.' I hear them. They hate him."

"Well," I said, bringing him close and brushing popcorn crumbs from his pajama top. "How do you feel about your daddy?"

He shrugged. He wiped his eyes. "I don't want to say."

"Okay. How about a glass of milk?"

"Can I have a cookie?"

"Only if you brush your teeth and eat cereal later."

He smiled and hugged me, a small gift from the heavens, each hug an assurance that he didn't hate me, blame me, for his not having a daddy.

"Mama?" he asked, dipping his cookie into the milk.

"What, precious?"

"When I grow up, will I be like Daddy?"

Kids always ask things a parent is never prepared to answer.

"Honey, you are a wonderful boy. You will grow up, and people will be amazed at your goodness and kindness. Daddy got real sick. Something was wrong with his brain. Let's brush our teeth and then I'm going to tell you funny stories, the funniest batch yet."

"I wanna hear them, too," Miranda squealed from the room. "I want the one about the pink bird that has drippy Popsicle wings."

"I'll be right there," I chirped, the happy mother with a troubled son and a screwed-up life. "We'll have a great morning. Hold your horses."

I'd give the children the impression of a calm and well-balanced mother, then I'd go in the bathroom, lock the door and read the letters, see what Satan's Twin was cooking up from prison.

# Chapter Thirteen

**Listen up, Prudy:** *Putting confidence in an unreliable man is like chewing with a sore tooth or trying to run on a broken foot.* ***Proverbs 25:19***

**Mama's Moral:** *Careful where you chew and step. I'll bet you and that Croc character have some repenting to do. I just hope you remembered your morals and didn't pull a Carla Tisdale. By the way, you're famous. All my bridge biddies love your radio show.*

**P.S. Here's a bonus.** *Don't long for the "The Good old Days," for you don't know whether they were any better than these!* ***Ecclesiastes: 7:10.***

**Mama's Second Moral:** *Don't regress. Go forward.*

After my radio show, which has been a sweet success, I got to work today in a horrible state of mind and tried to do my best to find a way to act friendly, not all hormonal and bitchy. It had been two weeks since my date with Croc, and I'd received nothing but a bouquet of roses the day after, yellow for friendship, saying what a fine time he'd had.

Nothing more. It was as if he'd taken one look at me and thought "been there, done that" and poof! Had no desires to return to the "good old days."

Maybe Mama was right. Putting my hopes in him would be like chewing with an abscess or trying to run on a boneless foot, which is more or less what I have.

If I had wanted relations with him, which I did not, because our date was about releasing feelings, not lust, then I might understand his sudden withdrawal from my life. All I could figure was he needed a shoulder to cry on and mine proved quite absorbent, so much so he wouldn't need it again. It's one thing to be rejected by Brad Pitt. It's quite another when the concave likes of Croc Godfrey, Ichabod Crane, Jr., won't even call you for a second date.

Well, his loss I told myself, unloading a few bags of beauty supplies left over from collecting toiletries here and there for the old women at the home. A beauty supply shop had donated a huge assortment of overstock and discontinued dyes and shampoos, brushes and sprays, hair dryers, just about everything a woman would need to recreate her looks and mood. I decided Top of the Hill's beauty shop needed a major upgrade, as did its wash-and-set residents who've been wearing the same shrink-wrap hairdos for the better part of 60 years.

Today, thanks to all the fine donors of beautification products and to my unbalanced mood due to Bryce's new lawyer's threatening letters about getting paroled, and my skeletal ex-true love dumping me, the women would get new cuts and styles straight from the pages of "Hollywood's Hottest Cuts," a magazine I'd picked up featuring the styles of the most glamorous stars. It is therapeutic doing hair when one has been slammed with a heaping serving of hell, first from Satan's Twin, then from Ghandi.

Oddly, the letters were addressed to me, not Jay, and they were type-written from some lawyer and threw out a bunch of legal terms I didn't understand very well.

I did comprehend the parts about Bryce's suing for "alienation of affection" and "seeking monetary damages" for his suffering brought on by the dissolving of the marriage. This fancy pants lawyer said in the letters that my "affair" with the professor, the poor old man who was trying to help me enter nursing school, is what caused Bryce's mind to snap and thus the ensuing carnage at BI-LO.

How in the world could he sue me from prison? Why wouldn't he just leave us alone?

I had called my attorney, hearing the dollar signs chi-chinging in my head as I sought advice.

He said Bryce's threats were nothing but legalized extortion and a tactic used to keep emotion stirred up rather than allowing "all parties to come to terms with the dissolution of the relationship."

"Stay calm, Prudy," he said, hearing my voice rise with emotion. "As a matter of law, he has the right to file an action against you if there is fact to support the claim. And, of course, assuming that he meets the procedural and substantive requirements to file for the lawsuit. Still, I really don't think he's going to follow through. He has no case. There have to be facts to support his claim, and you and I both know there aren't any. This supposed affair was two or three lunches eaten in pursuit of your education."

"What about this 'seeking of monetary damages?' How does he expect to get a dime from me when he left us broke?"

The attorney sounded irritated, as if I were just another woman who couldn't straighten out her own mess. I could tell he'd rather be chasing ambulances or other more lucrative cases, talking to Demerol'd up accident victims whose whiplash would pay for his new beach house.

"The plaintiff," he said, referring to Bryce, "is asking a jury to put a price tag on the value of the relationship, assuming the factual grounds even exist for a jury to decide alienation of affection did, indeed, occur."

"Well it most certainly did," I said, sounding exactly like Lucinda Millings. "It occurred on our wedding night, and if you've got an hour, I'll be more than happy to sit down and tell you all about what Mr. Jeter pulled the night and days following our wedding. He wants to sue for alienation? I'll give him some alienation."

The attorney must have sent his secretary their secret cue, for she cut in on the line and said, "Excuse me, Mr. Whittington, you have a client waiting."

"Mrs. Jeter, I have to run, but there's one more thing—"

"Millings. It's Millings. And it's Dee now. Not Prudy."

"Yes, pardon me, I forgot. In any regard, Mrs. . . . uh . . . Ms. Millings, I've been told there's been a pretty serious illness your ex-husband is fighting, so why don't you rest on it. Don't concern yourself at this point," he said. "If anything more is done legally or medically, I'll know about it and be in touch."

Serious illness? I wanted to ask more but the cheapskate had already slammed down the phone. What could possibly be wrong with Bryce?

Was it a scam? And here I was thinking prison would keep them away. The bad guys. I'd see court trials, similar to my own, families clapping and crying and carrying on when the guilty verdict is read, when the sentence handed down is the maximum as was served in my case.

Don't they know while they are celebrating, while they are spouting, "We can finally put this behind us and get on with our lives," and, "Justice has been served," when they say all this to the TV cameras and to friends and relatives, that the man or woman walking off in the orange jumpsuit has nothing but time. Time in which to plot evil schemes and revenge, time to rearrange the criminal events in such a way they come out in his favor. Time to concoct a "serious illness" defense. Or grounds for mistrial.

A lawsuit from Bryce was "unlikely," the lawyer had said. Unlikely. What was more likely was that my son needed more appointments with the therapist and that I had tons of work to do at Top of the Hill, which required lots of charm and chitchat. I'd have to shelve my own troubles because today was hair day and a half-dozen ladies had signed up for my unlicensed skills, including Annie Sue who wanted the Meg Ryan haircut to go with her new attitude and boozing ways.

"I'm going for Meg's choppy and casual look," she said when I showed her the celebrity cuts magazine and she chose her hairstyle. "I reckon it's time I lost the wig, and maybe

I could get me a few more admirers at Bubba's if I favored Meg Ryan. What do you think? You think all them fellers will swoon and buy me beers? You know I've been back twice more since you took me?"

"I took you twice, remember?"

"Thank God I don't," she said, mouth popping open, wig falling to the floor, hand slapping that jutting bone she calls a knee.

I had to run this haircut by Theresa Jolly, who ran it by Annie Sue's son, who said, "I don't care what you do with her hair. Keep her happy. If she's happy, I'm happy." Theresa claims the 80-year-old son stands to inherit quite a small fortune when Annie Sue passes on. Her husband, a doctor who died 50 years ago, had left her enough of a settlement that she'd built a fine lifestyle for herself. Plus she had saved and invested well.

This son, this only child from a previous boyfriend who refused to marry the pregnant Annie Sue, was well aware that as long as his mama held on, he would have less and less time to enjoy the benefits of her will. Might as well let her drink and ruin her health.

"Hurry her on out of this world so I can finally see the world," Theresa said, quoting the son's possible thoughts. I was in her office, showing her all the goods and supplies the stores had donated when she told me the plans Annie's son was probably making.

"He's waited longer than a patient old buzzard," she said. "I hope the woman lives to be 110. Hey, you look tired. You want some coffee?"

"Thanks. I'm all right. Not sleeping too well, I guess."

"This is my high-octane coffee," she said, stirring her cup with a pencil and pouring me a cup with a pack of Equal. "He can't wait," she said, returning to the subject of Annie Sue's son. "He's ready to go on a spending binge, though what the greedy old fart could possibly need to buy beats me."

"Guess some never grow out of loving money." I drank the coffee, the brackish Folgers Theresa leaves sitting in the carafe all morning, not making a new pot until after lunch.

"I hope she drinks away all her CDs and her pension and her savings. You wouldn't believe what she pays to stay in this place. It's outrageous, probably eating her alive financially. I hear they sold one of her two houses to front what they thought would be a two-year stint before death. Ha! That was over a decade ago." She opened her desk drawer and removed a box of Famous Amos chocolate chip cookies, helped herself to a couple and passed them to me. It was a routine we had—coffee, conversation, cookies.

Then she said with a mouth half full, "I don't know why he doesn't just take her in and save all that money. Or he could build her a small apartment onto his house. He must think every day will be her last. He'll come in and ask, 'How's Mother?' and we say, 'Healthy as a team of horses,' and his entire face droops. Listen to me telling all this when I have no business rattling my mouth. I know you'll keep it confidential."

"Sure I will. Annie Sue has let on to some of this." I stood to leave and grabbed two cookies, though I really wasn't hungry. I'd give them to Mr. Walsh down the hall. He liked to eat sweets when he wasn't too busy fondling himself. "Thanks for the coffee. I'd better hurry to the beauty shop."

"I hear they're lined up, excited as the first day of school." Crumbs tumbled from her mouth, settling in the goo of her heavily glossed lips.

I walked down the long hallway toward the nursing station, which resembled an island in the middle of isolation and exile. The center pod serves as the hub for each wing: nurses and aides and frustrated LPNs busy flipping open the metal lids of charts, scribbling notes and calling doctors, chatting amongst themselves about the goings on of the residents or the happenings in their personal lives. I loved this about nursing, even if we were in a place where endings are played out in a lingering, solitary and infantile manner.

I loved these old men and women. Most of the staff here, far as I could tell, was fairly decent in the treatment of the residents. With a bachelor's in nursing, which Bryce should have let me pursue, I wanted more than anything to legally care for them. Instead, he thought I was humpty-dumptying with the head of the department. My plan now is to go for two years and earn a B.S., then work part-time with the geriatrics who had no one to love them or touch their affection-starved flesh on a steady basis, if at all. The rest of the week I wanted to work in the Neonatal Intensive Care nursery where the smallest babies in the world, some weighing only a pound and born three and four months early, fight for life.

St. Mary's in Spartanburg has a wonderful NICU, known for its abilities to save those itty-bitty lives and give them decent futures. I didn't want to be a nurse in the middle of life's tapestry, tending those struck with the first chord of reality and bodily breakdown, taking care of the 45-year-old woman with cancer, 50-year-old men with blocked arteries and colon polyps. That was too emotionally tough. I'd learned this the hard way during the two years of pre-nursing in college, before like a fool I switched to psychology, but not before seeing first-hand those people forced to step out of their youth and dreams and straight into failing health and poor prognoses.

But to start from the beginning . . . when life first unfolds from the womb . . . and then to catapult directly to the end, when time is measured in months or a few years . . . these were the moments I'd wanted. Beginnings and endings. No middles. I didn't even want the middle of my own life.

The nursing staff nodded when I walked by, pushing a cart loaded with Clairol and curling wands, hair potions that smelled of professional salons, of watermelon and apples, the sweet scents of cherries. Oh, these ladies were going to feel good when they removed their wigs and hairpins and unleashed what few hairs were left for me to tend and tame with warm water. I can imagine how scrumptious it feels to be touched again when so many years had gone by with nothing but a few pats, *good doggie*, and maybe the obligatory peck on the cheek upon receiving visitors who watched the clock and counted the minutes until they could leave.

"Can't wait to see them after the big makeover," Loretta, an LPN with the crackly smoker's voice boomed out. "You gonna have to have a fashion show and let them all model for us."

I smiled, gave a thumb's up and wheeled my cart of cosmetic glory down the East wing where the beauty parlor was located at the end of the hall. Each room I passed was decorated like a grade-school teacher's, the name of the resident written on the door in the center of huge construction paper daffodils, tulips, pansies and the occasional needlepoint square typically referring to the beauty of Heaven and the Hereafter.

Many of the folks, behind the veil of confusion and the cobwebs of age muddling their eyes and hearing, knew full well they were in the final square footage of their lives. They bided their time in a box with two twin beds, blinds, a cheap ruffled valance, a dresser, maybe a chair from home that held them up for years and a few old pictures in dusty frames of relatives tied by blood but who rarely, if ever, dropped by to visit.

Of course, there were always the exceptions, the devoted daughter who came to feed her mother every evening and sit with her for several hours, the husband who arrived every single day, twice most days, to bring his wife the fresh gowns he had washed and dried himself at the local Laundromat. He would bathe her and talk to her and she would never say a word. If a tear ran down her face, he considered that an understanding between them. It was enough. For four years he'd done this, pausing only to eat in the cafeteria and sit with other older ladies or gentlemen, helping them cut their fried fish and Salisbury steaks.

I continued down the hall, slowing at each door, taking in the familiar odors: the soiled diapers and linens, the overpowering cleaning solutions, the Glade and Lysol giving the air a thick, almost suffocating quality—all a necessary arsenal of agents to mask the odor of decay and bodies breaking down before the heart would give up. I'd duck in and see ladies in cotton print nightgowns, all curled like children on the tops of the bedspreads. Some would wail, fling arms and legs at random. It was hard to witness, but Top of the Hill sure tried, with its perky activities director who organized bingo and old-time music, cakewalks in wheelchairs, anything she thought they'd enjoy. Most of them participated but wore sad, defeated faces registering utter indifference.

Twice a week I'd pass these doors with their cheerful preschool decorations and marvel at the sameness. Then one day, wham! An out-of-the-ordinary visitor would pop up and take me by complete surprise.

We have a woman on Kathy's floor, 94-year-old Martha Stradley who is 110 percent in la-la land and has a great-granddaughter, a sullen woman who dresses from head to toe in black and is covered in henna markings and piercings. She stays 10 minutes and leaves behind bumper stickers placed all over poor Martha's bed. The last batch said, "You! Out of the Gene Pool," "We Still Prey" and "Just Say No to Sex With a Pro-Lifer." We had to rip them off fast before the glue set and stripped the laminate from the beds and the inspectors came and ruled our institution unfit or cult-affiliated. One thing I loved about nursing homes was the way everything stayed unpredictable, especially the personalities of the residents. They could be talking about God and Glory in one breath, and in the next call you a mother-f'er.

"Good morning, ladies," I said as I approached the "salon" and the three old women waiting for me to unlock the doors to beauty. Two sat strapped in wheelchairs, the other tapping a walker. The rest who were waiting earlier must have wandered off, forgetting why they were there in the first place.

Annie Sue wasn't there yet but the morning was fairly young for her. She could be sleeping off a hangover, though I think the only time she drinks are the few occasions I've taken her.

"Who are we going to turn from regal queen to a nubile princess first?" I cooed to my octogenarian kindergartners. I fumbled with the key and cart and crammed everything inside the small room that had a shampoo bowl, a vanity, swivel chair, two ancient chair-type hair dryers, several drawers and shelves filled with shampoos, conditioners, pink foam and bristly curlers and assorted products from the past. There was also a handicapped-accessible restroom and a Coke machine, a bunch of old Reader's Digests and Guideposts, and two candy dishes, one for regular sweets and another for the sugar-free kind.

"Is that you, Lizzy?" a woman I never met in my life asked. She wheeled closer to me and picked at my shirt. "Is it you? Why, you ain't paid me the least bit of attention since you ran off with my husband." She scrunched her face up and the wrinkles multiplied. "You ain't gonna be stealing no man when I'm done with you. I told you that hooking up with a married man was bigamy."

I raised my eyebrows and said, "I think you're mistaken. I'm Dee, your unlicensed, happy-go-lucky beautician."

I glanced at the other two women and noticed the one standing banged her walker to the rhythm of her howls as she cracked up with that old-lady-like, wood-splitting laughter. The second, also in a wheelchair, said nothing, just moaned and stared at her poor gnarled fingers, each bent like bad road, curving this way and that, as if someone had broken them during an evening of torture.

"Come on and let's get you started," I said. "Here, take a look at this 'Hollywood's Hottest Cuts,' and pick yourself a favorite."

She snatched the magazine and clumsily pointed, beat upon actually, a style on page 11. Farrah Fawcett, circa 1977, with the caption beneath the winged and sprayed creation that read: "Go back in time when women looked like women. You, too, can have this feminine, sexy look. Farrah fashioned it, but anyone with hair below her shoulders can copy it."

"How long's your hair, Mrs. . . . Watkins? It has to be a certain—"

"Don't you dare refer to me as Mrs. Watkins. Mr. Frank Watkins got him another wife while I's still a married to him. Is that you, Lizzy?" she scooted up close as I tried to wedge her strong, bulbous head into the shampoo bowl. Before turning on the water, I combed out her gray hair and was surprised by its length and how it felt like a duckling's down.

"I've wanted to be Farrah since 'Charlie's Angels' first came on back when I was young enough to still have me a strong fancy for men. I liked what's his name, Bos. Bosley. That's the one them Angels was always talking to about this and that." She reached up and fiddled with her hair. "Give me some of them blondish flippy things that pouffed back off Farrah's face, since people tell me I favor her."

I bit my lip as hard as I could to keep from laughing and washed her hair in shampoo she complained of smelling like "boiled rat fat." I toweled her head and wheeled her to the booth, drying her hair and trying to comb out the soft wet snarls. She jerked and yelped and tried to swat me with her purply-bruised hands, every finger strangled in a ring swollen with large stones.

As I began cutting her hair, snipping and layering, creating much needed texture and volume with razors, she rattled incessantly about Frank and his big appendage and how I, Lizzy the man stealer, better make her look just like Farrah or she would see to it personally that I fried in a vat of hot Crisco.

She held Farrah in her lap, a veined index finger punching the picture, as if I didn't hear her the first time.

"You get me to that point and maybe Frank will leave you and come back to me."

"I don't even know Frank. What happened to Mr. Gentry?"

"Who? We talkin' about Frank here, not Mr. Gentry."

I finally managed to get the highlights in her head and stick her under the dryer with a magazine she couldn't read but would hush her up. While her color took hold, I turned to see Annie Sue who had broken in line and was grinning wildly.

"Annie Sue, I've got two before you, sweetheart," I said, noticing the other women were gone, replaced by Annie Sue and a wooly-headed woman I'd seen only in passing.

"You don't anymore," she said, slapping that thigh, jumping a few inches off the ground for effect. "I gave them both a $5 bill and they said I could go first. I have to get my Meg Ryan look today because there's a man at Bubba's who thinks I'm hot stuff." She winked and let that mouth pop open, showing those yellow but sturdy 104-year-old teeth.

"While that old thing's cooking under yonder, put a little Meg in me," she said, guffawing. "I don't want none of that heavy shampoo like you put on doflotchamajig or whatever the dingbat's name is. Give me some regular smelling stuff and then whittle away." I removed Annie Sue's wig and saw that the matted material left growing on her scalp was in horrible shape, and even a speck of harsh color would scald her head to skull and vaporize her remaining strands.

"Only thing for us to do is go black or brown," I said. "Bleach will kill you."

"Fine, fine, then give me this here Posh Spice woman's hair. I think that will be sexy on me, don't you?"

"Who is Posh Spice?" I asked, for it had been awhile since I'd been updated on current trends.

"Victoria Beckham," she said matter-of-factly, which made me wonder why in the world she couldn't apply her celebrity memory to the written test at the DMV. Then maybe she'd have a driver's license. She handed me a tattered photo of a scrawny brunette with a pixie cut. "Here's a picture I tore out of the *Enquirer*."

"We may can pull that off. You certain?"

"Sure as sugar. Posh is friends with Tom Cruise's people. You know she's in high cotton."

I got her in the shampoo bowl, and, after I'd put the cream rinse in and was about to help her over to the mirror, she sprang up like a wound toy and bounded from the chair, zipping to the counter to check her wet head in front of the vanity. She cast off the towel and the sight before me was shocking. There couldn't have been 100 hairs on her head. She reminded me of a dog we had when I was young, a fluffball that once wet took on a completely different appearance, not even resembling a dog but more or less a large and very wiggly eel. If Annie Sue had been a dog, she'd have been a Chinese Crested.

I snipped and cut, careful not to slice through her bared scalp and used a blackish/brown temporary rinse instead of a permanent dye. I was afraid the dye would kill off the rest of her hair and eat her tender pink scalp to bone.

After we got the color on, I took a razor, some mousse, gel and hairspray and finished Miss Annie Sue's Victoria Beckham hairstyle. She grinned at herself in the mirror, turning this way and that, finally adding, "I need some eyeshadow with such a short cut, and also I do believe, some rouge and lipstick."

"I need to get started on Mrs. Arrowood first and get Mrs. Gentry out of the dryer and comb her Farrah 'do out. You go on and show off your hair and come back a little later."

"Thanks, Dee. We still going for that beer tonight?"

"If I can get done here. I think four or five more are wanting their hair makeovers today."

"Let me know if you need me to pay 'em off to come another day." And with that she was out and down the halls, high-kicking and stepping like a majorette, hooting for everyone to "Come see the new me!"

Mrs. Arrowood was the steel-wool woman, a chubby curly top who seemed to be completely out of it, either zonked by medications or years on the planet. She let me do anything to her and didn't flinch when the hot water accidentally came rushing out of the faucet. I asked her what she wanted and she never said a word. I'm not even certain what propelled the woman to come to the salon in the first place.

At the station, I kept her in the wheelchair and worked from there, removing the towel, wondering what in the world I could do with her hair, stiff and unyielding as a Brillo pad. That hair had its own agenda, I'm telling you. When I couldn't get a comb through it, I had an idea. First, I needed to get Mrs. Gentry fixed, and then I'd return to this wooly booger.

"You ready, Mrs. Gentry?" I asked, taking her from the dryer and helping her to the chair.

Just as I was trying to placate her and assure her I wasn't after Frank, Theresa Jolly popped in and said I had an urgent phone call. My heart stopped. I thought of my children. Fear encircled me and I felt dizzy from a combination of anxiety and chemical vapors that weren't well ventilated in this small room.

"Here's the number. Use my cell." Theresa handed me the scrap paper and her phone. It was Aunt Weepie's number. I wondered what kind of emergency she could possibly have. She answered on the third ring, but it was hard to hear her because Mrs. Gentry was saying we all wanted Frank and "his thingamabob."

"He'll only set them roving eyes on me, Farrah Fawcett Majors Gentry," she shouted.

"Aunt Weepie? You all right?"

I heard great sniffles and gulps of air. She sounded like an upset 8-year-old whose doll had broken or turned up missing.

"What is it? Calm down."

"I'm coming over there, Prudy. Tony is a . . . a . . . he's nothing but an ass." She hissed the word. "Can I stay with you tonight?"

"Well . . . yeah." I wondered what he had done.

"Listen, I'm going to get under my bed for a while just to calm down and have a martini, then I'll stop by the Top of the Hill." I pictured her crawling under her four-poster and into the nest of blankets, books, Vermouth and mini bottles of gin. The only thing she'd have to bring was the ice and the olives.

"I may have to take Annie Sue for a beer first."

She paid that comment no attention. "Your mama has sided with Tony on this issue, this horrible thing they've cooked up, and I'm not speaking to her. I'll be over at 3. I want you to work me in. I've got something planned for that shit brain that's going to teach him the biggest lesson of his sorry life. You just get the Silver Fox hair dye ready. Get me that blue-tint look and make me look 108."

"Good Lord, Aunt Weepie. What happened?"

"He's an ass is all I can say for now. I'm too upset to rehash his HighnASS's shenanigans but I'm in 'Total Recoil.' I'll tell you more about it later when you're turning my hair gray as a goat's."

"I'm not about to turn your hair gray." I said, wondering what had gotten into her. She'd always been a redhead. Always. She dreaded gray like a dog dreads the vet.

"Your mama's all mad at me, too. You know how she can be. She got all hopping mad 'cause I talked up Croc Godfrey, and she said she'd found you someone better who had some meat on his bones and sense in his head. We had a big old fight. I don't have anybody in the world who loves me. I belong in one of those rooms at Top of the Hill, so at least I could have me a roommate, and maybe her groaning and carrying on would keep me company."

"I love you. Plus you have your children, your grandkids."

"They hadn't liked me in three years," she cried. "Since that Christmas I got all mad when they ate the ornaments off my tree."

"Well, they *were* candy. Did you say awhile ago that my mother had someone picked out for me?"

"Found you some boy y'all used to know. I can't talk about it now," she said, crying again, hiccupping gulps of indignation she claims were brought on by her fourth husband, the sweetest man I'd ever met. "I need to focus on me."

She hung up without any further trailing and lingering of the conversation. It typically takes us 10 minutes just to get all the goodbyes out.

Now, where was I? Whose head was I working on?

I turned back to Mrs. Gentry, took out her curlers and combed her hair, stiff and broken from the bleach and the heat. I flipped and teased, used the curling iron on her here and there and finished it all off with a blast of heavy-duty hairspray. The fumes of the room had me coughing and red-eyed. When we were done, she most certainly had Farrah hair. She looked like Farrah at age 95. It was quite frightening, but she smiled for the first time all morning and handed me a quarter, "for a tip," she said.

"Thanks. I'll let you know what I buy with this. I hope you like your hair."

"It's what Frank likes that matters. You sure look awful standing next to me in this mirror. Frank'll dump you permanently this time, Lizzy."

"It's Dee."

"Suit yourself." She wheeled away, blonde straw trailing behind her. Then from out of nowhere, Mrs. Arrowood moaned these haunted-house-like noises, and I'd almost forgotten about her sitting there with her wooly ram's head.

"I've got an idea for you," I said, trying to beat back all that thick hair. "We're going to give you some beautiful cornrows. I've got some beads, pearls I believe, and you'll have the Bo Derek hair that'll be the envy of all. Remember how pretty it looked that time on Miss Annie Sue."

"She's a whore," the woman said, the first and only words out of her mouth that day or for any day I could remember.

It took me 1 ½ hours to braid that mess, and when I was done, I tried hard not to laugh but couldn't help myself. I know it's mean and not very Christian-like, but I had to excuse myself to the restroom where I giggled for three entire minutes, tears streaming down my face. My sides were aching. Oh, Lord have mercy. Poor woman. I'd left her to face herself in the mirror. She hadn't said a word except Annie being a whore in the two hours she'd been in the beauty shop.

I returned, fairly composed, and put on a big cheerful act. "Look at you. Pretty as a movie star." Her ears stuck out like a mule's and her features were magnified and enlarged from the severity of the hairdo. The corners of her lips turned down and her mouth opened, then closed.

She slowly swiveled around and fixed her wobbly eyes on mine.

"I . . . I . . . I look like a jig," she said, reaching with a trembling arm for a braid.

"That's not very nice," I said. "There are just as many beautiful black women as white, and if you ask me, they age far better than we do and have much more personality, by and large."

She had nothing more to say, and I quickly wheeled her back to her room and tried not to snicker with the nurses who were doubled over with laughter as they passed us in the halls.

"I think you're going to like these braids," I said. "They are all the rage in Rio. Easy to maintain." She wailed and two assistants helped me roll her back into bed where she pounded the mattress with her fists, screaming about looking like "a jig."

When I got back to the shop, four more women were waiting for new hairdos. This was going to be a long day.

At lunchtime I met Kathy in the breakroom. She ate her usual tuna sandwich and Ruffles, three baby carrots and a pickle. I promised I'd help her with baths and beds after my last hair appointment, which just so happened to be Aunt Weepie, breezing in wearing the tightest outfit the law would allow without arrest, and enough perfume to fumigate six nursing homes.

She reeked of gin, Beautiful perfume and nesting materials. She smelled like something dragged from under a bed and then dunked in Estée Lauder as an afterthought.

"Prudy," she said, slurring her words. "Make me look wretched."

I stared without speaking. The world was cracking up. At least I wouldn't be alone.

"Let's hear it, Weep," I said, shampooing her loose head, shed of any muscle tone thanks to strong martinis. "What did Tony do to get you in this state?"

"He and your mother decided I needed nursing home insurance," she said. "Your mama and daddy have bought their fancy cemetery crypts, and then last week they go and sign theirselves up for nursing home insurance. They are so damned gung-ho on shriveling up and heading down the Interstate of Death.

"They got Tony all excited about this business of taking care of things before he strokes out or busts a heart valve. So he invites this giblet woman over who asked me all these damned nosy questions, and when I said, 'Why? What are you asking me if I drink or smoke or have anal sex for? What's it to you?' she goes on to say, 'We have to have this pertinent information in order to process your application for long-term coverage.' And I said, 'What long-term coverage you talking about?' and she gets all fired up and says, 'Winifred, your husband has signed you up for a policy in case you need care in your later years.'

"I said, 'Are you talking about a nursing home?' and she got all defensive and nervous, her glass of tea sloshing away, and she said, 'Your husband was trying to look out for your best interests.' I stood up and stuck my chest out at both of them, and I said, 'Do these look ready for the home?' and I shook my big old titties at them. Then I cut a perfect split, not one leg bent, and I said, 'Does this split look like it's ready for the home?' and they just sat there in shock, so I went ahead and did a front flip and topped it off with some nice walking on my hands and a back walkover.

"Once I finished my routine, I proceeded out the door. I told that woman, 'Stick your nursing home insurance up your own constipated fanny and his, too,' and I pointed right at Tony."

Weepie was in such a state that if I didn't agree to color her hair gray, she could very likely end up doing something much worse. "Ugly me up and then we'll go drink with that walking corpse you been talking about lately."

Within an hour, Aunt Weepie was a "blue hair," and she loved the new look so much she washed off all her makeup and clicked out her partial so that her mouth caved in where plenty of teeth were missing. She also removed her bra, so that her 38-D breasts hung like dead carp.

"I'll show him somebody ready for the nursing home," she mumbled, having a hard time talking over the missing front and side teeth.

Annie Sue met us in the hallway, and Aunt Weepie gasped upon seeing the ancient woman's jet-black pixie and bright orange circles of rouge, along with the outfit she was wearing. Annie Sue had taken a pair of her stretch slacks and cut the legs off, creating a pair of short-shorts that she paired with Control-Top suntan pantyhose, the dark girdle part showing beneath the ragged hem. She teetered on a pair of high heels and had hoisted her ground-sweeping breasts and stuffed them in a tiny black T-shirt that said, "Hottie," in giant letters, a birthday gag gift from one of the nurse's aides.

"I'm ready," she said, looking in our direction. She pointed directly at my aunt. "Is that old woman next to you coming with us?"

# *Chapter Fourteen*

**Up and At 'Em, Prudy:** *Being happy-go-lucky around a person whose heart is heavy is as bad as stealing his jacket in cold weather or rubbing salt in his wounds.* **Proverbs 25:20**

**Mama's Moral**: *My heart is heavy and to lighten it you will at least meet this man I've found for you. You won't be sorry. My load is heavier than you know. Now that you are a semi-celebrity with your radio show, I wish you'd up and quit cleaning other people's excrement.*

NEW BEGINNINGS ARE often harder than painful endings. The unknown vs. the familiar. It is along about the second or third week away from their abuser that the majority of women cannot tolerate the sobriety of life without him, cannot survive the unmerciful ache that bears down upon them. This is when they will risk suffocation or a fractured skull for a little of that love they crave, that poisonous crack cocaine of the heart. It happened to Kathy, who went back three times before the bullet tore through her skull and lodged into her left brain.

It is certain that in the beginning the victim becomes overwhelmed by thoughts of what lies ahead: the loneliness, the courts, the battles, the struggles of single motherhood and working to put food on the table and fillings in kids' teeth.

It is no wonder they go back. I shudder to think had I not come so close to dying, would I have returned?

***

I couldn't get Croc out of my mind, wondering why he hadn't called, if he had thought my butt was too large or did the scars scare him? This had been my first date in years, since meeting Bryce, and I surely deserved a callback. Do men not fully understand what the newly divorced and half-dead go through? That it's been so long since we've been repackaged and redistributed, put back on the shelves of love, we aren't sure how to act or what to do?

Maybe I didn't exactly need scorching sex, but a phone call would have at least taken the sting out of this pain, and a vase of Gerber daisies, icing on the cake.

I don't get it. I'm at least a solid 7, even an 8 on some days, and he came rustling in from the past as a 4.5 at best. Maybe less. Forgive me once more, dear God, for my mean comments. If he calls I'll bake some old woman a macaroni pie. Or at the least I'll bump him up to a 6 in the looks department. Please, God. I can't take any more rejection. Let him call.

***

I drove into my mother's circular drive, canopied with oak trees that seemed to bow like gentlemen. It was around 11 a.m., and Miranda and Jay were already in the pool, the final stages of summer evident in the darkness of the trees' greens. Mama was sitting under the cabana sipping a Diet Pepsi and watching them play. She wore a long blue-jean dress, straight fitting, and a pair of strappy blue-jean sandals. She looked right adorable. She smiled at me for the first time in a week. Even Jay seemed happy, taking off and springing into the air, firing human cannon balls and jackknifes from the diving board while Miranda stayed in the shallow end, bobbing along in her orange water wings and warning Jay about the dangers of hitting his head. Little mother. That's Miranda.

"Hello," Mama said rather coldly, the smile disappearing. She was still upset I'd gone out with Croc and that I'd told her I would under no circumstances date anyone she'd plucked off the streets. "He's not off the streets," she'd said. "You know him. But I'm not telling you who it is unless you say you'll go out with him."

We were gridlocked, neither saying much to the other. Aunt Weepie had called and wanted us all to try a new restaurant, having grown tired of funeral food and the Red Lobster.

She rang me yesterday at work, thanking me for housing her for two days. She'd slept the first half of the night in Miranda's bed, both of them nestled under the canopy; then along about 2 or 3 in the morning, I'd awakened to find Aunt Weepie in my bed, hogging the covers and snoring a song. I swear, she didn't just snore plain and regular like most folks, she added a tune and rhythm to her nightly breathing.

She said Tony had finally apologized and bought her a diamond tennis bracelet instead of the nursing home policy. "I told him to go ahead and keep his half of the policy 'cause I wasn't about to change his dirty Depends," she said.

She was also, much to our delight, back to wearing her partial, and her hair was once again the knockout shade of red she refuses to share with anyone interested. "My secret," she says, not wanting another woman on the planet to copy that trademark red color.

On the phone she reminded me about the new restaurant. "Oh, Prudy. Fresh Country Food, it says here in the ad. It's called 'Ma & Pa's Fresh Vittles' so you know it's gotta be good. I am missing a funeral to go to the grand opening tomorrow and was wondering if you and your frigid mama would join me. I believe it's kid-friendly."

"Why aren't you going to the funeral?"

"Heavens, Prudy. I got to thinking and the deceased is from a long line of horrible cooks. They will no doubt have a canned ham, canned green beans and those God-awful rolls that taste like the stuffing in a bad pillow."

We had planned to meet at Mama's at 11:30 to beat the noon crowd. I helped the kids out of the pool and got them dried and dressed while Mama sat there pouting and drinking her Pepsi until time to come inside. At 11:40, late as usual, Aunt Weepie pulled up in her Mercedes 450 SL, oozed out like a movie star and entered the living room like the Queen of England. When Mama's eyes were on her, she twirled around three times so we could all get the full view of her canary yellow pantsuit hugging every well-placed curve. She had the top four buttons open, revealing a gold lace camisole.

Diamonds glittered along her suntanned wrist. Her shoes shone gold and matched the buttons of her pantsuit. Everything was perfect. All accessories down to her . . . what in the world was she toting for a purse?

She clutched a dingy, enormous, drawstring cloth sack.

"You want to borrow one of my black or gold pocketbooks?" Mama asked, careful to say it sweetly so as not to set the woman off. Anything could fire Aunt Weepie's engines.

"No ma'am, I do not. I plan to put fried chicken in here and whatever else I can fit inside without having grease stains and spills. If the meatloaf's hard enough, like some of them can be, it'll go in nicely, too."

"I'm not going if you carry that old sack."

"Lucinda, my mouth's just a watering," she said, waving to the children and me but not bothering to hug us. Her mind was on food. "Suit yourself, but I can't wait. Ain't it wonderful that you and me can go and get us some home-cooked food and don't have to drive across town or to a funeral?"

Mama nodded and forgot about the cloth sack purse.

"Lord, I thought I'd died and gone to that big covered dish in the sky when I read a home-cooked diner was coming to our end of town. Hallelujah."

We all piled in my Accord because no one wanted to move the carseat and redo all its buckles. Mama sat in the back with the kids and Aunt Weepie scooted up front with me.

"You doing okay, Miss Prudy?" she asked.

"I've got a heartbeat," I said and laughed.

I cranked the car and began backing down the driveway.

"Don't hit our mailbox," Mama squawked. "See the flags we got rigged up on it. Our neighbors are Communists and don't have a flag so we got two of them to make up for their anti-patriotism."

My parents remind me of Archie Bunker, the way everyone who's not a Baptist or a Republican must be, for goodness sakes, an atheist or an Episcopalian.

"Prudy, Lucinda?" Weepie said, turning the attention back to herself where she was happiest. "I had to make Tony a list of things to buy at the grocery store while we're having our yummy home-cooked lunch."

I knew he did all the shopping where food was concerned. Aunt Weepie hated grocery stores. If a store didn't sell clothes or jewelry, furniture or something ready-to-go, she didn't bother shopping there.

"He needs to know what he has to buy to fix for our suppers this week. He can't cook a lick. Why, my first husband was the cook and so was my second. I tell all my husbands before I marry them that I don't cook, I don't put gas in my car or cut a blade of grass. If you want me, that is what you get. I can barely choke down a bite Tony throws together and calls a meal, but he's a good lover and makes me—"

"Winifred, there are children in this car," my mother snapped. "This isn't subject matter to discuss in front of children or anyone with any decency for that matter. I don't care to hear about Tony in the bedroom."

"I was just trying to make a point. That I am able to tolerate his cooking on account of his good lovin'. Get a grip. Get your A-S-S some Astroglide."

"What's Astroglide?" Miranda asked.

Oh, God. "It's toothpaste," I said. "Toothpaste for your privates."

"Prudy," my mother said, "turn around. Turn around right now. I'm not going anywhere with your filthy talking and your aunt's gutter mouth. She thinks these children can't spell three-letter words. Turn around, Prudy! You heard your mother." I flipped on the blinker.

"Come on, Lucinda, I was only kidding. Prudy, keep that car pointed straight toward home-cookin' and ignore your mama. Where was I in my story? Oh, yeah. I make Tony take me out a lot because his meals are downright depressing. Everything's always one color. If he fixes meatloaf, which is always black as a roach, he'll have it with some black-eyed peas and other brown or black food. If he fixes fried chicken, he'll stick with the yellows, adding corn and macaroni on the plates. I don't think I can eat another one of his dinners. That's why I'm so thrilled about 'Ma & Pa's' opening. If it's as good as the ad says, we can come here all the time and get those Styrofoam 'go' boxes.

"My goodness, I can just taste those veggies," she continued as I drove in silence, gritting my teeth as Mama squawked for me to watch out for this and that from her backseat post. "Mercy," Weepie said. "Tony fixed me something last night and I couldn't figure out what it was. It looked like one of my cat's coughed-up hairballs. He said it was made from leftovers. Lucinda, what am I going to do when he loses all his testosterone?"

"What's testosterone?" Jay asked.

"It's something you get when you're bigger," Mama said and told Weepie to nip the racy chatter.

"I want some tessyroni," Miranda said. "I like cheese on mine. Too much cheese will ruin your heart. They said that at school."

"All right, sweetie," Aunt Weepie said. "We'll all try to watch out for evil dairy products."

We were almost to the restaurant, maybe another mile, when Aunt Weepie wouldn't let the subject of her fourth husband rest. "I know you don't discuss your sex life," she said to my mother, "but my goodness you have been married 40 years and you do the cooking. The only way I can take Tony's cooking is to have two or three martinis before he spreads the mess on the table. Ooooh, I can't wait to taste those fresh, home-cooked vegetables. Aren't we there yet, Prudy?"

I saw the sign on the left, a hopeless pitiful hardwood sign that looked like someone's child had painted a few vegetables with watercolors.

The line was already out the door.

"My goodness, Luce. Look at that line. Why, this has got to be great. Everyone in town is here. Prudy, park over by that red Toyota. It's closer to the door."

We got out and stood in the sun that was heating up to 400 degrees and getting hotter by the minute. Aunt Weepie began her fellowshipping with all the strangers, and I figured at any moment, she'd offer to do a split or a handstand to entertain them as they waited on the best vegetables anyone had ever cooked on this planet, according to all the hype.

"I've been waiting weeks for this moment," she told people as the sun highlighted all her gold and freshly dyed red hair. The line finally moved into the restaurant and we waited to be seated.

Total chaos ensued as a madhouse of people rushed for the tables. Children shrieked and cried and the waitresses seemed in a state of mass confusion. Aunt Weepie couldn't take it. The restaurant was small and pitiful. "Rinky-dink," she said. "Looks like a hollowed out shell with some yard-sale tables and chairs.

"But, you just know the food in these dumps is always delicious," she added. "Now, if you'll excuse me, I'm going to relieve my bladder. If by some miracle this place gets its act together while I'm gone, order me the fried chicken, the fresh creamed corn, a batch of those turnip greens, a hot biscuit and a piece of cornbread for my greens. Tea with no sugar. Tell them I'll get my sugar in some fresh sweet peach cobbler. Tell them I like it warm with ice cream on top."

She sashayed off, pausing at various tables to spread and sprinkle her beauty dust around the joint. My mother sat defeated, once again ordered around by her big sister. She handed Miranda a crayon and she and Jay talked about his chemistry class. I sat there quietly until the waitress came, a plump young woman who had an overwhelmed cast to her face and body movements. She twitched and fidgeted while Mama gave her Weepie's order, and we managed to squeeze in our orders before the waitress lost eye contact and wandered off to the next set of diners.

Aunt Weepie finally floated out of the restroom, trailing a fresh cloud of White Rain. She was almost at our table when our waitress bounded from the kitchen carrying a huge tray of delicious-smelling home-made biscuits. The smells overpowered even my aunt's perfume and the crowd of people beamed with approval, stomachs growling left and right.

As soon as Weepie sat down we heard a loud crash. I peered around to see the waitress on the floor, writhing and epileptic-like, biscuits scuttling like scattered crabs. She hopped up and put every one of them back on her tray and ran into the kitchen.

"Lucinda," Weepie hissed. "I'll bet one of those will end up on our plates. Don't eat the biscuits," she said to the kids. "There were at least 40 on that plate. They *will* be served, so I will say this one more time: We will leave them intact and untouched with a Post-It note on top that says, *'We are onto your game.'* Y'all hear me?"

We all nodded and agreed to leave the biscuits alone.

"I was looking forward to a good old biscuit, Weepie," Mama said, clearly upset and growing more so by the minute. Something must be troubling her. She typically put on a good face, even when mad or nursing an inner wound.

"If you still want one after we eat, Prudy can stop by Hardees and get you one. From the way things are going, we should have gone there in the first place. Listen at that, would you?"

We could hear the manager fussing at the waitress from behind the flimsy kitchen doors. A few minutes later we saw the woman crying.

"In addition to carpet crud, there will also be tears on the biscuit," Aunt Weepie said. "If you eat one, you'll end up with a vile disease."

Finally, the poor waitress came lumbering along with our food, tray bearing down on her much in the way life was. The plates were small, food running over the edges and all over the waitress's forearms and apron—the chicken plopped on top of turnip green juice. The cornbread was burned. The tea tasted good. The waitress was sniffing and the only thing that smelled homemade were the biscuits, which we were instructed not to eat by Boss Weepie.

Aunt Weepie grinned and shimmied, excitement coursing through her veins. She lifted her fork and took the first bite. Her face bunched into an expression of disgust. "This food isn't fresh!" she said, loud enough to attract the interest of other diners. "It's frozen. Lucinda, it's awful. My corn niblets are still hard and half ice."

Mama took a few bites and agreed. Miranda started crying for a Happy Meal and Jay sulked and scratched at his face.

"Let's get out of here right now," Aunt Weepie ordered. "You leave that pitiful waitress a tip. I only have a hundred dollar bill." While Mama hunted a tip, Aunt Weepie shot from her seat and made a beeline for the manager who was standing at the cash register, a smug and greasy-looking man.

"I want to talk to you," she said, as he counted change, not looking up.

"Fifty-two, fifty-five, sixty—"

"You can put that money down and give me your full attention." He slammed the register shut and stared horrified at my blazing-mad aunt. I glanced toward my mother and saw she had grabbed the children and left the table; they'd sneaked to the back of the line, wanting to listen but pretending not to know Aunt Weepie.

"Can I help you?"

"You sure can. Now, just tell me how you can advertise fresh homemade food when all I put in my mouth was Campbell's or Stokely's, maybe even the cheaper stuff like Margaret Holmes's unseasoned offerings. Explain all this to me," she said as he stood transfixed, eyes darting about to see how many customers were listening to my aunt's rant. "Explain, please, and while you're at it, tell me why you haven't trained these poor waitresses to serve people. This is the most unorganized place I've ever set my size-6 feet in. Why, my husband can cook better than this and he serves hairballs!"

The restaurant's patrons began laughing, and the man turned redder than the hothouse tomatoes he was pushing off as vine-ripened.

"Ma'am, I am sorry you aren't satisfied," he boomed in a deep voice. "We will gladly not charge you."

"Listen here, mister," Aunt Weepie said, pointing a finger near his thin and scraggly mustache. "I didn't come in here for a free meal. I've seen enough low-class no-goods pulling that old trick. I pay for my meals, and I'll surely pay for my LAST one here. After we leave, you go on over to our table and read our biscuits. We left you our calling cards on top of those hairy, tear-soaked biscuits. I just may have to call the Better Business Bureau."

Mama hurried out of line and to the car, Aunt Weepie following us and saying to my mother, "What's wrong,

Lucinda? You ashamed to know me? Why didn't you come up there and help me out?"

"Weepie, what did you expect for $4.99? And by the way, you haven't seen a size-6 shoe since junior high."

"Can we go to Hardees?" Jay asked.

"Sure," I said.

While we ate burgers and fries, served hot and nothing plucked from the ground, Mama began to tell me about the date she'd found for me.

"If you agree to go," she said, "you won't be sorry. And I'll buy you a VCR for your room so you won't have to watch Snow White every day on the one in the living room."

"Thanks, Mama, but I have a VCR. Remember, my yoga routine?"

"Well, then we'll upgrade you to a DVD player. How's that?"

I bit my nails and thought for a moment. "Who is he?"

"That's the surprise. I can't tell you. He is going to pick you up tonight at 7."

"Tonight! Seven? I don't have clean hair and I have nothing to wear and I haven't started my diet yet. I have to clean toilets at the radio station, and I need to sanitize my squirrel's cage."

"You still have that varmint? That's sick. How come I never see it when I visit? I'm calling the Terminix people."

"Why don't you call this mystery man and say make it 7:30 or 8?"

"I might. So. Guess where we're going?" she asked.

"Where?"

"The mall. I'm going to buy you a beautiful outfit and have your hair done. It's been looking awful for months, long and stringy, and that last woman who highlighted your bangs made them look just like Linda Tripp's."

I stared ahead as I drove, feeling as if my life was out of control, my movements coordinated by strings woven through the deft fingers of Lucinda Millings' hands. What could a girl say? The out-of-nowhere rejection from Croc Godfrey certainly made me more willing to try out my mother's suggestion.

We were almost at the mall when I heard a wail from the backseat. I checked the rearview mirror and saw that Mama was having a fit. A full-fledged hissy fit.

"Good God," Aunt Weepie said. "What's wrong with you?"

Mama boo-hoo'd louder than I'd ever heard Weepie sob at a funeral. She grabbed her head and shook it, stomped her feet into the car mats.

"For shit's sake, pull over, Prudy," Aunt Weepie said.

I turned into an Exxon and parked, leaving the air-conditioning running. My children's faces were like those coming out of a morgue. My mother howled and stomped some more, kicking the seat with her clompy shoes.

Aunt Weepie reached back and popped her on the leg as hard as she could with her open hand. "Snap out of it, woman. There are children present."

Mama lifted her head. Her face was red and swollen, puckered in spots like when you blow something up and the air spreads out unevenly.

"Mama," I said in my most soothing voice. "What is it?"

She sniffed and blew her nose on a Hardee's napkin.

"It's Amber. She's moving ba . . . ba . . . back home," Mama said, trying to speak and melt down all at once. "First, you," sniff, sniff, "nearly get yourself killed and come home and take up again under my roof, then your little sister ups and marries herself a big old homosexual and is coming back to roost in my peaceful nest, and I've already raised you one time and don't have it in me to do it again. I'm tired. Where's the good life? Where are the golden years of travel and freedom from your children's bad decisions?"

Aunt Weepie and I sat in total shock. No one seemed to breathe. I finally asked, "Why is Amber coming home?"

She looked at me with that red, puffed-up face, smoke all but curling from her nostrils, that chin in full jut. "Her husband prefers fannies. Men's fannies. Is that all you need to know, Miss Prudy, or shall we go into great detail in front of these poor children who have no F-A-T-H-E-R?"

"They can spell, Mama."

"I got a daddy," Jay said, his ears bright red with anger. "He'll kick your ass, Mama Millings."

"Oh, take me, Jesus," she sighed and collapsed against the door, her face splatted against the window, streaks of Revlon on the glass.

"I'm not sure who Jesus is about to take, but I'm going to take these kids in for a candy bar," Aunt Weepie said, unbuckling Miranda and telling Jay to hop on out.

"Candy's bad for you," Miranda said. "I don't want any because it rots the teeth." They went inside while I waited for Mama to finish her massive fit.

"I'm too old for this. My blood pressure was 150 over 98 the other day at Eckerd's. Your murder nearly killed me, and now your sister's husband is running off with a male stewardess. Those poor twins. Not a tooth in their infant heads. And her 4-year-old. Three boys with no decent daddy. Five grandchildren with no male influence. What in the world have I done wrong to deserve these pathetic statistics?"

"What do you mean, statistics?"

"What I mean is this. Two children. Several divorces. The records show 50 percent of all marriages end in divorce. But here I got two children and three or four divorces. Oh, lawsy, what are my bridge biddies going to think? I'm ruined. I tried to be a good mother and teach you two girls right from wrong. Look at this. You're poor as white trash and your sister may have AIDS."

"AIDS? Just because he likes fannies doesn't mean he has AIDS. For God's sake Mama, calm down or I'm taking you home."

"You won't have to," she said. "I hear the Lord calling me home."

# Chapter Fifteen

**Rise and Shine, Prudy**: *A gift does wonders; it will bring you before men of importance.* ***Proverbs 18:16***

**Mama's Moral**: *Give this important man a chance; and think of me while watching movies, hopefully nothing rated R, on your new DVD player.*

AT PRECISELY 8:16 P.M., as I stared for the twentieth time at my new hairdo in utter horror, there was a knock at the door, and this time, it was Mama, not Aunt Weepie, who ran down the stairs to let more of my past inside.

"Coming," she trilled, and I heard her heavy shoes on the stairs. I wished she had made him wait. As it stood, he was exactly 16 minutes late for our date, not quite the impression decent men care to make.

"Oh, he probably got caught up in traffic," she said, and I wondered when in the world Spartanburg ever had traffic after 6 p.m. Even during rush hour, the delays never amounted to more than a few extra minutes.

I heard the door creak open, the old wood giving way once again to visitors, to this mystery man. My mother had been so excited the past couple of hours, ever since her meltdown prior to visiting the mall. She had smiled and become almost giddy, a mother who'd at least temporarily forgotten her daughters' troubles: the gay husband, the jailed husband, the five might-as-well-be fatherless grandchildren and the assortment of uncertainty her grown children faced. It was her hope, at least I assume it was, that I should fall madly but not lustfully in love with the man knocking on the door.

How in the world could I possibly let her down, especially after her mini-breakdown in my Honda? It had taken a Reese's Cup and a Diet Pepsi to rouse her into enough of a state of normalcy to proceed with my appointment for beauty and new clothing, so that I might impress this creature now entering my rental unit with the Pier 1 and Bed Bath & Beyond accessorizing.

Once the man got a load of my hair, which was crow-like in both color and feathery bang, he would run right back outside, bumping into the plastic pool on his way out of a potential nightmare. The hair was the disaster du jour, the handiwork of a Northside Mall stylist who treated me as walk-ins are often treated. No appointment, no pleasantries or juicy conversations. If a woman wants any of the above, she best have an appointment, keep it to the minute and have chosen a trendy, privately-owned salon with a name like Rumors or

A Cut Above where they offer customers bottled water and even glasses of wine.

Mall stylists are often in a league of their own. They are either fresh out of beauty school or fresh out of options, or just love the Gap so much they'll work anywhere to be near one. Sometimes you get a great one, other times, well . . . you don't.

Another thing about mall stylists or any stylist without ideas, is that they'll likely whip you into a mirror image of themselves or who they fancy being.

My particular hairstylist from the Northside Mall had hair blacker than a moonless night, and I had repeatedly told her, "Just darken mine enough to get rid of the Linda Tripp look. Please, spare my light brown shade and highlights, at least the more subtle ones."

"Sure, whatever," she said, not a bit more hearing me than Miranda did when I told her no more videos for the night. The beautician reached over me, pressing her $6,000 inflatables in my face and began mixing color.

The result of her hidden agenda to transform everyone into a version of herself stared back at me in my antique vanity. Tomorrow, if only the mystery man Mama had summoned waited one more day, I'd have had enough time to redo my hair and get my natural shade back, whatever that was. Too late now.

"How in the world you been?" I heard Mama saying in her high, sing-song, "I'm-just-a-classy-Joanne-Woodward-type" voice. In return, I heard a deep, unrecognizable muttering of clichéd responses.

I scurried quickly into Jay and Miranda's room to hide, find comfort in my babies' presence and sneak a better peek than I would have been afforded from my own room.

"Hey, darlings. What are y'all doing?"

Jay actually looked up from his book and waved at me and my heart soared. He was doing much better. I believe the basketball camp was helping, plus Grampy was taking him to sporting events and the golf course. In addition, Jay had met a new friend at camp whose daddy had died after being struck by lightning and this seemed to even life's score, so as not to appear all the bad had collected only in our court.

"You look like the Addams Family lady," he said. "Cool."

Miranda stuck out her tongue and made a face. "You look like a pooh-pooh. That stuff on your hair will give you lice bugs." I tried to hug her but she backed away and grabbed Jay, hiding behind his shirt. Both of them pretended I was the mean monster lady and squealed and shrieked with delight as I played the part chasing them around and making ghoulish noises. Despite the nightmare they had actually lived, pretend fear for some reason comforted them.

I heard the voices in the kitchen. "Y'all be quiet just for a second," I said, opening the door a crack and seeing a pure-T hunk that the good Lord must have dropped down from heaven just for me on account of past pain and suffering. Thank you, Fortuna, Mother Mary, St. Francis of Assisi and every other goddess or saint in this world.

This man was adorable, tall and curly-headed, kind of long-haired and foppish, a chiseled-faced thing with a suntan and wearing jeans that fit him like a Calvin Klein model. He had a fanny that shouted "Amen!" to me as my heart pounded, not with fear but with the most impure thoughts I'd had in a long, long time. I could show that man some Serta hospitality for sure. I thought Mama said he was a man I knew. I'd never laid eyes on this six-feet, three-inches of glory in my life.

I gave myself another once over in the kids' mirror. Whew, I was one ugly looking woman. Thank goodness for the wonderful white peasant blouse and slimming jeans Mama had bought me. Even my large arse could pass for an 8 in these well-cut pants. I wished turbans were in so I could cover up this ghastly crow hair. I'll bet Aunt Weepie or Annie Sue had a turban, but it was too late in the game to round one up. I had an idea, though, and rummaged through Miranda's drawer and found a thick white headband and pulled my black hair from my face, applied some pink frosted lipstick (which as I've noted previously will cure any beauty problem) and decided this was an improvement, despite the fact that an iron-on Barbie danced in ballet shoes on the side of my head. Maybe he wouldn't notice the tiny figure emblazoned on the headband.

I promised Jay a baseball game and Miranda a new Groovy Girl if they'd let me get through this one date without a hitch. "You guys behave for your Mama 'Cinda," I said. Jay gave me a big hug. Miranda once more told me I was ugly but that the headband made me "one ounce better looking."

When I walked into the kitchen, my mother's hand flew to her mouth. She'd zoomed right in on the Barbie headband. "Prudy, sweetheart, don't you look pretty," she lied, and I felt

12 again. Instinctively, my hand went to my neck and chest where the huge silver necklace, a woven pattern that took up a lot of space, covered most of the scars.

The unbelievably attractive, throw-down-on-the-ground gorgeous man next to her nodded approvingly and winked. How vain I thought. He winked! Yuck. "You remember this fellow?" Mama said. "Be sure and think a minute before you answer, Prudy."

"It's Dee. Tonight, it's Dee." I checked him out, and there was something oddly familiar about him, the eyes, the thick unruly hair. Maybe I did know him. I searched my mind and couldn't place him, though I knew he was there, lost in the gray folds of living and too much information crowding those things I should have retained.

"We're not going to tell you. You have to guess," he said. And then it hit me, the dimples I hadn't seen since. Since . . . 1980. The image of a little boy, at our supper table, eating like it was his last meal, hair damp from our washing him in the bathroom sink, slammed into me. I couldn't believe what I was seeing and hearing.

I shook my head and said, "No. No way. How did you find him?"

My mother smiled victoriously. So did Landon. The little boy who all but lived with us for a couple of years. The muddy neighbor boy whose mom had died of cancer, whose empty eyes had searched ours to fill his, whose precious dirty face was a staple at our kitchen table for nights of chicken casseroles and green beans with potatoes. I remembered his dimples, how he smiled when we put him in the sink and let the warm water rush through those thick curls. How we'd lather him up, singing while we suds, then fed him home-cooked meals and taught him about love and family and the etiquette of the South.

Mama, as I recalled, had wanted to adopt him. And here was Landon . . . Landon . . . what's his last name? . . . in my kitchen, drinking one of my Miller Lites and having himself a grand old time with my once sane mother who in the past 24 to 48 hours had turned from the stable branch of our frenetically fed family tree to the shakiest of all. Her behavior of late made Annie Sue and her "Hottie" T-shirt and naughty bar jokes seem almost blasé. She had soared above even my Aunt Weepie's madness.

In this state, this frantic condition, she could and would do anything. She was a woman whose daughters had plummeted from grace. She would take life by its choking collar and unleash what was rightly owed her of the good life. And here he was: Landon . . . Landon . . .

"Tell me, because for the life of me I can't remember," I said, "What is your last name?"

"Kennedy," he said. A Kennedy. My mother had gone out and found her daughter a Kennedy. Who cared if he wasn't anymore related to John-John than old Myrtle Monroe down in Seneca was related to Marilyn. It was a last name. Oh, but to my mother . . . She could tell the bridge club that her daughter, the one nearly murdered at BI-LO, has hooked up with a Kennedy. She might even dare whisper to a select few that he was a "distant cousin of the real thing," and then sip her coffee in utter triumph.

It takes a Southern daughter to understand the inner workings of the Southern-mother mind. I had her number, although it hung around my neck like a noose she could tug and pull at will.

"It's really wonderful to see you again," I said to Landon, and he lifted his beer and took himself an introductory swig then released his grip on the bottle with a satisfied sigh. No return greeting. Where were the manners we'd taught the boy? My, to look so fine he was as rough around the edges as a pair of Annie Sue's pinking-sheared short-shorts.

"Prudy, you'll never in a million years guess what he does for a living." Mama was beaming. Any more endorphins and she'd have ascended to the heavenly kingdom she's been awaiting since buying her mausoleum.

I thought about potential careers for vagabond, motherless boys who liked dirt and sopping gravy with biscuits.

"Got me."

"Guess, Prudy," Mama demanded, opening the fridge and helping herself to a beer. My mouth dropped open. My mother didn't drink beer but maybe once a year. She twisted the cap off with the tail of her silk shirt and held the beer to the light, then put her mauve lips around the opening, not even bothering to pour it in a glass. She tilted the bottle and swallowed six or seven times without pause. "Lord, have mercy, that's delicious."

The world wasn't spinning correctly; it had shifted, reversed, and nothing had been going right for the last two years in our family, particularly these past few months since I'd finally gotten a place of my own. "I can't tell you how I met him or that would give it all away."

"Mother, it would be my best guess, given his physique and head of hair, that whatever he does definitely doesn't involve the banking industry, the law profession or anything that requires conforming attire and mannerisms."

"Just talk plain, Prudy," she said, finishing her beer and reaching for another. "I done told him you got yourself a B.S. degree. Ain't no use putting on a pretense." She was doling out double negatives and "ain'ts," which she'd never done before. It was the beer. And now it's back to the two basic types of women in the South. The classy preppy types who join sororities and service organizations and talk with proper grammar and a lovely Southern buttery drawl, and the redneck types, the hicks who have a certain beauty, granted, but one that is buried beneath tons of makeup, hard living and the unfortunate habit of smoking cigarettes, which can suck the prettiness right out of a girl.

If say, a woman happens to fall somewhere between the two types, due to a generation or two of family members finding education and higher rungs on the social ladder, then it's a sure bet that after a few beers she'll land right back where the family originally began. She'll be twanging and ain'ting and acting like she'd never in her life shopped anywhere but Wal-Mart at 2 a.m. on a Saturday night. My mama was 12 ounces away from becoming an aging redneck.

I eyeballed the handsome man in front of me and secretly broke a few commandments. I figured he worked outside, given his muscles and bulging pecs. I was dead wrong.

"You are tanned, well built . . . I would say you are a building contractor or an outdoor fitness instructor. Or maybe you're a student. You can't be more than 32."

"Close," he said, grinning, those dimples sending my thoughts into the bedroom, a kitchen table, the woods, any surface would do. I did some figuring. If I slept with him, which I very much wanted to do in spite of his unpolished ways, this would put me well into digits that weren't acceptable. I was already at 12 to 14, (my memory fuzzy about two of the encounters), unless one believes the lie I'd all but convinced myself to believe, the measly four men I'd told Bryce about. Going one more couldn't hurt. It was too late to pull out of the double digits, and an extra lover would not bump me from the teens and into the super-slutty 20s. Why, I could even go up four more. No use sweating over adding him to the list.

"Prudy, come on and guess, hon," my mother said, sounding exactly like Wynonna Judd, not that there's anything wrong with Wynonna, it's just that usually Mama sounds more like Naomi or Ashley. The Judds, by the way, are perfect examples of the two factions of Southern women. All the Judds are pretty. One simply decided to stay on the lower rung, and, in a way, I had to admire her for doing so.

"Pruuuuuuudy?" Mama licked foam from her top lip.

"Tell me please, before I have to go find some fun on my own, leave you two here to reminisce and pretend to be Jackie and John-John splitting a sixer."

"Hush up, Prudy, and act sweet. Listen to this," she shouted. "He's a vet! A veterinarian! A man who takes care of—"

"I know what a vet is, Mama."

Landon was smiling as if he'd finished Harvard at the top of his class and received the Nobel not long thereafter.

"That's great. Really, you must love working with the animals. We have a pet squirrel if you're interesting in taking its pulse."

"Prudy, Wuudy," my mother slurred, deep into her second beer, getting sloshed on a mere 24 ounces just like Annie Sue. "He's a D-O-C-T-O-R."

"Are we still spelling, today? I realize vets have their doctorate degrees," I said. "Did you tell him about my squirrel and how I'd brought it back to life with some good old mouth-to-mouth?"

Mama ignored me.

"It's really a tough profession to break—" Landon was saying when Mama cut in.

"I mean it ain't, *isn't* rather, the highest rooster in the pecking order of medical doctors—no offense, Landon, hon—but at least M.D. comes after his name. M.D.!"

"Actually, Mrs. Millings, "It's D.V.M., Doctorate of Veterinary Medicine."

Mama thought for a moment, eyes red and cheeks flush with drink. "Do they call you Dr. Kennedy?" she asked in a voice like a squealing pig getting ready for a fine cob of corn.

"They sure do," he said, basking in my mother's appreciation of his accomplishments.

"Hear that, Prudy? You hear that? I had taken Kitty Bitty to get her shots and there he was, old Doc Newsome's new partner. There he was. I couldn't believe it. I ran out of there and forgot poor Kitty Bitty I was so beside myself. Are you aware of this man's talents?"

"I believe I understand them." And I'm hoping he has others, I wanted to add but did not.

"He cuts open baby animals and fixes their little intestines and stomachs and things. All those tiny parts must be much harder to operate on. I believe this makes him smarter than a doctor with bigger organs to fix. Makes him a genius. You know, Prudy, here? She's got herself a genius back there in the back bedroom. Bona fide."

"I'll have to meet him soon," the Great Neutering One said, as if he'd do my child a favor by offering an introduction.

"You ready to go?" I asked, but he and my mother were having another beer, his second, her third, before I went to the fridge and took the last one out and opened it myself, drinking it just so my kids wouldn't have a sloshed babysitter.

After about 30 minutes, during which time the kids ran around wild and hyped up on Mama's insistence that Little Debbie's were part of a major food group, the phone rang. I lunged for it, as if whatever was going on inside the receiver was better than the turn things were taking in what Mama likes to call my "rinky-dink rental."

"We really hate to bother you," said the old woman downstairs that we'd rarely seen since moving in. "But Fred recently returned home from having by-pass surgery and he needs his rest. Could you have the children play a little more quietly?"

I covered the receiver with my hand. "It's the neighbors," I said to the children. "Y'all please tone it down. She says we're too loud . . . I'm so sorry, Mrs. . . . uh—"

"Give me that phone," my newly brazen mother said, grabbing it from my hand.

"Can we help you?" she snapped. "Well yes, I'm well aware of that. Uh-huh, I'm sure he is . . . that's really useful information we'll have to keep in our memories . . . all right . . . do what?" Mama tucked the receiver under her arm and said to Landon and me, "Old hag says she'd almost had enough when she come home one day and seen the house all pink.

"It's not pink," Mama said into the receiver. "It's salmon," and she pronounced the L. "I thought you were from Florida and would appreciate a colorful house, 'specially one the color of a fish. Isn't that what y'all do down there? Go wild in that hot sun painting your houses an assortment of pastels? The owners gave us permission, if you recall, which it appears you don't." There was a moment of silence on Mama's part. She frowned and swigged her beer. "Uh-huh. I figured you were Jersey. Figured it right off the bat . . . say what? . . . I have you know I paid $3,200 to have the house painted for you so you ought to be sending me a Hallmark 'Thank-You' card. You want my address so you can send it?"

"Mama!" I shouted, snatching the phone. "I am so sorry about her," I said to the woman. "She's not herself. We're sending her in for testing tomorrow, so please excuse this behavior."

"No one ever asked me if I wanted a pink house," the old woman said, her memory dusty.

"What color would you prefer, ma'am?"

"One without . . . without . . . such goings-on above us. It's like a bowling alley up there with all the racket."

"I'm sorry, really. I'll try to remind myself and the children not to flop about like a herd of T-rexes."

I hung up and turned to Mama. Landon wasn't paying this scenario the least bit of attention. He'd gone into the living room and cut on the TV, flipping all the channels, which we now had since I am rising up in the income world due to the radio gigs and can afford the better cable offerings. Men will retreat to any area of a house as long as they don't have to witness the dramatics of domestic friction.

"Prudy," Mama said, finishing beer. "You don't need to live above them Yankees. I'm going out tomorrow and finding you another place. This is no kind of—"

"I'm starting to like it here and the kids are adjusting. I'm not about to move them again."

"Fine . . . get your purse and you and what's his face go have some fun." She wiggled a long finger in the direction of the living room, her eyes watering from drink and mirth. "Don't drop your drawers, Prudy. I know you'd like to. Lord, if I wasn't such a good Christian I'd be tempted to—"

"I'm going to fix you a sandwich before I leave you with my children," I said. "A club with three pieces of bread to absorb some of that alcohol that's got you talking crazy."

"Oh, it ain't the alcohol," she said. "I've had these thoughts in my head for years. I've held them back from you and Amber, trying to act decent and upright so you girls would defy the statistics. You defied them all right. Up and exceeded the 50 percent single-parent household rate. Not one daughter's gonna stay married. Where did I go wrong?"

I gave her the sandwich, a big scoop of pasta salad and a hug. "It's okay, Mama. None of this is your fault. We picked wrong. People do that sometimes and there doesn't have to be some deep underlying reason. All those therapists who say I'll never get well because I don't get angry enough, they believe every choice a person makes is indirectly or directly based on her raising. I think there may be some truth in that, but only a little. I picked Bryce. Amber picked the chicken man."

We talked for a few more minutes, Mama growing more coherent and rational, giving me the confidence to leave with Dr. Kennedy and see where this date was headed.

We did a last-minute check on the children who had grown quiet, which is never a good sign. They were giggling and watching a PG-13 movie Aunt Weepie had loaned me. Cuss words flew, and I couldn't handle Miranda hearing such, not with her convent-like mannerisms.

"Don't let them watch this movie, Mama."

"You're the one with the filth in this house," she said. Good. She was becoming an old stiff prude again. The food did the trick.

"Well, all right," I said, replacing *Ferris Bueller's Day Off* with *Shrek.* "I guess I'll go see what Dr. Kennedy's been doing to entertain himself during all this lunacy."

"Prudy," Mama said. "Remember your morals. I know you must have the itch. Please, don't go using this youngster to scratch it. Not until you're married."

"Married? I have no plans for that again." I left her standing in thought and discovered Landon asleep on the couch, hands folded in his lap, mouth ajar. "Not on my time, buddy," I said and kicked his foot to rouse him. We decided to try the new oyster bar in town where a classic '70s rock band played on weekends. The radio station had been promoting the new place all week and the band, a group called the Boomerangs, was supposed to be great according to Landon and all the hype. It's just the ticket for people like him—younger than I with no dependents, men who say things like "cop a buzz" and "chill." Those were his exact words, the language of a man with four years of vet school and internships. He was set on going there and that was fine with me.

The parking lot was packed, mostly newer cars, sporty and youthful, not many wagons or SUVs, a sign this place catered to the market everyone was after: 18–34. As usual, I was a few years past the expiration date, and no one was courting my "market" these days.

We went inside the stucco bar with a Spanish tile roof, a former Mexican restaurant that had gone out of business. The place was freezing cold and smelled like a pier. I shivered, my flesh rising and neck stiffening. Men in khakis and polished girls with good skin and white teeth sat on tall barstools as they cracked oysters, peeled shrimp and drank imports.

Farther into the room, where the light grew dimmer and then brightened around a small stage, was the band. I paid them no attention. They fiddled around onstage, warming up, tuning and checking equipment. I turned my back to them, focusing on Dr. Kennedy. The place was loud, and even though the smokers were relegated to the bar, the clouds floated like blimps into each room. We were all as one, breathing the same air, blending all factions of Southern society on the basis of a common interest in classic rock and shellfish.

Landon ordered a Blue Moon with an orange slice and I sipped a glass of Zinfandel, what Annie Sue calls "pussy wine." A few minutes later the band started and I could ignore them no longer. As soon as the first words came out of the singer's mouth—though my back was toward him—I froze. The male voice was in perfect pitch and sounded like the lead singer from Ambrosia. I'd know that voice anywhere, any time. I couldn't swallow, couldn't talk, could not even turn my head 180 degrees to see that at the microphone, singing his heart out, was none other than Croc Godfrey.

He belted out "You're the Biggest Part of Me," my favorite Ambrosia tune he used to sing to me in the clubs when we were young and first started dating. The voice, the singing, skinny Croc Godfrey moving his body with the music, caused a corner of my heart to fall away. The tears poured without warning. It wasn't time for my period. I wasn't hormonal and yet they spilled anyway, falling into my bar napkin. They went unnoticed by Landon Kennedy who was grooving and guzzling and trying to absorb every single woman as she walked by. His head swiveled like a gyroscope, and he couldn't stop checking out everything with breasts that came within 50 yards of him.

Eventually, he got up and roamed around, told me he'd be back "in a while." I sat there and cried, drank my wine and heard one song after the next. Pablo Cruise, Zeppelin, Electric Light Orchestra, Doobie Brothers, Foghat, Steely Dan—all of them until the set ended and Landon returned from wherever he'd disappeared, hands in his pocket, probably to make sure the phone numbers and business cards from horny women were still in there.

"Want another wine?" he asked, not even seeing me, speaking into the dark bar air, over the voices that had risen since the music stopped.

"Why not?" Nothing like drinking pussy wine alone while your heart flaps on the floor, and your ex-ex boyfriend (who dumped you twice) tears it up onstage.

"There're a few pool tables in the next room. You play?"

"We used to have one in our house, remember? Seems you played when you were a little kid. I used to beat you then, might as well do it again." I smiled, and he didn't return my gesture.

We walked into the next room, a cloud of cigarette smoke hovering, not moving, just growing larger like a lifeless Portuguese Man-of-War. I felt feverish from the wine and the tears, the music that peeled the years off, even if only in mind and spirit. Landon broke the balls, and I went first, leaning over like a vixen, making my shot, landing the pocket I'd told him I would hit. I stood up and raised my eyebrows.

"Not bad," he said. "Let's see you do it again."

And I did. Four more times the cue ball smacked the target ball, sending it into the chosen pocket, then rolled and spun its way into perfect position for my next shot. This felt good. Bryce had never allowed me to shoot pool, said it was "skank's play."

"Pretty impressive," I heard someone say. Croc's voice. I didn't know whether to feel mad as hell at him for rejecting me or for daring to come to Spartanburg to play a gig without letting me know. This was certainly a major slap in the face. Had he the slightest bit of interest in me at all, he would have called to say he was coming to town. But no. He hadn't. So I could either play it mean, as if I didn't give a flying hoot, or I could be all nice and cool, just like Holly Golightly from *Breakfast at Tiffany's*. I'd be charming and indifferent. I'd be anybody but the insecure and indignant woman I really was at the moment.

"Nice to see you, Croc," I said, smiling, thankful I'd thought to reapply my pink frosted lipstick moments earlier. "I don't believe you know Landon. Landon, this is Croc Godfrey. My ex."

Not missing a chance to be pretentious, Landon said, "Hi. I'm Dr. Landon Kennedy. Animals. All sizes and breeds. Nice to meet you, Crotch."

"It's Croc," I said. "As in crocodile. His real name's Edward, but when he was young he kept baby crocodiles for pets and the name stuck with him. Plus, he really doesn't look like an Edward. Or kiss like one from what I recall, but naturally a girl's memory fades after 19 years."

Croc grinned, and it appeared his teeth had lightened since our date weeks ago. Maybe he'd discovered Crest Strips. He seemed amused by the scene I caused, and I noticed him checking out my rude but beautiful date who did not remotely resemble Gandhi, God love him. My escort for the evening weighed more than me, which certainly raises the score in most women's books.

"Take good care of that one," Croc said. "She's a winner on all accounts." I couldn't believe the words from his lips after this recent rejection.

"Say, Prude, or Dee, rather," Landon said, finally noticing I had a pulse. "What's with the limp? Your leg hurt?"

"No," I said, hating being called Prude. "Hard to have a hurt leg when you don't have a bone." I died laughing. I couldn't help myself: the wine, my mother, the strange tilt of the bizarre world. "Did you not hear about me? Did Mama casually 'forget' to tell you? I'm the woman married to the preacher who went nuts and ran over her with the church van. See this?" I pulled my necklace to the side to reveal the holes in my skin, the gray dented scars, deep as his dimples.

"Christ Almighty," he said. His expression formed that look I'd seen on so many men's faces. It reflected a blank screen, the flicker of eye and the pause in animation when a woman knows what he's thinking. That he's in over his head. That even a divorced woman, or say, a woman with a kid or two was baggage enough. But this? A divorce, two kids, a near-murder, boneless leg and pierced chest? He morphed into a cornered dog, hunting a way out of the room.

"She's been through a lot, but I've never met more of a survivor or wonderful mother," Croc said, knowing I was on the edge; he'd seen it many times even if it had been 19 years ago. He patted my shoulder, a there-there type of affection similar to the comforts we dole out at Top of the Hill.

"You a big or small animal vet?" Croc asked, trying to steer the conversation back to neutral ground. Landon was not biting and instead his mind was on how to get away from me and my heavy-duty past. His eyes were transfixed and staring another hole in my chest.

"What the hell did he use to make those kinds of wounds?" he asked as tactlessly as I'd ever heard a question put by a grown-up with any amount of decency.

I ignored him and focused instead on Croc's question. "His specialty," I said, "is neutering. Small animals. Large ones. Humans, too. I do believe he's trying to neuter either you or me right here in this nightclub. What do you think, Croc? You think he stands a chance?"

"Not with you, sweet girl," Croc said. I thought he was so classy and precious the way he behaved that I almost forgot he'd had me on a blanket in the dark and never called back for an encore. Landon, on the other hand, fidgeted and prepared himself for a quick exit. Both were confusing me to the point it was hard to remember who to be mad at, so I decided to be aloof and a bit mean with each. That's the strategy Aunt Weepie used to get 11 marriage proposals, four husbands and a giant jewelry chest crammed with gemstones.

"Croc, it was nice seeing you," I said, noticing my date was inching toward the bar. "I appreciate your not giving me the time of day since our little 'Lake Date,' seeing as how I didn't have it anyway due to my super busy schedule. I was telling Dr. Kennedy just the other day while we were eating a romantic lunch at The Gardens Café, I said, 'Landon, hon. There's a fellow who broke my heart 19 years ago when he left me for a Miss Georgia finalist with dentures.' Remember her? Before your wife? I said, 'If that's not enough, a few weeks ago he breaks it all over again. Could you fix him for me, sugar pie?'"

I grinned and tried to wink at Landon, to let him in on the secret, but he had glanced away, eyes on a tall blonde with obvious saline lifting her to new heights and the only scars on her chest the small slits where the surgeon had stuffed in her new "milkies," as my daughter Miranda calls them.

"I've meant to call you," Croc said. "A lot has happened, I'm so glad to see you, and truly, you look gorgeous. I've missed you so much."

"Spare me, darlin'," I said with sarcasm.

"Now, listen, Prudy. Please. I really—"

"I have a phone. I have a mailbox. And tonight, if you'll excuse me, I'll be having a heaping serving of Dr. Kennedy here who has other specialties besides animals. If you know what I mean. Come on, Landon, time to go home."

"I'm not leaving." His eyes were all over that blonde.

"You'll take her home like a decent gentleman," Croc said, getting up in Landon's face.

"Yes, you will," I said. "You can always return for the kill. She's not going anywhere. Just to be sure, I'll run tell her you're a doctor and a Kennedy. That ought to do it."

I was on a roll of rejection, not knowing how to behave. It's bad enough when one man doesn't call, but when another doesn't jump on your suggestive remarks, the humiliation is more than unbearable. I then took a higher road and did what Mama does, pulling compliments from thin air.

"Croc, your voice has never sounded better." He was smiling, a confused daze in his eyes. "You have more talent than I ever knew possible. I was too young to fully appreciate it then. Never, ever give up your music." I flashed him a classic phony Southern-woman smile.

"Prudy, wait," he said as I was heading for the door. "Prudy!"

Inside my soul, I was completely undone by the rejection of both men but not about to show it. I would pretend all was great in my world. If there is one thing I do know about men it is this: They are driven 100 percent cuckoo over women who seem to have lives and interests outside their relationships with them. The women who chase and pine are going nowhere. They'll get nothing but society's backwash and leftovers.

Even the homely girls who act like they have it all together drive men crazy as long as they seem slightly detached. The plain Janes with exciting lives never lack the attention of available and genetically normal-to-superior males. That's why you see so many giblets married to hunks. They've fooled them with fabulous hobbies and interests. Yes, that's the secret. A social calendar squeezed and overbooked with marvelous events and activities.

I would try this strategy with these buffoons.

"Croc, once again, and perhaps never again, it was nice to see you. I must rest up. Got an early morning at the airport. Flying lessons. Gotta be sharp. While we're up in the air, we're going ahead with the skydiving training from last weekend." I didn't tell him my real plans: a minor league baseball game with Jay, then last-minute preparations for the big dance I'd cooked up for a week from tonight at the old folks home, complete with a D.J. from Bubba's Hideaway Bar and Grill and a pack of bikers who'd agreed to cut the rug with the golden oldies. I'd promised Annie Sue a complete makeover to go with her Posh Spice hairstyle. It was to be quite a busy day, but nothing in it glamorous, risky or smashing enough to entice wonderful men to seek my company.

"Hmm. You are one busy woman," Croc said, not buying any of it.

"Say, you skydive?" Landon asked, getting in on the tail end of the conversation, the part that interested him.

"Easy as shooting pool."

"Cool," he said.

And I thought, *How can men this verbally and socially challenged ever get into vet school?* Maybe he's much better with animals, pups and kittens that wanted only two meals and a stomach rub. Conversation, especially witty exchanges, not required.

"Prudy," Croc said as Landon beat a path to the bar. "Make sure Doctor Boy treats you with the respect you deserve. I want you to know I had a wonderful time with you the other week."

"Yes, Croc. I can tell."

"I'll call you, sweet girl. There's a very real explanation as to why I had to back off for a while. I'm so sorry. Please. Just take my call."

"I may. Good seeing you." I walked away, managed a weak wave as another piece of my heart sank and the tears threatened to fall from eyes already burning from smoke. It was a long drive home. Mama wasn't going to be happy about this at all. I had tried. That's all a girl can do.

***

Two days later on a cloudy, almost breathable Monday morning, I remembered I hadn't checked the mail. In the box was another letter. Bryce Jeter's Charlotte address. A letter, it seemed, from him to me, directly. I shoved it in my pocket and went inside to make the children breakfast before dropping them off at Mama's and going to the radio station for my show to discuss the subject of how whiny children end up conservative and confident children somehow become liberals. This radio job I loved almost as much as the work at Top of the Hill.

Once I got to the station, I slipped into the ladies room and ripped open the letter, my hands damp with fear and shaking. My stomach twisted and I felt sick. I entered a stall and sat fully clothed on the edge of the toilet seat, the proper place to read a letter from Satan's Twin.

It was typewritten, once again.

*"Dear Prudy: I love you and am so sorry for what I did. I'm not sure what it was that caused me to snap, other than the fact I was driven insane by constant thoughts of you cheating on me. I wish it didn't have to be like this, but there is no other way. You put me here, so now I'm going to put you where you belong. If you know what's good for you, and you never have before, you will move to Virginia immediately and allow my parents to have meaningful relationships with my children, their grandchildren.*

*If you don't move, I am not at liberty to say what will happen to any of you. I have plenty of connections, if you know what I mean. I guess you heard I'm gravely ill. I won't go into that at this time.*

*Yours, Bryce."*

This was the first time I hadn't seen his letters signed, "Yours in Christ." Maybe he realizes he is evil. But this very mention that he would hurt me or my children again, was the last straw, the one he'll never pull again. I sat there, the hard plastic of the toilet seat causing my legs to go to sleep. I sensed the approaching anger that hadn't come since the accident. I trembled and my entire body began sweating and then shaking violently. I threw up, a vile sickness in my stomach, a deep and darkening edge closing in on my vision, the entire world zooming in, zooming out, making no sense at all.

I had just enough strength to stand up and walk toward the studio for my show. After that, it was time to pay my ex-husband a little visit. Way past time to drive to Charlotte and see what he's been doing with himself these past two years.

# Chapter Sixteen

**Hey Miss, Prudy:** *A man with hate in his heart may sound pleasant enough, but don't believe him, for he is cursing you in his heart.* ***Proverbs 26:24-25***

**Mama's Moral:** *Watch out for the smooth talkers. Like Satan's Twin. And probably Croc. Give Landon Kennedy one more chance. Please.*

BY THE TIME I was done taping, the room was spinning and I held the edge of the chair until my fingers hurt, pressing my feet harder into the floor, trying to anchor stability that threatened to disintegrate.

"Dr. Dee!" Mr. Hammer, Chuck's boss boomed, calling out my on-air name. "Are you with us? As I've stated twice, the show's over."

"Good morning," I said, barely whispering. "This is Dr. Dee and I'm here to . . . to . . . may I help you?" *Care for some fries with that? Would you like to supersize?* I wasn't thinking straight.

"Dee you're OFF the air. Are you listening?"

In my mind I could hear a caller, someone's voice fading in and out like a speaker with a bad connection. "I'm going right now to get that parenting book . . . you'll be . . . then let's see what you think you can . . . just put him in time out if—"

I sat there until the station manager shook my shoulders and hooked one elbow under mine. "Let's go into my office," he said. "We need to talk."

When life begins tumbling as it had for the last two years, it keeps rolling until it hits bottom. I was about to smash into mine.

"Dee," Mr. Hammer said, settling me into a cold leather chair in front of his desk, the chair for minions and hopefuls and subordinates. His smooth radio voice boomed deeply, a tuba of tones, a voice that could make the unaware rush out to Bojangles for a biscuit, hurry over to Haverty's for a new loveseat. It was an advertiser's magic carpet ride to sales. It had taken him to the top of this radio station in a fairly large market for rock stations. He was going places. He had honors and framed awards on his wall and heavy glass trophies lined up on a shelf.

"I'm terribly sorry," he said, cracking his chubby fingers. "You have a certain audience, the moms, granted, but quite frankly, I'm not sure about their buying power. Appears their husbands have control over everything, including the finances. Bottom line," he was no longer making eye contact, "bottom line is we don't have the budget to keep the show going. We're going to have to let you go. You were great and funny as hell, but parents don't really think they need an expert. They think they ARE the expert."

Let me go. Let me go? Go where? Where does a woman go who has plates and screws in one leg and a chest full of holes? This is where I thought I belonged. No matter what was going on or how many letters Satan's Twin sent, flip on the radio and there I was, every morning at 8 a.m. I wondered, but didn't ask, if I could still clean the restrooms and perform housekeeping duties. My mouth filled with what tasted like quarters, dimes, nickels. I tried to swallow the bitterness.

I was speechless. All I could say was, "Why?"

"The audience we're targeting is much younger. The demographics have changed. We're courting the 18 to 34s. It's the way of the world. We're changing the show to a dating format to meet our audiences' needs."

Everything was about the demographics. The world loved Gen X. Gen Y. Baby Boomers had done their spending, were now sucking off the system they'd bought into, reaping their interest rates, paying off their mortgages, buying power on pause, a group feeding off savings and purchases made long ago. "And the kids want more music, less talk. We could cut you back to $50 and put you on at night."

"I have small children. It wasn't even my idea to have the show, but since it started my whole life was getting better." By then he had quit listening and I could feel the edges of anger broiling and approaching the surface of my mind like a raging fire.

"Dee, it's just the way it is." I kept hearing a Bruce Hornsby song in my head after he said it then repeated it. "That's just the way it is. We'll do one more show to wrap things up. Give you a chance to direct the market elsewhere. Oh, and you can still serve as our housekeeper."

"I don't fully understand, if you could—"

"No ad dollars. Nobody's paying for the programming. People don't want to advertise their new cars when a bunch of women are calling in yakking on and on about their juvenile delinquent children."

"Please. We could do another type show. I could help women who've been through spouse abuse. Just think. It might work and really help—"

Mr. Hammer turned red as a hot pepper. "They shouldn't have married the bastards in the first place."

So this is how he saw it. This is how the world saw it. Men beat up their wives and girlfriends and that's just the way it is. It's been happening since man's beginnings and we'd better damned get used to it. Take our punishment. Shut our mouths and wear our pretty underthings and fix a decent meal and act like when he's inside us that it's the grand prize, that all that cooking and cleaning and the putdowns about our fat asses and our cheating and our ugly stupid minds and terrible driving and parenting skills don't matter. Throw all those verbal and psychological abuses out the window and suck it up because now . . . now . . . you're getting the big one. The golden spike. Lay down woman and submit. That's just the way it is. The way it will always be.

Women try to leave, over and over they try to leave and the bad wolf brings them back and dumps them in a pot of boiling water, cooking their souls and frying their resolve until nothing is left. He promises to kill them if they don't stay. And when they stay, like good dogs, he'll beat them and rip their skins and break their bones but he won't kill them. Not usually. He reserves the knives and bullets, vans and screwdrivers for when she gets brave enough to take out a restraining order and show a little power. This infuriates him. He decides to put her in her place. Once and for all. That's just the way it is. The way it will always be.

The anger, the missing link to my life according to the therapists, was marching to the front of the emotional lineup. I felt it, the way it heated my skin and scalded my veins: tapping drumming pounding. It had to get out. It begged for release. It had simmered for two years, and suddenly, with this news, rushed to the surface. I reached up to feel my cheeks and they were flaming.

I saw flashes of light, of Bryce, his chrome bumper dazzling against the sun before ramming into me, sending my body reeling through the plate-glass window. Before anyone came to help, Bryce pounced, straddling my bleeding and broken body as I tried to thrash and fight back on the hard sidewalk. I felt his smooth manicured hands around my throat, squeezing tighter, then releasing me while he fumbled with a six-pack of Phillip's screwdrivers, choosing his murder weapon as an afterthought. No one did a thing but stand gawking, mouths agape.

I remember smelling French fries, the kind at McDonald's, hot and right out of the oil. I looked around for heroes when the first screwdriver entered with a sharp, intense pain, over and over, until it didn't hurt anymore, and I was using one hand to cover my face and the other to shield my heart. Instinctively, I knew if he struck my left chest it was all over. No more life. No more love from my two babies who were with Jenny and had no idea their daddy was trying to kill their mommy with the same tool kit he used to put batteries in their Fisher Price toys.

My eyes flew open and didn't blink. I stared as the dead do while Bryce held up a small screwdriver and jabbed it into my neck, shoulders and the breasts that had fed our babies. Again and again the screwdriver plunged and I felt nothing, only the dullness of an object, like someone poking a finger to get your attention and the warm wetness of blood and a body unplugged.

After eight or ten blows with one of the smaller screwdrivers, he threw it aside and picked the biggest from the bunch and stabbed it into my chest twice, nicking the ventricle until I lost my breath, choking for air, and felt consciousness slipping and the entire world cut off its light. I saw the yellow plastic handle of the screwdriver, I saw his purpled face, the blood. All the blood. My blood. I saw my leg, the tibia bursting through skin and panty hose and foot bent like a wrung chicken's neck. Someone in the grocery store had called 911, a giant man was on top of me trying to pull Bryce off, and the crews arrived seconds before I'd have died.

My anger was now out of control as I stared at Mr. Hammer and reached for the first object I could find, the cell phone, hurling it across the room, aiming for floor, but accidentally hitting the glass framed awards case and listening as it shattered into hundreds of splintered shards. Instead of feeling guilty and apologetic, I took it a step further and threw the chair into the bookcase, a hot river of adrenalin surging up my spine. I began to scream and couldn't stop. The station manager picked up his desk phone, sweat on his upper lip and around his armpits, and called for security. I crouched behind a sofa in the corner, nothing moving but my shirt, the fabric beating from the marathon pace of my heart, which had become a live animal, an eviscerated creature, skinned and raw and trying to escape. My mind was gone . . . sailing to BI-LO, in the parking lot, dead unblinking eyes on the display window. Silver Queen Corn, six ears for a dollar.

I couldn't stop the flow or pace of memories. They rushed without direction and all I could do was watch. I saw Bryce's tanned fingers, wedding ring glinting gold in the sun the first time the sharp tool slashed the skin and, then later, when there was no pain, only heat, like a few drops of splashed boiling water. My eyes rolled back and I saw other feet, feet of human beings standing far enough away to watch, but not moving toward me, not helping, not pushing the beast from my body. He held his hand up again and I reached for his face, my nails digging into his perfect cheeks, tearing and scratching as hard as I could, only the weapon plunged down again and again. This time, my hands let go and cupped my heart, one across my face. Consciousness was flickering, blinking. On and off. Alive. Dead. Heart beat beat beating. Flatlining.

And now in the radio station, lights flashed, maybe sounds. I was no longer in the world of functioning beings. Men and a couple of women arrived in navy pants and thick black boots. They carried red crash carts and medical kits. Police cars squealed into the station parking lot, blue lights splashing the afternoon with intrigue. The paramedics asked questions but it was dark in my head, and I was unable to separate the voices, just heard them melding together like indiscernible jazz and couldn't make out the questions. It was like a choir, only everyone singing different songs. Two of them lifted me onto a stretcher and eased me down the four steps leading from the station's front door and into one of two waiting ambulances. I saw faces—people pointing, and someone, someone . . . laughing.

The ride was different from the one I'd had after Bryce ran over me. For the first time my brain had jolted into remembering details of the crime, not the pain or the rampage, but the ride. I remember the interior of the rescue vehicle, the freezing cold feeling of losing control, the warmed blankets the EMS crew draped around my legs while they ripped away my shirt and tried to prevent the holes in my neck and chest from spewing any more blood. There were needles and nervous, loud voices. Equipment flung and discarded and piercing my body, paddles and rapid heart flutters, then no flutters then darkness, light, a face, a woman's startled blue eyes opening mine and looking in. Is anybody home?

The white sheets crimson with streaks of bright red blood. Candy canes. Barber poles. Latex gloves. "We've got to stop her bleeding . . . need to get the blood pressure up . . . losing her . . ."

This time I wasn't bleeding. Not on the outside. They asked me questions, what is your name, what day is this, what year is it, can you hear us, do you understand where you are, that you are in an ambulance? Everything is going to be all right, we're going to call someone for you, could you tell us who to call? Who do we call Ms. Millings? Do you have a number for someone—

We are taking you to the hospital and need to get in touch with next of kin. Next of kin. Who are your next of kin?

We were suddenly in the emergency room. I wasn't thinking clearly and slipping farther into a place where there was no ladder out. A nurse with long acrylic fingernails forced a gown over me, and I could feel the tips of the nails, cool and scratching along my bare back. She tied the two loops and eased me onto the stiff white pillow and hard gurney. I don't know how long I waited for a room or for next of kin. They injected me with a tranquilizer to stop the shaking and trembling. It calmed me, liquid Valium that takes women places they're normally afraid to go.

It took me back to Kiawah Island, my wedding night, the gray cedar beach villa, ocean breeze playing hide-and-seek in my flowing, billowing dress. I was this new bride, legally wed to Rev. Bryce Jeter, the most beautiful man I'd ever seen and made more so by his connections, his gold sashes to the kingdom of God and to forgiveness, what I wanted most. Forgiveness.

God, forgive me. Forgive me for the sin you know I committed when I was 22 years old and forever ashamed to face myself in the mirror, a woman who hated her own eyes, her body, what had occurred within. I'd thought Bryce could extend his Jesus glow and encircle me in the robes of forgiving cloth. Show me the way. Show me how to ask and receive the peace of a God who promises redemption.

And now I lay on the steel bed padded with sheets where others had bled and died, sheets sterilized in industrial washers and dryers, bleached and sanitized and holding yet another victim. I lay there all Valiumed and loose with a mind opening enough to allow all of the Rev. Jeter inside. I would not have married him, this much I know, had I lived a life free of this one sin I couldn't bear, a sin without absolution no matter how many times I'd fallen to my knees and begged for God's mercy. I'd visited Catholic churches and pastoral counselors, confessing and crying and all of them pointing to Scriptures that showed without doubt I could be sin-free, but in my eyes the act I'd committed had been murder. All I had to do was ask God for release and it was mine, they said, because Jesus had died on the cross. He hadn't died for nothing, they told me. Just ask. Ask in sincerity and you shall receive. Peace, the sweet peace of forgiveness.

I had never felt forgiven until I met Bryce Jeter. He could get me there, the conduit to complete reprieve from above. If I married a man of God, then maybe, quite possibly, what happened would disappear and bury itself with the sins of others who'd stepped forward and released inner demons. The tranquilizers in my blood brought everything back so clearly yet impersonally, as if it were happening to another woman.

A lens in my mind zoomed in and focused on a day sixteen years ago, the red brick clinic in a rundown part of the city, the hard, unpadded metal table, the stirrups, the doctors who seemed as cold as their mysterious jars of specimens and solutions. The nurses who had cigarette breath and fatigue and boredom in their eyes. I might as well have been a woman going in for a root canal. Line us up in the waiting room. Give us old magazines wrinkled from sweaty hands and the passing from one nervous woman to another. Day after day. In they go, filled with life—out they go, empty and dead-eyed.

Two hundred and seventy-five dollars. A couple of Tylenol, a shot in the cervix that burned like a hot poker, and then the rods, one after the other, opening what needed six, seven or eight more months to rightly yield. Prying and pulling and suctioning and scraping what women were meant to nurture, sucking it all out with hoses and nonchalance while I lay in agony and tears, crying for what was lost and what would never be.

"You have no choice," a doctor had told me the week before, when I had learned. "You've been taking Accutane plus birth control pills. This child is severely deformed. Why weren't you using protection?" More guilt. Yes protection, protection. Lots of it. Pills. Did I forget one? A condom for backup. And then almost three entire months of not realizing something was wrong, that my breasts were growing huge and my periods—yes, I had them—were irregular. The news. A baby. A deformed child, 12 weeks' gestation, a sonogram that showed limbs unformed from the teratogenic effects of Accutane and estrogen. Oh, God. Please, help me God.

The pain was more excruciating than any I'd ever endured, more so than actually giving birth or the shattered bones from Bryce's van, the sickening tear of flesh, the striking and chipping collarbone and sternum.

I stirred from this memory back to the present and the faces above me, the ones asking about family and kin. I couldn't stop trembling and a nurse left the room and returned with a syringe she pumped into the IV tubing. More Valium. Truth serum. Memories flowing faster and sharper as other edges dulled—the shame at the clinic, the hidden torture of the secret and deciding to tell Bryce on our wedding night, needing desperately to tell him, knowing he would lead me to amnesty. Knowing he would forgive and make me feel better, or so I assumed. I was as attracted by his wires to God Central as I was to his body and his perfect face.

I held Bryce's hand as we walked the white sandy beach at sunset on our wedding day, the Kiawah Island wind like warm arms around me, whispering, *Go ahead. It's safe. Tell him.* Bryce, of all men, would understand what I needed. We sat on a blanket, my head against his muscled shoulder. He stared at the water as it lapped gently, caressing the shore.

I told him my story, how I'd sought pardon in every church I could find. How right now, before we went inside and brought the marriage toward a union of flesh and love, I wanted him to know. I told him the entire truth and left nothing out. He made a noise, a low grunting sound and turned the dark furious color of day-old blood. He stood and walked to the edge of the ocean and screamed out toward what seemed like infinity, as loud as he could. The beach was almost deserted, but the few who were there scattered far away from the wailing man calling out into the ocean. He stayed there for at least 10 minutes before diving in, wearing all his clothes, as if he needed the water to cleanse him of what he'd heard. Baptize him in salt and foam and rid him of sin by association.

When he returned I was crying on the blanket.

"Let's go inside," he said, grabbing my hand a bit too rough and shaking the sand from the blanket. He released my hand and led me by the elbow, squeezing, seething. I could see the color still heating his face. His jaw was set. This was my new husband, my honeymoon. Why had I told him now? Why had I ever told him?

We went inside and dressed for dinner, he in the bathroom and not allowing me to see his body. I felt such shame, such a dirty guilt that I wanted to run out of there and get on a bus and go home. We drove to dinner in silence. There was no champagne, no toast to a happy future, only a piece of blackened tuna I couldn't eat and a solemn minister who was showing me the first taste of what my life would be like for the next six years.

I tried to hug him and even put my arms around him when we got back to the villa. I told him I had no choice—that the child was deformed but he wouldn't look at me. "There are two bedrooms," he said. "I'm taking the one closest to the beach."

I cried myself to sleep and awakened before dawn to find him gone. He did not return for two days, and I was beside myself with grief and confusion. I called Aunt Weepie who swore never to tell a soul.

"I'm coming to get you," she said.

"All right. Tomorrow. I'll call and tell you when and where to pick me up. I can't think straight right now."

Bryce had come back on the third night, sparing Aunt Weepie's rescue mission. He wouldn't tell me where he'd been or what he'd done as he led me to the bedroom and stripped off all of his clothes and ordered me to undress.

I froze with a mix of revulsion and fear. I stared at his nakedness, which was no longer an attraction but the form of someone filled with hate and rage in each flexed and quivering muscle.

"Take off your clothes, whore. You heard me." I should have left but I didn't. I slowly removed my jeans, T-shirt and faced him in a bra and panties, lingerie from a shower my friends from the gym and Steak & Ale had thrown. He pushed me onto the queen-size bed. He was heavy and on top, letting all his weight crush me instead of holding himself up. He kissed me, hard and his teeth tore my lip . . . the rusted taste of blood ran down my throat. His hands were on me, hot dry hands, tearing off my bra, twisting and ripping my new underwear, wrangling them down my legs, never taking his lips off mine and the blood continuing to trickle.

"No, Bryce. Please."

"You whore. Shut up. Your sinning soul is mine now, you Jezebel, you cunning Delilah." He grew hard and didn't wait. He pushed himself into me and growled like an animal. I stared at the ceiling as it moved back and forth with Bryce's forceful rhythms. I hated my new husband. Hated him. It only lasted a few minutes.

Strangely, after he'd had his way, he scooped me into his arms and cuddled me like a child. He cried and told me, "I forgive you, Prudy. God does too. I love you." And all the evil left him almost as quickly as it had entered. The eyes—trick eyes—had changed, and in an instant he was a different person. I prayed and hoped I'd never again see the man who turned my honeymoon into a nightmare.

My prayers were answered. But only temporarily. The evil man from my honeymoon would slowly begin to re-form and rebuild himself into something beastly and capable of killing.

***

At some point during the late evening, a swollen, pink sun bled through the window. I opened my eye a crack and immediately felt my head pounding. I stretched and tried to fully awaken and shake the webs of tranquilizers from muscles and mind and come to terms with where I was and how I'd gotten here. Mama curled herself into the vinyl visitors' chair, the chair that held sweat and worry and tears of death and defeat, the chair that held grandmothers who rocked and purred over brand new grandchildren. She was dozing, the sun like brass in her strawberry blond hair.

"Mama," I said, my voice breaking.

Her eyes flew open and she jumped, sitting straight up in the chair. "Prudy, honey. My heart can't take any more. This is IT!"

She didn't ask or mention the troubles that had landed me once again in a hospital. "You and Amber are killing me. One incident at a time. I took my fanny to Eckerd's when I heard about your little fit at the radio station and my blood pressure was 161 over 90. That's high enough to send me stroking. It won't be long till my brain blows a tire. Total blowout, Miss Prudy who can't seem to stay out of trouble."

"I'm sorry. The therapist said this would happen."

Mama bolted straight up in her chair. "Screw that woman," she said, the second time I'd ever heard her use that word. She then closed her eyes, letting the last of the sun sweep the lids and her face, a shadow settling in the hollow of a high cheekbone. We were quiet for a few minutes, and then the door opened and in waltzed Aunt Weepie with a big bunch of flowers and a stack of magazines. She surveyed the gloom and focused on my mother who wasn't speaking or offering even a remote greeting.

"I've been to funerals happier than this," she said, setting the vase on the windowsill, closing the blinds to block out a sun she found irritating. "Perk up, people. Nobody's dead. Of course if they were, I'd at least be eatin' good. Well, let's hear it. What happened?"

"Prudy showed her ass at work," Mama said, tiredly, as if she'd been drugged. "They carted her over here in an ambulance. She goes around talking about men and their violence and look at what she pulls. How in the world am I going to live this down at bridge?"

Aunt Weepie glanced at me, and I rolled my eyes and shook my aching head.

"Oh, spit on those uppity-tight asses," she said. "Half of them have gay husbands and the other half haven't had sex in years 'cause their men are off screwing younger women. I'm sure they themselves could benefit from time in the hopper. Gracious, Lucinda. Everybody's got problems."

"My children have nothing but."

"Phooey. You watch those soap operas. They oughta make your life seem like the sweetest piece of cake in the bakery. Let's pay some attention to poor Prudy here. What did the doctors say? Prudy, what's wrong, hon?"

I couldn't tell my mother about the letters from Bryce. Her gaskets would fire and I'd have a funeral on my hands, though to hear her talk you'd think she wanted nothing more. She was predicting her death within weeks, "due to the recent events of my sorry children's pathetic lives."

"I've got two dresses for my service," she was fond of reminding us at every opportunity. "I'm going to wear the green rayon with the real pretty collar for the visitation and the white silk with the lace inlay for the service and subsequent meeting with Jesus followed by Elvis."

"Prudy," Aunt Weepie said, ignoring Mama. "What's wrong?"

"I got fired from the radio station and it didn't sit well with me."

"Sit well," my mother yelled. "It didn't *sit well* with her. Let me tell you about sitting well. Nothing in life is going to sit well with people. We make our own cushions, feather our own benches. If you want to sit well then you line the bench with decency and goodness. You don't go crashing and busting up a man's office just 'cause you can't help a woman whose 8-year-old son won't quit wetting the bed."

"Jesus, mother."

"Wouldn't hurt you to call out his name more often—and on your humble knees."

"Aunt Weepie?" I pleaded.

"Can't do a thing. She's been like this since birth."

"Where are the kids?"

"Oh," my mother shouted, "So you remember you have obligations and responsibilities. If you really care, they are with your father and Landon Kennedy."

Landon Kennedy? Wonder where he came from? "Why are they with them?"

"Landon drove his BMW convertible over and agreed to go to the park like you promised them kids before you decided to become a rock star and trash someone's office. Such a nice man. He said you were quite witchy while on y'all's date and wouldn't stop talking to your ex. Said his name was Croc and that's all I needed to hear."

"He's an egotistical ogre."

"He's a Kennedy."

"Oh, Lucinda," Aunt Weepie interrupted. "He ain't nothing but a hairy has-been. I saw him at your Mama's, Prudy, and he may look good for a long-haired hippie, but he's dumber than wood. I wouldn't let him operate on a stuffed animal much less a real one. He's got the wit of a gerbil. I tried to tell him my husband was fond of cooking furballs and the dumb ass actually thought I was serious and went into a textbook lecture about feline fur and the dangers of—"

"Shut up, Weepie," my mother said, her head in her hands.

"Don't you talk to me that way."

Mama looked up and jutted that chin way out. "I'll talk to you any way I please. I'm going to check Prudy out of here before the whole town hears about this latest fiasco involving my oldest. She can go back to her pink rental and we'll sort this out there."

They both talked about me as if I didn't have a mind, an opinion or a say in the matter. It had been this way since Bryce Jeter burned rubber on my body.

"You know, Luce, I believe it wouldn't hurt her to stay a few days. Maybe if you had let them take her last time, she wouldn't have had this breakdown that damned therapist correctly predicted. "

"I am the most wonderful mother," Mama yelped. "I have lived my entire life for my two girls, and now they're sucking the remainder of my years right out of me. Look. Look around. They are the walking wounded. Well, one can't even walk good."

"I walk just fine," I cried. "I even wear high heels a lot of days so you don't need to—"

"Hon, they can't help it," Aunt Weepie said. "Life gets hard when a woman hits her mid to late 30s. I told you it's the Uglying Up years. The wrinkles come and the arm fat. The hangy-down thing on most necks. I'm just fortunate to have bypassed that trait, but Prudy, here, she may well have a neck thing if she don't—"

"I will NOT have a neck thing!" I shouted.

"Weepie, why don't you go on home," Mama said.

My aunt put her hands on her curvy hips and said, "I'll go when I'm ready. Prudy here, needs me because I don't force her into things."

"And I do?"

"Yes, you do. You keep telling her to get a man, then refusing her good mental help when it seems advisable. You have been running her life now for the past two years, going to that apartment every day and calling in those proverbs with your ridiculous morals attached."

"She has needed me. And my proverbs. That's what decent mothers do. If you'd been any kind of decent mother—"

"Please," I said. "Both of you, please leave."

A quiet fell. They stared at each other then me. "I want to be alone. I need to think. The best thing you could do for me is make sure the kids are okay. Tell them I'm all right and don't give out too much information. Please."

By the time the room grew dark, except for a fluorescent light over the sink, Mama and Aunt Weepie had respected my wishes. They promised to take care of the kids, but were first planning on grabbing a bite at the Red Lobster because after their rough day they deserved a Bloody Mary and coconut shrimp.

Sleep came in cycles, broken by the nurses and aides who rolled squeaking machinery in every four hours for vital signs and medication adjustments.

Even with the interruptions and little sleep, I awakened the next morning feeling refreshed, cleansed and focused, knowing what I had to do, needed to do to get my life back from Bryce Jeter. To get it back from the sins of the past that had trapped me and kept me from thinking I was decent enough to have a normal happy relationship with a man. Flawed or not flawed. Everyone was flawed and I was no worse off than anyone else.

For the next four days I stayed in the hospital, resting and listening to the therapists, even taking their suggestions and not focusing on their teeth or facial features. I asked one of them, a man with a sweet gentle quality to him, why he thought my husband would want to kill me.

"It wasn't you he wanted dead, Dee," this man said, leaning into me. "It was himself he wanted to kill. This is just how it all manifested. It would be my guess he had an undiagnosed mental illness or even a physical condition of the brain."

"I want to go there, the prison, and find out why he's sending the letters."

"Then go."

I walked the entire hospital, up four floors, down three, stopping to see the new babies and pushing the elevator buttons to a floor where the sickest old men and women from nursing homes are transferred.

On the fourth day when I was due to check out after lunch, Theresa Jolly came to visit and with her was Annie Sue, her Posh Spice hair in need of some gel and reworking, her eyes sad and confused. She was wearing old lady clothes and no makeup. Her spark had dimmed.

"You dying?" she asked, reaching up to feel my dirty hair. "You missed the dance. We didn't have no dance matter of fact or is it tomorrow?"

"I am really sorry, Annie Sue. I'll make it up to you. We'll have that dance. We'll have that and more, wait and see."

Theresa nodded and walked toward me with cautious steps. She stood at my bedside, her face set with concern.

"Am I fired?" I asked as she handed me a beautiful flower arrangement stuffed with pink roses and orange Gerber daisies.

"Never," Theresa said and hugged me. "You're actually hired full-time if you want it. Name your hours. You've brought new life to everyone in the place. Let me tell you something . . . Kathy, who's eaten nothing but tuna salad and Ruffles for years, actually ate a turkey sub yesterday with Doritos. I couldn't believe it. She wanted to come with us but said she didn't want to cry and upset you. What do you think? About full time?"

"I'd love it. Jay and Miranda start regular school in a couple of weeks. Miranda's going to preschool five days a week." This gave me time to take care of business with

Bryce, to drive to Charlotte and put a stop to his threats and twisted control.

"One more thing," Theresa was saying and smiling. "It's a pay raise and new position. I don't care if you have a masters or not. I've got it budgeted for a year. 'Social Rehabilitator.' I think I can get a grant, and I know in my heart nobody's made more of a difference with these old people in such a short amount of time as you have."

I felt a lump of gratitude in my throat, and as I was fighting tears, Annie Sue scurried around to the other side of the bed and tapped me on the shoulder, diverting the attention from employment and employer. "Guess what?" she said, not waiting on an answer. "There's a new fellow at the home and he's sweeter on me than them stinkers at the bar. I may give up my boozing for this one," she said, winking, mouth popping as she slapped her thigh. "He said if I didn't quit going out drinking, he'd send me to rehab with Lindsay Lohan."

The spark had returned as soon as she heard I would be back, and not only back—but on the campus every day of the week for the entire day. "I was eating the fried fish in the cafeteria and you know how good it is," she said, "the slaw and them hush puppies. In walks this old geezer hobbling along and dragging his walker behind him instead of using it to aid in the business at hand. I said, 'Come over here and join me,' and sure enough he abandoned the walker in the middle of the mess hall and sat right down in front of me. Before we even had an introduction he says, 'Lord help me. My genitalia!'"

Oh, God, I thought. Here we go. I had noticed over the years when some women reach a certain age, say 80 and older, all pretense of decency flies out the window. They began to speak in streams of unedited commentary, most of it a combination of religious quotes followed by the bawdy and shocking.

"I say to him, 'What in the world you talking about?' and he says, 'I'm afraid it's shriveled up to nothing. I used to have some starch down there, but I ain't got nothing left but a useless nuisance that does nothing but dribble and draw up.' I tell you it was right impressive that he got down to business, and we didn't have to warm up like the young people with a bunch of chatter that does nothing but tiptoe to get to the real business. Which is always the genitalia now, ain't it?"

Theresa winked and I let Annie Sue prattle on.

"See, this man had it all figured out. He's learned to skip whole chunks of courting, knowing we ain't got time left on the clock to monkey around with such banal chitchat as 'How's the weather?' or a big old list of our ailments."

I couldn't help it and cracked up, causing Theresa to join in as Annie Sue grinned, gold flashing in her teeth. "I let him go on about it because the information he was sharing could prove right useful at some point. I'm starting to have them feelings down there again. I may ask him to lay down in the back seat of my car and put another kind of mileage on the thing since I can't drive it no more according to the law."

After about an hour, they left and I dozed, a smile on my face. It would be wonderful working at Top of the Hill full time. With only one job to juggle, it'd be that much easier to get my nursing degree, steps closer to the dream. I could do this; it was looking more possible every day.

I must have slept for a couple of hours. When I awakened I glanced at the visitor's chair expecting to see Mama and instead saw Croc Godfrey.

His eyes were closed. He'd been waiting for me to wake up.

"Croc?" I said. "Croc!"

He raised his eyes toward mine and didn't blink, not for the longest time.

"I'm here," he said, walking over to my bed and stroking my hair. He leaned over and kissed me on the forehead, on my eyelids, then on my cheeks . . . soft, sweet, loving. "There's no more room for fear in either of our lives. It's a waste, Prudy. A waste."

The way he was looking at me, I knew he had more to say. He'd better have more to say after what he'd put me through. A bouquet of "Thank-you flowers" followed by weeks of silence doesn't cut it. Then again, he'd been so nice during my awful date with Dr. Ego, defending and taking up for me. He'd promised to call, and he probably would have, or maybe he'd tried and I'd been cooped up here in the nut ward of the local hospital.

Every time I saw him, I died inside, wanting to be as close to him as possible, so close I could smell traces of Irish Spring on his skin.

# *Chapter Seventeen*

**Hop on out of bed, Prudy**: *Even honey seems tasteless to a man who is full; but if he is hungry, he'll eat anything.* ***Proverbs 27:7***

**Mama's Moral:** *I suggest if you aren't going to date Landon, you best find someone who's neither hungry nor full. Croc looks like a refugee, sugar. What does that tell ya?*

CROC JUMPED INTO our lives as if he'd never bowed out. He conveniently forgot he'd dumped me for three weeks, not even a measly e-mail, and was pretending he was some kind of Fairy-Godfather swooping in to make us all better. I wasn't about to ask him why he hadn't called. He'd just have to think I never paid it a bit of mind. Too many activities such as skydiving and flying lessons and whatever else exciting and interesting women who didn't need men did with their time.

One day out of the blue, about a week post my mental breakdown, Croc announced he had a big surprise. He drove to my apartment shortly after Mama had left her morning Proverb.

"Get dressed," he said, presenting a bag of bagels with honey-nut cream cheese, my favorite. "I have something for you." He reached deep into his blue jeans and pulled out a velvet box, not the ring size, but a large rectangular version covered in dark green cloth. I felt my heart turn a flip and skip two beats. "Hold up your hair, please," he said, opening the box, not giving me a chance to peer inside.

He stood behind me and looped a silver chain around my scarred neck. Dangling at the bottom was a small tortoise encrusted in emeralds. He must have sensed my reaction—why a tortoise?—while carefully hooking the necklace.

"Giant tortoises are great symbols of survival," he said. "They go through so much and always make it on top. I figured I'd get a small one because it might look weird to have a giant turtle hanging from your throat."

"It's beautiful," I said, touched by the sentiment but not too fond of having a turtle on my neck, no matter its symbolism. With a sudden movement, not too unlike those Croc and I enjoyed while christening all the golf course holes with our love, he spun me around and kissed me softly on the lips, progressing with each kiss until I felt his tongue searching mine, wanting that connection lost all those years ago. Almost as soon as the kissing started, it ended, the fire burning in my belly and loins extinguished.

"Prudy, I'm taking you somewhere long overdue, but don't worry, jeans are fine."

"With this?" I asked, holding up my emerald tortoise. "Where's Sam?"

"He's at a friend's," he said, kissing the top of my head, my cheeks and my lips once again. "The tortoise is meant to bring you courage. This is going to be one place you're going to need some." He waltzed into the kids' room to help Jay find his decent clothes, a pair of Gap khakis and blue striped Polo Mama had bought while we were at the mall having my hair dyed crow black for the tragic date with Landon Kennedy.

I dressed Miranda, gave her one of Annie Sue's old purses, and we dropped the children off at Mama's where she couldn't wait to take them to her church. "Heaven knows it's about time they got reacquainted with a decent version of the Lord," she said, refusing to come outside or even wave hello to poor Croc from her window.

"Where are we going?" I asked as he backed out of the driveway like a 95-year-old man, a trait he'd probably never get over since his wife's death.

"Charlotte."

"Charlotte?"

"I understand there's a certain prison there. A certain asshole of an inmate."

God, it was really going to happen. I inhaled deeply. "Oh, well . . . good . . . fine, I guess. How did you know I was planning on going?"

"Your Aunt Weepie told me you wanted to face the felon. It's not like your mother has suddenly found me loveable and offered up info. The necklace is because when a woman goes to visit her felonious ex, a mighty turtle can't hurt."

"Kind of like a Ninja Turtle," I said, thinking Croc might be borderline loony and Mama at least ought to appreciate that quality—the notion of a big-ass turtle for a prison visit to see a man who'd tried his damnedest to polish me off.

Croc said he'd written the Charlotte prison and requested Bryce put his and my name on the visitor's list.

"That's the only way we're allowed on the premises."

"I can't believe he actually agreed to all of this."

"I didn't want you to do this alone," Croc said. "I know you feel like you have to go—and I don't blame you—but I'm going, too. Just to be on the safe side."

It took nearly two hours because of Croc's ultra-cautious driving and my frequent trips to convenience store bathrooms to puke my guts out. This would be the first time in two years I'd seen Bryce, since he sat in his state-issued jumpsuit and shackles in the courtroom. I poured an Alka-Seltzer into a Diet Coke, hoping for a settled stomach and full control when I had a face-to-face with my would-be killer.

The prison featured a sprawling set of facilities—a two-story structure with fencing all around and another one-level unit silvered up with razor wire spiraling and threatening to turn escapees into sliced ham. Several guard towers rose high in the air where armed corrections officers kept watch and smoked cigarettes.

When we entered, after I'd hyperventilated by the car and Croc had handed over a brown bag to breathe in, we were searched and zapped, much like during airport security where they all but stick a wand up one's hoochie. After an eternity we made it into the visitor's area, and as soon as I realized we were there, really there, I had to run to the bathroom and throw up again.

"Prudy," Croc said. "Once this is over, you'll be free, sweetheart." He held my hand, rubbing my knuckles with his thumb. He was looking more handsome each day. The nicer he acted, the cuter he grew. I think he gained a pound or two. Probably not.

The doors clanked open and for a moment my heart stopped. I waited for my body to fill with bitter hatred, but as I stared at the stooped and thin figure before me, the shell of humanity with flat, greasy hair, I was thrown off track. Bryce's gait was unsteady and he stumbled as he took a seat. For a moment, he didn't raise his head, and when he did, I saw the eyes, the trick-card eyes, boring into me for a long, never-ending moment and then vanishing, lost somewhere in his own brain. My hand instinctively fingered and held the tortoise.

He jerked up suddenly, as if alertness had kicked in. He grinned and waved, like an idiot. He had cheese crackers in his teeth and the crumbs dusted his stained white prison T-shirt.

Croc spoke first, soft in his approach. Any initial thoughts that we were going to barrel into the joint and lay down the riot act were quelled by the pathetic appearance of the source of these threats. Bryce didn't seem capable of tying his own shoe, much less finding loopholes in laws and sending hulking cons to take care of his "unfinished business."

Croc continued talking, increasing the firmness in his voice, but he lacked the malice I'd predicted as we drove to Charlotte. "We're here to tell you that if you send another one of your sick letters, we *will* press charges. We've saved copies of them all."

Bryce grinned and nodded, as if Croc had been discussing the weather. "Hey, Prudy," he said, slurring. "Whatcha been up to?" Oh mercy, this man was either drunk or zonked on high-octane medicine of some sort. I'd seen it enough in the nursing home. "You look so pretty. Did I send you a letter?"

Before I could answer, Bryce addressed the officer and said, "I need an ace. Can you bust me down with an ace?"

I didn't understand, until the officer said, "No smoking right now. Maybe later. It's not going to help your condition to be smoking."

Smoking? Bryce smoking? What condition?

My head dropped into my hands, and I smelled my own sweat and vomit breath until I felt someone tap my shoulder, the same officer motioning me to follow him.

"Excuse me," I said leaving Bryce and Croc alone.

The man led us to another section of the room where no one could hear what he was about to reveal. He had Skoal in his cheeks and pores on his nose that looked like tiny ice-pick holes.

"He's out to lunch," the officer said. "Gone. A Bam-Bam. They're trying different stuff, seven or eight meds."

"What's wrong with him?"

"You've not been notified? He has some brain tumor the doctors said had been growing for years. He's been over at state hospital going through a bunch of tests. They even paid, his folks did, and took him to Duke. That's about all I'm allowed to say due to all these medical violation laws. It was weird because when he first came to us, he was all in control and working out and preaching. Now, he is almost infant-like some days due to the tumor."

"Tumor? For years?"

"They say it's only a matter of months. Six if he's lucky. He's going to another doctor end of the week. He won't eat, 'cept crackers, just lays in his bunk or plays cards in the activities room. He makes collages out of magazines. Tears them out with them big hands of his for hours and hours, gluing it all to a posterboard. You ought to see them posters. I'll bet he's done made a dozen of them and all have pictures of pretty ladies with children and families. He'll cart one around and say, 'Look at my wife and kids,' pointing at six or seven different women and sets of kids. Most the time, he's wantin' to get up a gang to play cards."

"Cards? He never played cards."

"Go Fish's the main one. Got him a pack of Old Maids, too, and threw a fit one day when he drew the hag. Thought you might want to know. Hard to believe he's the same man who—"

"If that's all, I'll head on back," I said, quickly shaking his hand so he couldn't finish his sentence. "I assume there will be no more letters?"

"Nope. Far as we know, he never sent no letters. Musta been somebody else. Regardless, once the tumor got so big, he forgot all about revenge and other things men in here typically talk about."

When I returned to the visiting area, Bryce held up an arm and waved like a child delighted to see his mom.

"I know you," he said. "Don't I?" His perfect-phony-preachery smile, those big white teeth, had turned gray with neglect.

Croc gently put a hand on my shoulder and said we needed to go. I leaned into the partition and tried to find Bryce in the face staring back. I waited for his eyes to turn, wanting to see the trick eyes. But they weren't there. No one was home. Maybe that's a good thing, the place people flee when they can't stand their own minds.

"Prudy?" he said, but I stood and began walking, my heels echoing in the cold hallways of the prison. "PRUDY!" I stopped but didn't look back. "I'm sorry. I'm sorry I hurt you."

For a moment I couldn't move. These were words I never in my life expected to hear. I reached for my neck and tried to swallow. Slowly, I turned back one last time.

"It's over now, Bryce. I forgive you. So does God if you ask." As I said these words, cinderblocks of weighted pain and horrible memories lifted, and I felt as if I could fly. I smiled and threw my hands up in the air and let out a whoop.

I felt satisfaction that my husband wasn't driven to hatred because of himself, but a tumor—because somewhere within his screwed up head or DNA everything got all mixed and wired wrong and brewed up a malignant mass. Like when a house burns to the foundation and they rule the fire "electrical." Not arson.

Croc tried to hold my hand in the car but I pulled away. I wanted to feel nothing but my own body, my own thoughts, uninterrupted.

"Whip into that Shell station," I said. "I need to celebrate and could sure use a beer."

"I don't drink and drive," he said.

"That's true. You're not drinking, I am. I'll pour it in a cup." As an afterthought and to prove there remained nothing but sweet bones in my body, I said, "It meant a lot to me that you would do this, drive to Charlotte and everything. The necklace. All of it."

"I love you. I always have," he said, and turned into the Shell station, popping Allison Krauss in the CD player. He loves me. What could I say? What should I say? Oh my God. He said the words. I. Love. You.

I bought a six-pack of Blue Moon and poured one into a cup printed with a Diet Pepsi logo. Life was good.

***

With school having started, summertime feels shorter than ever, most of the children already back the second week of August. As soon as the voters approved the bond referendum for central air, officials have been herding the flock to their desks with the dirt of summer still clinging to their newly shod feet, their arms and legs brown as pecans.

Jay had entered second grade in a gifted program at a well-respected public school on the north side of town. We decided it was as good as the private school he'd attended earlier. Several people wanted him to skip a grade, but I wouldn't hear of it and wanted him to be a kid as long as possible. We'd found this public school a few miles away that had a program for what Mama calls "bona-fide geniuses," allowing them to remain in their regular grade and study a more advanced curriculum. This meant when recess came around, Jay would run around on the playground with his peer group, not a bunch of 9-and-10-year-olds who already knew the F word and more about sex than my Mama did on her wedding day.

The school also had a wonderful pre-kindergarten program, and Miranda was excited about going to "big-girl school." She couldn't wait to strap that giant Hannah Montana backpack on her tiny little shoulders (she'd finally decided granny purses were no longer fashionable) and carry peanut butter and jelly sandwiches in its matching lunch box.

This morning I dropped Jay off and made sure he got to his room all right. I opened my arms and was surprised he let me hug him. His hair smelled like watermelon shampoo and he was wearing a new shirt from Old Navy that Croc had bought him. His feet looked huge in new shoes that were a size too large because I was afraid if I bought them to fit, I'd have to rush out and get another pair in a few months.

Watching him disappear into a stranger's care, I had to push back the tears so I wouldn't embarrass him. I nodded to his teacher and waved goodbye. I had met her during orientation and liked her philosophy and the plans she had to nurture gifted children without making over them like freaks. She had been gracious and calm, not once prodding me for information about Jay's past or how that might affect his learning. She had simply allowed us to enroll, eat the cookies and drink the punch, sign the forms and leave like ordinary people. Not people who'd entered and exited nightmares.

With Miranda it was different. I'd never had her in a full-time program, only half days at Mama's church. I wondered if this was too much. She was accustomed to family taking care of her, a mother who alternated between the great waves of energy and laughter and long stays in hospitals or the bed. The pre-K wing was a newer addition to the school, and I'd heard nothing but good feedback from the mothers who make it their mission to evaluate every school within a 20-mile radius. This was my new way to make friends, joining the PTA and chittering about children's needs and issues, even though I was no longer getting paid to do so. Thank goodness the radio station dropped its charges after I'd made several trips there to apologize, going as far as offering to clean the toilets free for a week. Thanks, but no thanks, they'd said, which was fine by me.

Though armed with this positive knowledge about the school, dropping Miranda off at the classroom and seeing the ABCs on the walls, the 1-2-3 choo-choo train racing across the borders, my heart felt as if it were an anchor about to sink what was left of me.

Miranda shook herself free of my hand, which had held hers too tight. She marched as jauntily as Annie Sue in a pair of clunky tennis shoes, diva style, straight into her classroom and right up to her new teacher, a young woman of about 24 or 25. She never looked back. Not once.

"Miranda," I called out as children and mothers exchanged tears and goodbyes. "Miranda!" I couldn't get her attention. She was giving it all away. I smiled at the back of her hair, gathered in a pink clip, my eyes lingering on her ankle-length ruffled skirt, the thick-soled shoes, the fringe blouse that had come back in style and was the big rage of my own grammar school days. I wanted to run and bury my face in her soft brown hair before I loaned her to the world. Instead, I turned and walked down the hall, through the doors of the elementary school and to my car where I sat and laid my head on the steering wheel and cried for 20 minutes.

Afterward, I was fine. My personal motto is "Cry it out. Tears are God's Valium." A good cry drains a person of all stresses, leaves her limp and cleansed. I blew my nose, patted my face with powder and drove to Top of the Hill where I would begin my stint as a full-time worker with salary and benefits, enough money to pay the rent, put a few dollars in savings and have extra so that when Miranda wanted a Barbie I didn't have to go to Goodwill to get it. Nor would I have to shop at the Junior League's thrift store where women like Kippie Murray were always right around the next corner, flames dancing from tongues rather than the ends of batons.

***

Kathy was making beds when I arrived. She needed help getting the residents in the shower for their weekly baths, the soothing spray of warm water massaging old arthritic bones and aching muscles. As soon as she saw me, she moved forward, reaching out her arms to hug me. She'd never shown me or anyone else affection since I'd known her. She said, "I'm glad you're back."

"Plan to stay that way, too," I said, helping her lift a heavy, immobile woman into the shower chair and trying to remember as I rolled this 220 pounds of patient in the center of the bathroom that she was once someone's mother and grandmother. She'd had a life and people who loved her.

They'd just forgotten about her, put her here and rarely, if ever, returned for visits. I sprayed the warm water on her bare skin and she moaned with pleasure. You never knew what the elderly could feel or hear.

Beginnings and Endings.

Those are the places I could make a difference. The middles were too difficult.

As we lathered the patient and the shampoo bubbled in her hair, the door burst open and in clacked Aunt Weepie, off-kilter in a pair of super-high heels and a magenta suit, white silk blouse trailing a wet stain from neck to second button. She was buried in enough Beautiful to sicken a farm animal. Her face twisted itself with angst, white as paper except for two drawn-on circles of pink blush splotched unevenly on her cheeks.

"I have done a horrible, awful thing, Prudy," she wailed, and the semi-catatonic woman in the shower chair turned around and stared with fright in her otherwise blank eyes. "I will never balance this sin. I'll never live it down. You're going to hate me forever."

"What, Aunt Weepie?" I said, massaging the shoulders of the old woman under the water, drops of hot water splashing my face and arms. "It can't be that bad."

"It's so bad you're going to have to let me wipe a lot of wrinkly butts today," she said. "Give me all the Depends to change. Every ass to wash."

"Aunt Weepie!"

"Oh, Prudy, no one in the family's going to ever speak to me again. Your mother will nail the final screw in the coffin she's been custom building for me in her mind for years.

Lord, I'm a horrible, wretched woman. Give me an old butt. Give me a dirty man to bathe!"

"Excuse me, Kathy," I said. "Could you finish up here? I need to escort my foul-mouthed aunt to the break room for a few minutes."

"I can handle it," she said, looking my aunt up and down with her right eye.

We walked down the hall, me holding Aunt Weepie up as she clicked and swayed, martini-breathed and bumped into several of the residents who were parked in the Geri Chairs, strapped into safety and their own worlds, cruising the halls with God knew what going on in their minds. Aunt Weepie's sporadic obscenities blended in with the outcries of the residents, men and women who never swore in their early lives but had morphed into viragoes with the mouths of drunken sailors as soon as age tightened its grip, squeezing out their censors and memories. It was common to hear M.F. and G.D. and an assortment of vulgarities one typically expects only from Eddie Murphy or Howard Stern. Aunt Weepie's talk of dirty behinds went unnoticed by everyone but me.

As we proceeded toward the break room, she made faces when the odors I was accustomed to hit her. She fanned the space in front of her nose. "Shoo, Prudy. How can you come to work here every day? Smells like the bathroom after one of Tony's furball meals."

"I need them. They need me."

"They need the Estée Lauder counter and a potty trainer. Seems to me if you can train dogs and children, you could at least get them to ring a bell before the shit starts flying."

"Lucky for them, the potty trainer is here today. Wearing hot pink and silk. I'll show you where you can start when you're ready."

"What? You're serious? In this outfit?"

"It already has a stain."

"You aren't even going to say, 'Oh, it can't be that bad.' Or, 'Tell me, Aunt Weepie, what in the world could you have done to give yourself over to diaper duty?'"

Aunt Weepie slumped in a chair and threw her head into her arms on the Formica table where Kathy ate her tuna salad sandwiches and Ruffles, carrots and pickles. My aunt convulsed with tears and hiccups of agony. I patted her back.

"I'm ruined. It's over. Even your Mama will never speak to me again, and we'd finally patched things up enough that I could go over there and she'd mix me a martini. When she finds out about this, I'll have to drink forever up under my bed. I shouldn't have come out. I should have stayed under there, but Tony said since we had company I needed to crawl on out and do some chores."

"What company?"

She wailed louder and louder. "I can't tell you. You'll hate me."

"I'll be madder if you don't tell me what in the world you're talking about."

She lifted her head, face a mess, eyes blackened with Maybelline Great Lash and puffy from crying. "Pauline's here," she said, sobbing and grabbing her chest, as if she were Fred Sanford and the 'big one' was about to strike her dead.

"Pauline who?"

"How many do you know?"

It hit me. I knew only one. Pauline Jeter, the giblet who jumped around like a subservient squirrel, that nervous little thing springing around at the wedding. The woman who joined in when everyone thought I'd birthed a Mexican, who'd sat in the back row at her son's trial, away from her husband and boy, but not uttering a peep.

When I testified I watched her; I took the stand and focused on her because I couldn't bear to place my eyes on Bryce or his daddy or my chin-jutting mother or my Aunt Weepie who'd cry like a banshee. I honed in on Pauline Jeter as I told of the van speeding toward me and the few details I could remember. To add to the horror, the district attorney suggested I wear a scoop neck so the jurors could gawk at the purple-red scars and zigzagged, Frankenstein-like stitches.

"I don't understand, Aunt Weepie. Why is Pauline Jeter at your house?"

"She heard about your episode, the hospitalization. She was coming down to bring the children a bunch of stuff for back-to-school, and when she couldn't reach your mama, she called me and I'd had a few martinis and she starts boo-hooing about Bryce dying of a brain tumor, and before I knew what I was saying . . . oh, I felt so sorry for her I asked her to come on down, but to wait a week or so until you got better. She showed up today. I'd forgotten all about inviting her. I must have a drinking problem. Is there rehab in this facility?"

"No. You have a thinking problem. Why didn't you tell me about the brain tumor?"

"I was planning to. I've been writing to her on and off because she loves those grandkids, and I just thought it was the Christian thing to do. Anyway, I thought for sure she'd drink the coffee I poured her, eat one of Tony's cement cakes, then hightail it to a Sheraton somewhere down the road. But noooo! She put her bags down and said, 'Which room is mine?' And I could have died right then and there. I was about to call Tony in, and I guess she sensed I was panicking about her being there so she started telling me all about those letters and something about you marching down to Charlotte to see the murderer in person, only she didn't call him a murderer, of course, she calls him, 'my poor baby.' You never told me about the letters, Prudy."

"What did she say about them?" Shock was too mild a word for all I was hearing.

My aunt ignored my question entirely. "She's left him. She's shed herself of her husband who she said would rather bed down the young women coming in for braces than sleep with her. She said he'd cheated on her their whole marriage, had treated her like dirt so it was no wonder Bryce was screwed up. She told me her husband said she had, and I quote, an 'unfixable, ugly-ass overbite.' This is what she said last night after she got to our place. Said that mean man point-blank told her she had the bite and bone structure of a chimp. Bless her heart. Tony fixed her a plate of food and the woman gulped it down like a starved dog. It was one of his uglier meals, too."

"Aunt Weepie, how long is she staying?"

My aunt wouldn't face me. She rummaged through her purse for lipstick and her fake Chanel compact.

"How long?"

"She's moved in."

"She's what?!"

"Prudy, you need to listen before you go getting all upset," Aunt Weepie said.

"Those letters you thought Bryce and the attorney were sending . . . they weren't from him. Pauline told me. She found out old Peter Jeter was typing and mailing the letters to you 'cause he didn't think you were suffering nearly as much as his baby boy. Pauline's on your side, hon. She said Bryce was out of it in prison, diagnosed with a vicious tumor. She said he's so medicated he doesn't know what he's done or who he's done it to."

"Oh, my God, please!"

"That husband of hers is the villain this time, Prudy. She ain't going back. What could I do?"

I tried to digest all this new information. Dr. Jeter sending the letters, at least the violence-oriented batches that had been typed. Pauline the giblet, just another Jeter victim.

"Hate me all you want, Prudy, but I need to clean the elderly and get on with my business. Me and Pauline's going to a funeral at 2."

"A funeral?" I could not believe a thing I was hearing.

"I told her she could cry it out there, all her pain about her husband and no-account-but-sick-and-dying son—of course she still loves him but we agreed to disagree on that one and not bring it up. I figure with her crying and carrying on . . . I can't cry twice in a day and I've already cried all morning. It'll be up to her to get us invited to the covered dish. I told her when she set her Louis Vuittons in my guest bedroom, 'A meal around this place is something one works for and plans carefully. It ain't always easy, Pauline.' Then I explained to her what to do at funerals and where the pots and pans and cookbooks were located in my kitchen. 'The louder you yell like a scalded animal, the better our chances for the post-burial spread,' I told her. So see, I'm putting her to work, Prudy."

"And I'm also putting you to work. You run along and find Kathy," I ordered. "Tell her I said to show you where Mr. Walsh is, and you can go and change him and give him a nice bed bath. Clean out from beneath his toenails. Clip his nose and ear hair. He might even show you the new trick he can do with his privates since you seem on to that subject today. After that, Mrs. Holcombe needs changing, too. She also could use an enema if you know how to give one."

My aunt stood to leave, tucking her white silk blouse back into her magenta skirt.

"I'm only trying to help, Prudy. Trying to be a decent person in this world. That pitiful giblet shouldn't suffer and miss out on seeing her grandchildren because she married a senior ass and gave birth to a junior ass."

"You find her a place to live. I'm not saying a word to her. She never sent me but one card following what her 'baby boy' did to me. I remember the card well. Had a woman, one of those cartoon-drawings on the front, with her leg up in traction, then the words, 'Sorry to hear you're back at the factory.' You open up the inside and it said, 'Must have made you on a Monday,' only she crossed out Monday and put Sunday, the day of my near demise."

"Prudy, she was trying to be funny or else she was confused and not thinking right. A lot of people don't know how to be funny, the subtleties of classy humor."

"Aunt Weepie, how in the world could she send such a card? 'Must of made you on a Monday?' You realize the card is referring to the general and overall defectiveness of products made by hung-over workers on Mondays? You realize the jackass that sprang from her giblet loins tried to kill me on a Sunday and that's why she scratched out Monday and added the Sunday part? So, I'd say she was in her right mind to know the exact day of the week. I wrote to the card company and gave them a piece of my mind for putting out such trash. They sent me a free assortment box for my 'troubles.'"

"Wasn't that nice?" Aunt Weepie said, checking over her face in a compact. "If you don't mind, I could use one to send to a friend if there's a Happy Anniversary card in the—"

"Aunt Weepie!"

"I'm in a hurry and need to—"

"You go down to room 104 then 116 and get busy. Kathy's probably still in the shower room and will give you a pair of gloves, unless you prefer to get it all over your pretty hands."

"Prudy, I swear you can be a carbon copy of your mama when you take a notion to it."

"You tell that jumpy squirrel at your house that this little town isn't big enough for both of us."

"She's flush with cash, Prudy. Loaded. Ready to spend, and it's all flying from her authentic Chanel bag like loose birds. Said the courts gave her everything but Peter Jeter's underpants when they learned he couldn't keep his paws off the patients. He's lucky he still has a license. She got everything, drives the most darling Lexus you ever laid your eyes on. Said she's going to be the best grandmother in the world and wants to meet with you to go over a few things."

I could not believe what I was hearing. "Go over a few things?"

***

I left Top of the Hill in a state of disbelief. Pauline Jeter has moved to town. Not only to town but into the guest room at Aunt Weepie's. What next? Lord, could you please move along to another sinner? Surely there's a hussy or drug addict you could focus on for a while, tilt the world back a smidgen in our favor, shove the black clouds farther to the north or south of us. Please.

I put these latest events out of my mind and drove to the Northside School of Elementary Advancement where my cherubs rushed from class with their backpacks and excited faces.

"How did it go?" I asked Jay's teacher as she helped him into the backseat. Jay gave me a quick smile and began fidgeting with the door locks.

"He's one smart young fellow. Got quite a talent for art," she said and winked. Art? I never knew Jay had any interest in art. In fact, that was the one subject he had always avoided, breaking Crayons since he was strong enough to crack and hurl them.

I drove around back to the Pre-K wing, and we met Miranda in the commons area. She was delighted, showing me her finger paintings, her handprint, the ABCs she was learning to form. The teacher said, "What an intelligent girl, such a way with language, and her lectures to fellow classmates on the advantages of recycling and avoiding alcohol were priceless." When we returned home, I noticed a moving truck in front of the house. The Beckers. The neighbors downstairs were loading all their worldly goods onto the yellow and green

Mayflower moving van. All that dark brooding furniture, the medical supplies and beds, the formal paintings, piano I'd never heard.

I ran into Mrs. Becker as I released my children from the car and sent them toward the apartment. She was thinner than last time I'd seen her and had dark bags beneath her eyes.

"Hi. How are you?" I stood there and waited for her to speak.

"We're leaving." She offered nothing more in the way of explanation.

"I'm so sorry." What could I say?

"Fred thinks Florida would be better for him. I'm afraid I have to agree with him. We need more peace and quiet, no offense." She motioned for the movers to be careful with her dining room chairs. "Don't nick the legs," she ordered. "When Mr. Franklin told us a couple of days ago he'd had a buyer and couldn't resist the offer, we didn't have much choice. The buyer wants to remodel the whole place. I take it because of your . . . um . . . circumstances, the buyer will live downstairs until you can make arrangements."

I was not believing my ears. A buyer. I wondered why Mr. Franklin, my landlord, hadn't called me with the news.

"Well," I said, not knowing what to say. "Good luck in Florida." She smirked and said nothing, and I rushed upstairs and noticed the light blinking on the answering machine. Three messages.

**Aunt Weepie:** *I've cleaned filthy fannies and old crust from toes, I've made my peace and amends. Call me. Pauline was fabulous at the funeral. Cried from start to finish. We had the best meal. I don't think Heaven could've put out a finer spread. She's a natural.*

**Mama:** *Hi. You never call your poor old Mama anymore. I was hoping to hear from you. I miss my sweet Prudy. I'm proud of you, honey. You held your head up high even when the newspapers wrote that story about your business at the station. Oh, guess what? Amber and Landon are dating. Isn't that wonderful? We'll have a Kennedy in the family yet.*

**Croc:** *Don't go anywhere tonight. I need to stop by. It's important.*

***

Croc had rarely left my side since the four-day stay in the hospital. He and his boy, Sam, a couple of years older than Jay, had become fixtures in our lives.

He'd quit the recording industry shortly after my hospitalization. Said he had made enough money to retire and was renting a condo in Spartanburg, playing music on weekends. Mostly, he was living as a single father, trying to take away the pain and empty places his child must feel after losing his mother. We were walking the same road, filling potholes and trying not to fall in. I was already falling. Straight into a tempered love with Croc Godfrey—a quiet love that is comforting and sustaining, like soup. Not the kind of hot jalapeño love that burns out long before it ever has a chance for sweet embers.

However, if he had intentions of fooling me again, I'd put him to work before he fled like the time before. May as well get some use out of men before they dump you. Have them fix the leaky faucets, caulk the tub and tile, stain the deck, especially when you feel they are about to bolt for the door.

Croc's first mission from me wasn't a paint job or a few gutters to clean. My plan for him, as long as he stuck around, was to elicit his help with my first important event as the new "Social Rehabilitator" at Top of the Hill where I'd organized a fantasy "Day at the Waldorf Astoria" for the residents. The staff and I had spent most of the week scraping together enough money to turn the home into a resort and spa.

We'd hustled businesses into donating everything from AstroTurf putting greens to bubbling foot spas and transformed every room meant to park people for naps, crafts and bingo into beauty stations, massage centers, relaxation parlors stocked with every King-and-Queen-For-A-Day amenity I could think of.

We decorated the cafeteria with wall-to-wall canvases of the New York skyline, lending an authentic touch to our Day at the Waldorf. It was my intention that for at least one day, every resident with a strong enough heartbeat and semi-functioning brain would know what it felt like to be pampered instead of Pampered.

We planned manicures, pedicures, foot and shoulder massages, putting on the greens, shoe-shines, hand massages, makeovers and hairdos.

When the day arrived, residents entered through an archway of gold helium balloons. Soft music played and little white lights flickered in the room instead of the usual overhead fluorescents. The place had an intoxicating aroma of nail polish and scented candles, the delicious fragrance of cakes baking in the kitchen.

The band, Croc's old group, agreed to lend its talent for an afternoon of music, playing mostly oldies for the crowd.

As a huge surprise, he'd called Lewis Mortuary and arranged for two limousines and drivers to escort the men and women around town in style, a short sight-seeing excursion that included trips past the new Wal-Mart Superstore, which delighted Annie Sue to no end, and a quick stop at a bakery for those with a sweet tooth, compliments of Croc, who'd also bought orchids for every woman, which must have cost him a couple of hundred bucks.

As a final gesture of his kindness, about an hour before the dancing was to start, Croc and Theresa Jolly took two cars and drove to Bubba's to round up a half-dozen men sober enough to stand, wanting to make sure all the ladies got a turn or two on the dance floor. Croc was smart enough not to recruit them in advance, as I had tried to do, knowing any plans made would be forgotten with the morning sun and worn-off booze. He'd strike while the taps were flowing, promising each volunteer a case of beer for his troubles.

Later, with Annie Sue's Posh Spice hairstyle restored, she and her new geriatric boyfriend with the penchant for discussing his genitalia hit the dance floor with some fairly exotic moves on Annie Sue's part. She'd borrowed one of Amber's many bridesmaids dresses, this one a lavender column style, a backless and plunging gown that made her favor a purple swizzle stick. She enlisted one of the nurse's aides to Banana Boat every inch of exposed skin and, amazingly, not much had streaked.

Over and over she kept saying, "Would you look at us, Prudy? Aren't we something?" popping that big mouth open, the gold dental work shimmering beneath the slowly spinning mirror ball Croc borrowed from a local nightclub.

As for the elderly men willing to forget bad knees and other problems, the staff and I got all dolled up in taffeta and satin and danced with them. Aunt Weepie even performed an acrobatic routine in a tight leotard that caused one man to have to return to his room for medical care.

She cut the rug with men who weren't accustomed to double-Ds sitting high on a woman's chest. Most of them were used to scanning waistlines for such business.

"They sure are sweet to me," she said, between dances. "I think if Tony's ever negligent or stops cooking, I've found husband No. 5." She pointed to a man sitting near the door, cussing up a storm, shouting about the filthy vulgar dancing, repeatedly yelling, "This place needs to be shut down for its fucking indecency." Thank goodness Kathy, dressed in a long black formal and wearing a double pearl choker, had the good sense to wheel him out of the "Waldorf" and back to his room.

As I waltzed with a man who smelled of cologne that probably hadn't escaped its bottle in 20 years, I heard a woman's hissy voice and felt an elbow jabbing me.

"Is that you, Lizzy?" Oh, Lord. Not her. "You think that slutty dress is going to bring my Frank back to you, is that what you think?"

I did not feel like repeating the same conversation we'd had in the beauty salon.

"Yes, ma'am. That's what I'm thinking."

"Think again, you . . . you . . . bawdy strumpet." I hurriedly found her a semi-sober tattoo artist from Bubba's to dance with, taking her mind off Frank for at least three full minutes.

Croc was amused the entire day, saying he understood why I loved my work, why it was so important to get that nursing degree. Afterward, we took the kids and went to Mr. Gatti's for pizza and games in the arcade.

And that's how it continued with Croc and me. We were just two single parents meeting in friendship and occasional kisses to offer support and give our kids a serving of happiness. He was turning out to be a much more available babysitter than Mama who was busy with Amber in the house, trying to deal with the twins and her older boy, and all while playing another game of matchmaker—only this time with a candidate who had a better body and leg than her first. Amber could have six kids and four ex-husbands and no one would ever say she had any baggage.

Croc dropped by the apartment every day with plans for the children, with flowers, videos, my favorite junk from fast-food restaurants. He'd mow the lawn or sit on my couch and hold my hand, laugh at the TV and tell me I'm not a bit fat and could very well be the prettiest woman he's ever seen. I figure if a man doesn't mind a lumpy butt and a few ripples, some abdominal overhang, a stretch mark or two, then his testosterone levels are high enough to deem him a safe bet. The men who liked their women to have the starved, lanky shape of an adolescent boy . . . well, there's where the worry should come to play.

Croc Godfrey could not care less that I had cellulite on my thighs, even a bit on my upper arms if I stood in fluorescent lighting, which I tried to avoid at all costs. He never told me, "Hold off on the ice cream," like gay chicken man had told Amber. He never said, "Maybe you ought to join a gym," or "I hear kick-boxing's a real fat blaster." None of this from Croc Godfrey. My only regret is that by my best estimate, I weighed 33 percent more than he did.

While there were those random kisses, I wasn't sure what was happening, whether he was dating me or my children. It didn't matter; life was better.

I have discovered the one thing that can cure a person of the miseries of her past, the daggers that had hung over my head and heart since I was 22 and lay on the gurney in the run-down women's clinic.

That one thing is love. Not sex, not lust, but the love of someone who expects nothing in return. I wanted to believe this was real, and it was what I was hanging onto, my hands white-knuckled on the edge of the cliff. This time if I fell I had a safety net—a job, my babies and others who loved me, others I loved in return. It's when a woman has nothing but a man that the fall is often fatal.

***

Later in the afternoon after picking up the kids from school, I settled them with snacks and games and opened their backpacks where the teachers said all important papers and information would be stored. Checking Jay's folder, I noticed a white piece of poster-board sticking out. It must have been 18 inches long. I tugged on the corner and gently pulled until the entire drawing sat in front of me. My head began to lighten, the room sway. I checked the portrait closer. The instructions. "Draw Yourself in Old Clothes." Jay had colored his hair yellow and brown and was wearing a pair of overalls and a red scarf around his neck. There were holes in the pants, a few patches, a shirt with a missing sleeve. Boy, he was descriptive, that teacher was right. I started to put the drawing back in the folder when I noticed the . . . the . . . OH, MY GOD!

The shock took my breath and then I doubled over with laughter. I laughed so hard my sides ached and I rolled off the couch and onto the hardwood floor, howling and hee-hawing, writhing with the insanity of life.

When I had completed this fit of hysterics, I dialed Mama.

"Hey."

"Hey, hon." Ice clinked in glasses. She was cooking supper. "How was their first day?"

"Great. Jay drew a self-portrait."

"Isn't that nice. I didn't know he liked to draw. Parker, did you hear that, Jay drew a picture at school today." I could hear my father in the distance, from his green chair, bourbon always next to him.

"Mama."

"What sugar?"

"It was anatomically correct."

"Well of course it was, hon."

"I don't think you understand."

"Well, maybe I don't."

"His drawing was anatomically correct. It had a huge, pink-colored wee-wee hanging from the overalls and he'd put a purple tip on top like a circumcision."

Mama hooted and the phone slammed onto the linoleum. Her laughter echoed throughout the kitchen. "Parker," she shouted. "Jay drew himself with a wee-wee at school today."

"Did he do it justice?" my father boomed, and right then, I'd never been more grateful to have been born into a family of kooks. They made life so much easier to swallow, even the parts that were speared with fish hooks.

"Prudy, hon," Mama said when she'd finally composed herself. "Did he say why he'd drawn a wee-wee on his picture?"

"Yep. He said the boy next to him had four hanging off of his. He said he needed at least one."

As soon as we hung up, the doorbell rang. Jay ran downstairs to answer it, eager to see Croc and Sam. I put on a kettle for the tea and took out some chicken for supper.

Croc entered the kitchen and put his arms around my waist as I stared at the white stove and the blue flame beneath the kettle. There was no way I could have predicted or prepared for what was coming.

"Prudy," he whispered into my neck, giving me chill bumps. "I got you a little present."

# *Chapter Eighteen*

**Hey, Prudy:** *A friend is always a friend and relatives are born to share our troubles.* ***Proverbs 17:17***

**Mama's Moral:** *No more morals. You have plenty as it is. And relatives will always be here to share your troubles. Please, for my blood pressure's sake, don't have any more troubles for a good long while.*

IF SUMMER IN the Upstate of South Carolina is an insufferable blend of heat and humidity, then fall is its apology, wrapped in breezes and an easing of temperatures. You'll find more friendliness and waving, more, "Hey, how y'alls?" in mid September than about any other time of the year unless one counts Christmas, which I don't. Christmas is in its own league.

Finding grouches after Labor Day, when fall begins to peep from summer's hot curtain, its head in plain jewel-toned sight, is rare indeed, and if you happen to locate one, best run. Because if a person cannot be happy in a Carolina autumn, then forget it. Enjoyment just isn't part of the poor soul's makeup.

It's strange how life doles out ups and downs and how each individual handles these hills and valleys, the highs and lows. I have to hand it to Pauline Jeter. She is a woman who can flip sides faster than an IHOP pancake. She goes from giblet to treasure in one month, everyone adoring her, even me, on occasion.

She has devoted her entire remaining years on this earth to uplifting what her son tried to destroy. I have to give her some credit. Most relatives, no matter how much they loved their grandchildren and wanted to be near them, wouldn't go to these lengths. We'd always allowed Pauline and Peter to see the kids, though he rarely made the trip for the visits. When she'd come, I made sure to stay far away from the scene. Occasional visits hadn't been enough for her, which led me to believe the woman had a real heart beating in her squirrel chest.

"Those grandbabies and your aunt here, unusual as she is, are my only peace," Pauline had said when we first got together at Aunt Weepie's for her to "go over a few things with me," as my aunt informed she'd be doing. What that entailed was her opening wide her giant Louis Vuitton purse and taking out a big leather checkbook and calculator combination. "I will never have a restful moment in my life," she said, scribbling with a pen, "unless you take this money. If not for yourself, take it for the children." She thrust a check toward me, but I backed up, fearing the implications behind the zeroes.

"I can't possibly accept this," I said, grasping my hands behind me where she couldn't put money in them. "Pauline, I appreciate what you're trying to do, but I—"

"Take the money, foolish woman," my Aunt Weepie screamed from beneath her four-poster. She'd gone in there to drink martinis and hide, to give me privacy while meeting with Pauline. "She ain't ever going to be right in the head unless you take it. Tony and me took our share. I'm hoping he'll take a cooking course. Your mama got a cut, too. Some women wipe asses for sin's sake. Others write checks."

"My mother would never take a dime from—"

"As pure as she either *is* or *pretends* to be, all her Proverbs flew out her proper and righteous fanny when she extended her hand to accept one of Pauline's seashelled-embossed entitlements, let's call them."

"My mother would rather roll in hot coals than take that money," I said. "She has pride."

"Pride has a sister, Ms. Prudy. It's called Greed."

Pauline sighed. "Prudy, I insisted every one take a check. I can't begin to repay what all my people have done to cause you and my grandbabies grief and harm, starting with Peter, who is really to blame because when you think about things, my baby boy—"

"Watch it!" my aunt yelled. "Don't even say his name. Remember, that was House Rule Number One until we can digest everything better. Maybe after a while we'll let you add him to the prayer list, but that day's a ways off, hon."

"Pauline, you are much too generous," I said, rather uncomfortably. "But I'd feel indebted forever. Like I was always having to pay you back or something."

"I'm the one trying to pay you all back. And this is the only way for me. The jerk I married at least had some ASS-ets," and the way she said it caused her and my Aunt Weepie to roar. What a pair. I never thought that jitter bag of a woman had a shot at humor and fun, and look how wrong I was. If I was wrong about her, I wonder how many others I'd misjudged? Maybe my mama was right and there was at least a kernel of decency in everyone, it just took the right timing to make it pop.

"I got $550,000 in cash from the beast," Pauline said, her growing boldness a nice change. "I also made off with half the value of both houses, the one in Virginia and the other in the Tennessee mountains. You know how much that is? It's more than I'll ever spend. I don't even like to shop. Nothing fits me. Nobody but Ann Taylor makes a zero, and I can't wear those clothes. I have to special order. It's not a pleasure, I'll tell you."

"Well, it's a great pleasure for me," Aunt Weepie said, crawling out of her nest to find more olives for her martinis. "She gave me and your Mama $50,000 apiece, and I plan to go to Jamaica and sit on the beach and let the natives braid my hair and bring me piña coladas. I'm ready to get my groove back."

"Prudy," Pauline said, "the money is for anything you need, but if you want to call it an education fund for you and the kids that is fine with me." Pauline surprised me by making eye contact. This was new. "If you don't accept it for any other reason, do so for education. I know how much you want to be a nurse. This will help pay some of the bills while you're in school. Plus, Jay's so smart, I'll bet he goes to an Ivy League college. I'm afraid this bit won't pay one year's tuition at Yale."

I didn't know what to say. In the South we never accept gifts we feel we didn't earn. I told her I'd think about it, but a not-so-quiet voice deep down told me I deserved it. That I'd more than "earned it."

Pauline reached eagerly for the martini my aunt had mixed her and sipped like a flitty hummingbird at the feeder. "My offspring would never accept a cent from me, so please." She extended her tiny bird arm with the check.

I finally took the check, folding and putting it in my back pocket without looking at the amount.

"Thank the good Lord above you remembered to say 'offspring,'" Aunt Weepie said. "You're learning, darlin'."

What I did next came as natural as breathing and felt as right as saying a blessing before a big meal. I bent down and embraced little Pauline Jeter, her sharp, child-like bones pressing into me, into the scars. I was unable to let go and held her tightly, the way Jay and Miranda hold onto me when they're terrified. I broke into tears and, no, it wasn't because of the money. No, it wasn't that at all. I cried because finally this woman was acknowledging I was a worthy human being and that I didn't deserve what had happened to me. As I wept against her pointy shoulder that smelled of baby powder, I knew she didn't deserve it either.

"I never hated him, Pauline," I said, dabbing my running nose with the back of two fingers. "They used to get mad. The therapists. I couldn't punch their pillows or throw a fit. They always said I'd never heal until I expressed anger. Maybe I never hated him because somewhere deep inside, someplace buried in the mind, I knew he was sick."

I released Pauline, who remained silent as I led her into Aunt Weepie's living room, all ornamental and festooned in formality despite the green shag carpeting from 1971. I turned to her and said, "We're all different. Nobody has to be a textbook example of the stages of grief and recovery. No mother has to fault herself if her child does what others can't forgive. Your son . . ." and I whispered his name, "Bryce," into her ear so Aunt Weepie wouldn't hear, "he was very sick and still is. I saw him, Pauline, and I hate what he did to me, to us. I really despise it when I see myself in the mirror or in my babies' eyes. But as far as hating him, how can I? Look what he gave me. Jay and Miranda. I wouldn't have them if I'd taken any other road."

"Prudy, you don't have to say all this." We had taken a seat on Aunt Weepie's formal, velvet sofa. Pauline's hands rested in two tight fists against her lap and clutched a clump of shredded tissues.

"I promise, Pauline, whatever it took to get them on this earth . . . if I'd known before—had held a crystal ball and seen what the future had in store—I'd have said, 'Let's get on with it.' I wouldn't have used that knowledge to change courses. These children, I honestly believe, are the ones I was born to have. I couldn't have had them without . . . him . . . without Bryce."

Pauline let out a succession of shoulder shakes, the tremble before the massive rumble and flood of her tears. It was a long while before the shoulders quit moving and the voice found itself, the crying Aunt Weepie was so proud of at funerals—the tears that ushered the two of them into the dining rooms of brick ranchers and Georgians where dish after dish of CorningWare released the homey smells of Campbell's Cream of Mushroom soup, melting cheese and whatever vegetable happened to find itself bubbling beneath cheddar heaven.

"It's okay," I said. "Let it out." I patted her. She was frail, a broken ballerina in my arms. "It'll be all right, Pauline." I tried to think of what else to say, what might possibly comfort her enough to stall this torrent of tears and silence her heaving upper body. The more I tried to soothe her, the more she wept.

"You have a new family now," I said, amazed at my own words. "We're here for you." She cried even louder. Aunt Weepie rushed in with another martini sloshing from the stemware.

"Pauline, suck it up. We got a funeral in two hours and I don't want you to use up your reserves over Miss Prudy. No offense, Prude." She stood in front of Pauline, gin doing a Hula-Hoop in the wide-mouthed martini glass.

"I already invited you to Thanksgiving and Christmas. Surely you realize a person doesn't get such invites unless the family actually likes them enough to digest a meal in their presence. I'm not even inviting my oldest daughter this year. Surely this gives you an ounce of confidence." She lifted the gin to her lips and sipped, struck a classic Aunt Weepie pose, then excused herself and crawled back into her nest. "Get me up when it's time to crash the fune," she said.

***

Mama and Aunt Weepie live two miles from each other, and this is fortunate when a woman runs out of gas, which is exactly what happened after leaving my aunt's place, a check for Lord-only-knew-how-much folded in my jean's pocket and fresh tears of forgiveness damp on my cheeks. I was surprised how good I was feeling, how a heart could swell if a person found the capacity to excuse and release acts of people she never dreamed possible.

The magic of near-autumn in the Carolinas wasn't holding back, and today's sky bathed itself in a shade of blue so intense it was startling.

The day spread gorgeous, a postcard afternoon, temperatures in the low 80s and perfect for walking the remaining mile to Mama's to bum enough gas to get home.

I strolled at a leisurely pace, taking in the way the air felt when all the humidity had been squeezed from it. The trees were growing a deeper, dull green, the color before the first frost brings a slow and beautiful transition into fall's capes of red and gold and pumpkin orange. I thought about Croc as I walked, hugging the side of the road to avoid the teenagers who sped by in trucks and sports cars. I thought of the day the Beckers had packed their faith and furniture and put them at the mercy of the Mayflower and a second go at Florida. That was the night that changed everything. The night that turned living into loving.

Working and taking care of my children had taught me how to live and that it was worth it to get out of bed every morning, that a lot of people had problems worse than mine, that I was lucky to have survived and am not in a wheelchair. After a while, a woman can find the satin edges of grace in tragedy's wool blanket.

It was Croc who taught me how to love. Really love. He taught me love in its beginnings, when we were young and in a hurry and fueled by out-of-control hormones. And now he was teaching me about the kind of love that could pace itself, a 26-mile-marathon love as opposed to sprints and dashes.

I wasn't seeking salvation in his arms. I did not long for him in a lusty sort of way (on most days). But I loved him—a steady kind of love like the older people I've come across over the years.

"He's my best friend," they'd say. "He's my greatest companion." These people knew the secret. That if friendship were a major part of the union, the sex would always be the seasoning, something to spice it up or make it sweeter. And that if a devoted friendship wasn't there, sex would, even on the best of days, be nothing more than an exercise of meaningless movement.

I'd always, without question, figured a girl needed seasonings before she could cook the meal, and that love without spices and the zing of heat couldn't be real or lasting.

Now I understood better and knew love didn't have to hurt. I know when I hold Croc's thin hand, fingers calloused from guitar strings, when I allow him to trace my scars and tiptoe along the quieter paths to my heart, that this is right. That this is the kind of easy love I want. Not the kind Amber is getting from Landon, the scorching sizzling sex, the fights, the intensity of a brush fire burning fast and all-consuming.

***

"I have a surprise," Croc had said a few days ago when the Beckers moved out, the day I learned the roof over my head had been sold. I was at the counter, coating chicken breasts in a mixture of Special K and Parmesan cheese.

"Come on, Croc," I said, "I'm trying to cook. Might be one of the last meals I get to cook in this kitchen, so I want it to taste decent. The owner hasn't returned my call, but I'm sure we'll be put out just like the Beckers. It's only a matter to time."

He wrapped his arms around mine, led me to the sink and cut the water on, rinsing raw chicken and crumbs from my hands, toweling them off with a Bounty, then kissing each finger until he came to the ninth, holding that left finger in his hand. He dug into his pocket and pulled out a teeny box wrapped in silver paper, no room for a bow. Oh, God. He was proposing. My heart raced, picking up irregular beats that rob a woman of breath and firm footing. I had not prepared for this, wasn't even wearing lipstick or a decent coat of mascara. I had on ugly clothes, too. My breath was oniony. A woman doesn't want to get engaged in the kitchen of a rental unit with raw chicken on her hands and onion breath. But who can be picky these days when a good many men fear death less than marriage?

"Go on," he said. "Close your mouth, take a breath and open the box." He nudged the gift into my damp hands.

I unwrapped the silver paper, slowly removed the black velvet box and lifted the lid. Inside, tucked in the slot where the ring should have been, was a piece of paper, a pink Post-It exactly like the kind Aunt Weepie had stuck to the biscuits she'd thought had been served from the floor. I unfolded the paper and read the block print, the careful lettering, almost as if professionally written.

"MY DARLING PRUDY. WELCOME HOME. FOREVER, CROC."

I was puzzled. Welcome home. What was this? I smiled and started to go right back to my chicken, pissed there wasn't a big old diamond in the appropriate section, where instead had been the Post-It note. I grew madder than a wet cat that he'd duped me into thinking he was proposing. Not, mind you, that I'd have said yes. Not by a long shot. Maybe. Possibly. I don't know.

"Prudy," he said. "I bought this house. I'm the new owner."

I turned abruptly back to dinner preparations and rolled another breast in the mixture and plopped it into my Pyrex. Great. Wonderful. He owned the house and therefore he owns us. Could treat us like tenants, march us around like soldiers for the all mighty rent dollar.

"Did you hear me?"

"What are we supposed to do?" I snapped. "Fall on our knees? Say, please, Mr. Godfrey, have mercy on us poor folks and add 'rent control' to your high-falutin', property-owning vocabulary?"

Croc stood stunned as men will do when they've once again, for the millionth time, misread a woman and what she really wants in life. I wonder how many women expect to unwrap rings at Christmas and Valentine's, then have to put on a big old fake smile and say, "What a lovely bracelet. Please, help me fasten the hook."

"Prudy, I don't get it. Don't leave me here to fill the gaps in a woman's mind. I can't do it. I admit I'm from Mars, Pluto. I want you to spell it out for me. Please."

I didn't budge from my silent stance.

"Okay, all right," he said. "I'll spell it. I L-O-V-E Y-O-U."

"G-R-E-A-T!" I spelled, opening the oven and shoving the pan into the heat that bathed my face, already hot with anger.

"Prudy?"

"Does this mean I'm your Jezzie, your $550 a month hooker, or do I get a discount because we're finally French kissing and copping a feel or two?"

He offered a lopsided grin, an exasperated smile that you see in 1950s movies when the befuddled man can't figure out what the zany, wasp-waisted female is doing. He was Cary Grant, Humphrey Bogart, Hugh Grant, Brad Pitt. All mine.

"I'm going to be living here, too, Prudy."

I threw down the potholder and jabbed the air with a fork.

"Is that right? You think a little black box with a major chunk of jewelry AWOL is going to get you in my queen bed, will entitle you to my Serta hospitality, my overall Sunday afternoon zest for the big act? Is that what your Lesueur pea brain is thinking?"

He quit smiling. "I'm not moving into your bed," he said. "I'm going to be living—"

"What? What? I'm too hog-like for you. You a bit put off by a few cottage cheesy ripples? Well, I may be a size 10 to 12 but at least, at least . . . I don't have that neck thingamajig hanging.

"Show me a dozen 39-year-old women who don't have a neck thingy, and I'll show you a piece of ocean front property in Oklahoma."

"Go to your room," he ordered.

"Excuse me."

"You're ruining my whole plan. Go to your room."

"I'll not have you talking to me like your 8-year-old child."

He grabbed my waist and led me into the bedroom blooming with an enormous vase of 24 red roses and another box, this one much bigger than the first, sitting on my vanity. I picked it up. It weighed at least a pound or two and I figured it held a lead crystal candy dish or a clock or some other impersonal, non-committal type gift.

"Go on and open it," he said as I switched the box from hand to hand, figuring, guessing. "Before your chicken starts burning."

"It's only been in there a few minutes."

"Fine. Please, Prudy. Go on and open it."

I untied the white velvet bow and carefully lifted tape from the same silver wrap that had been on the first package. The first object I came to was a rock, a big Charlie Brown rock with dirt and moss still in its crevices.

"Keep digging around," he said.

I found it. Another small, black velvet box, same as the first one. I opened it quickly with an expression of "another Post-It?" I saw my face in the vanity, flushed as a teenager's, Croc behind me, expectant. Nearly 20 years may as well have been erased in that one moment, that single window of time warping—when we were both 18, 19 and love was new and possibilities endless.

I looked into the box and staring back at me twinkled a beautiful diamond, emerald cut, at least 1 ½ near-flawless carats. He'd remembered, remembered all those years ago when we'd made love on the Hillbrook Golf Course and he'd asked, "What kind of diamond do you like best?" and I'd said, "There's only one kind. The emerald cut."

He reached for my left hand, slipped the ring on and said these words:

"I've loved you all my life. If you'll marry me, I'll give you every bit of joy you could ask for. The kids, too. Remember, fear no longer has a place in our lives. Regrets either."

My throat closed with emotion. I inhaled, smelling the flowers, the chicken, Croc's Prell shampoo. I could hear the children in the next room, fighting, laughing, then fighting some more.

I thought about the house and the kindness shown by this skinny man, this man as good as Gandhi and equally deserving of a peace prize. As I'd rebuilt my life since the radio station breakdown, he'd been there, the mortar for every brick I'd stacked.

"Me too," was all I could say. "I mean, I've loved you, too, and yes. Yes, I will . . . well, maybe not. I really want to, but I have a question to ask you, if you don't mind."

He shrugged his shoulders, giving his ribs a more gaunt appearance.

"I have been wondering about this for quite a while," I said, picking a rose out of the vase and working it like a prop. "Remember when we dated earlier this summer? You know, I don't understand and you've never fully explained why you didn't call for three whole weeks."

"I did call. I sent flowers."

"That was the day after," I said, twirling the rose absentmindedly. "You never called again until I ran into that trouble at the station. Even after the oyster bar, you didn't call."

He sat in my vanity chair, crossed a leg and picked at his blue jeans. "It's a long story," he said.

"I've got nothing but time, 45 minutes until the bell goes off and says my Parmesan chicken is cooked to perfection."

He decided to stand, then changed his mind and sat again. No wonder he was thin—all that motion he put into his regular daily moves. My mother used to say he was wired all wrong. "Too many volts give a man the wiggles," she'd said.

"I was dating someone else." The words fell out of his mouth. They floated from his face and sailed toward my heart, ready to spear me. I wanted to inhale and blow them out of the room. "It was a mistake," he said. "I met her about a year or so after Shannon died and thought I liked her enough to pretend to be happy and give my son stability. Sam never grew close to her. Neither did I, really. I guess it wasn't meant to be."

"I'd say not." I tried to process this information but was having trouble. "How long did you say you were with her?"

"Nearly three years. Right up until you went to the hospital."

"Oh, so my going to the hospital is what lit the fires of your heart," I said. "Got those ventricles pumping." My voice was stern and the stem of the rose snapped in my hand, but I kept holding on, feeling the flower's sharp thorns digging into my palms.

"It was the night at the bar. Before then, really," he said. "I'd already broken it off, told her I was moving back to Spartanburg. I wanted to be near you. I swear, Prudy." His eyes were so big and sad they would have sunk had I put them in water.

"Then she was your transition woman?"

"My what?"

"Cushion. Rebounder. I don't know. The relationship people always say a person has *betweeners.* The warm-up woman, the filler, the pinch hitter, the sub."

"More or less." He saw my unsmiling face. "Yes. She was my shock absorber. I felt kind of bad about breaking up with her, but I could sense she wasn't fully invested in us either."

I broke the limp portion of the stem off the flower and reinserted the rest in the vase, trying to rearrange the petals so everything was even and balanced. Croc put his hand on my neck and the warmth of it sent me spiraling into him, holding and kissing his face, his hands, his forehead.

When we kissed, I tasted all the flavors of love, the spearmint gum, the nerves behind it, the future ahead of it.

Suddenly, I had a crazy thought. "Oh, no, Croc. I haven't had my in between, my rebound person yet."

"That's okay. Maybe not everybody needs one."

"I guess the fact I've had 14 lovers, you being the first and hopefully the last, counts for a good deal of cushioning and rebounding."

"Fourteen?" He was grinning. "You sure it was only 14?"

I reached for the pillow and threw it at him. He caught it and we both landed on the bed, falling into the soft down comforter, the bed my mother had made for me when we'd moved into the apartment. He pressed his body into mine and I realized the signs were there. He wanted me. His heart, his hands, his body.

"Purrrrrrdy," he whispered into my ear and neck. "Sweet Purdy."

"Umm . . . let's wait," I said, as he continued his moves, a hand slipping into my jeans. "I want to pretend to be a virgin. Let's wait till our wedding day. Want to? I mean, we could at least *try*, given the fact I've gone way over two years without sex. Also, I need to let you know right now I'll do it with you any day of the week but Sundays. I'm not ever having Sunday sex again."

"I'll bet you will," he said, putting a hand on my breast, giving it a gentle squeeze.

"Don't count on it."

"When do you want to run off?"

My romantic veil vanished. "Excuse me? Did you say run off?"

"You don't want a big old wedding do you?"

"Does a Dachshund bark? I sure do want a big giant wedding. With friendly guests and a band, not some harpist and non-alcoholic punch."

He raised his shoulders in an I-give-up pose.

"Miranda will make an adorable flower girl. Jay and Sam junior groomsmen." The plans swirled in my mind, and I jumped from his arms and dashed into the kitchen and called Mama right away. Even though it was Croc I was marrying and she'd have preferred almost anyone but him, she'd grown tired of worrying about her newly-single daughters and shouted, "Thank you, Jesus," when I told her the plans. "Tell him no more shenanigans. You know what I mean. My yard?"

"I've already picked out my dress, and it's as white as when snow first falls."

"Prudy," she said. "You absolutely cannot wear white. Everyone and his brother knows you've had relations."

"I sure will wear white. The whitest I can buy."

"But you're not a . . . a . . . you're not a virgin, Prudy."

"I believe I am, Mama. About as close as you can get. Kind of like those Chanel watches you get in New York and those Gucci bags. They aren't exactly real, but they're close enough."

***

After running out of gas at Weepie's and walking a mile or so, I arrived at my mother's slightly out of breath, hot enough that I decided to cool off in the pool before going in and announcing I'd need some petro from the lawn mower. The parents were never thrilled when I'd done the irresponsible, and I wasn't big on telling them. Maybe a good swim before the colder weather arrived, a last swim before fall became official would be nice. A hearty lap swim. Good for the fanny. Good for the mind. I saw my mother's Town Car and my dad's van, but Amber and her brood weren't there, and I didn't want to ring the bell in case my parents were napping.

It was Saturday afternoon and odd that I didn't hear a TV, only the music from the outside speakers aimed at the pool. I entered the combination on the gate, fumbling then remembering the last number. I took a chaise lounge under the cabana my father had built and removed my clothes down to bra and panties, which could have passed for a swimsuit should a repairman or delivery truck arrive.

I was about to step into the cold water when out of the blue, the clear blue of a painted sky and the quiet-as-a-tomb house, I heard a noise that was unmistakably that of a woman having delicious and riveting relations. I bolted from water's edge, grabbed a towel, my skin rising with chill bumps. I waited. Then heard it again.

"Ohhhhhhh, my Looooooord . . . Crank it up, crank it up! Myyyyyy, Sweet heavenly daaaaaaaaayyyyys. Yesssssssssss! You are the kiiiiiiiiiiing! The man!"

I froze with mortification. The screams of pleasure belonged to my mother. My frigid, un-horny, proper and stiff mother was having a wild romp, the ride of her life.

I couldn't help myself and moved closer toward my parent's bedroom window at the back of the house. There was laughter, more sounds of hot sex, followed by a squeal a pig couldn't have matched and then a high-pitched, "V FOR VIC - TOR - Y!" bellowing from the screen of the open window.

I rushed back to the pool, cheeks red, the unsettling reality that my parents had sex and had enjoyed it running through my fuzzy head. I dressed as quickly as I could and practically jogged all the way back to Aunt Weepie's to fetch a gallon of gas so I could go home and pretend none of this had happened.

By the time I stopped by the pizza place and Blockbuster, preparing for a night of lovely solitude, a message flashed on the answering machine.

**MAMA:** *Prudy, this here's your mother. I'm more than a little concerned that you and Amber are living with men and don't have marriage licenses and the bands of gold around your fingers. I know you're both planning to get married, but it's not good for your reputations to have taken up with men. Shacking up is what you're doing. Everyone knows you're having relations. Prudy, call me. I know you and Amber get the itch. I think Pauline's getting it, too, 'cause Weepie said she flirted at the last funeral with a man who had two teeth in his entire head. She told Weepie she never wanted to see another perfect mouth in her life. Prudy, sex isn't good before marriage. Remember that, hon. It's a service to the man, a duty and chore for the woman. Don't service him without the legal documentation."*

I picked up the phone and dialed my parent's number. I was mad that she'd pretended all these years to be such an ice queen. She answered on the third ring.

"Don't you go telling me about your 'pretty patch's' *dreaded* duties and everyone else's having itches and urges," I said, hearing a squeaking sound from her throat. She tried to speak but nothing emerged from the tightening vocal cords. "I know you got a wild what-not in your panties so please, please quit trying to pretend you don't heat up for relations. Why, everyone in Spartanburg heard your zest for the wand this afternoon. Wifely duty? You always made it sound worse than scrubbing toilets."

Mama gasped, finding her voice. "How dare you talk to me like that? I'm your mother!"

"Well? Isn't that what you've been doing all day?"

"I've been cleaning and getting ready for Monday's bridge group. It's my turn to host and I had to steam clean the carpets, polish the silver, make a pie . . . "

"Be sure and tell the bridge biddies how much you enjoy it," I said, feeling naughty but justified. For years I'd had to listen to her lectures on morals and chastity, but after today, the cat was finally out of its howling, horny bag.

"Enjoy what? What is wrong with you, Prudy?"

"Tell them you are one hot mama. If today's any indication, sounded to me like you chased and hog-tied a suitor to the bed. Why, between you and Annie Sue and Aunt Weepie, every mattress coil ever made is getting the workout of a lifetime."

She sucked at the air, tried to form a word, then gave up and slammed down the phone.

I ate my pizza and stayed up late watching movies, followed by listening to my favorite Dixie Chicks CD, *Fly*, and singing out loud the words to "Goodbye Earl" and "Sin Wagon." At 2 a.m., pumped up and still not tired, I ran a tub of hot water and lit a few candles, the smoke rolling toward the ceiling as the fan tried to stir the night. I thought about Croc telling us all that everything would be all right, his favorite saying in the world.

At 3 a.m., relishing in the thought that my mother was normal but trying hard not to replay her delight in my head, I forced myself into a bed that had all but sucked me in like quicksand for a year.

The fact was, I didn't want to go to bed tonight. I was afraid I'd miss out on something. Anything. After a while, I gave up fighting the cotton sheets that were twisted in fitful bunches around my legs. I got up and found my blue jeans, reached into the pocket and took out the check from Pauline Jeter. One

Hundred Thousand Dollars! Oh . . . my . . . God. I held onto the bedpost to keep from falling to the floor. I was expecting a lot, but this was twice as much as I'd bargained for.

I rummaged through my Goodwill nightstand for a pen and paper, locating a few sheets of blue-lined loose leaf from one of Jay's many packages. I grabbed a thick-tipped marker. "One Hundred Ways to Spend $100,000" I wrote across the top of the page.

1. Private School.
2. College.
3. Ballet School.
4. Genius School.
5. Graduate School.
6. Medical School.
7. Nursing School.

This time next fall, I wrote in the margin, I'd be a student in the RN program, studying to take care of the world's tiniest and sickest newborns, the premature infants in the neonatal intensive care units. And those at the opposite end of life's journey—the white-haired men and women at Top of the Hill or any other nursing home. I'd usher new babies into a world that stretched and loomed endlessly, and then I'd lead the elderly out of a world that had held onto them as long as it could.

I thought about this, my daydreams so real I could feel the two-pound babies in my arms, wires and tubes sustaining their breath and bodies. I thought about Annie Sue and her new boyfriend and how they were the talk of the home, inspiring others to seek companions, or, as in her case, lovers.

I thought about Croc and how good he was to the kids and me, and then I thought about how all those women looking for sizzling nights under the Laura Ashley's were missing the whole point.

The next thing I knew there was a dull thud at the side of the house.

The newspaper. The Sunday paper. I believe this is what I've stayed up waiting for. And here it was—downstairs, in the dewy grass of what was almost another morning.

# *Final Chapter*

THE SUNDAY PAPER, even in small Southern towns, weighs more than most full-term babies. Every major advertiser stuffs the paper like a Christmas turkey, and it can take a good while to dig through the insides to find the Lifestyles section.

Could it be in there, already?

There on double pages in black and white, stood all the beautiful brides and brides-to-be in poses of innocence and expectations, thinking the moment the camera clicked, the flash popped, their lives were going to be a series of rising pedestals on which their husbands were sure to place them.

They have no idea as they grin into the future that the man by their side could end up one of the thousands like Bryce Jeter. Never satisfied with the meat loaf you make, the hips you've tried to tame and tone, a man who doesn't want to see your morning face. A man who builds a barricade with Chex and Raisin Bran boxes so he can eat in peace.

For these women's sake, for the sake of honesty and accuracy, most men aren't like Bryce Jeter. Many are good and decent, as much so as Croc Godfrey or my daddy or other men who bend over backwards with kindness and respect. Otherwise, you wouldn't see so many brides with optimism shining on their faces, white picket fences reflected in their eyes.

There is hope. Like my mama said, 50-50. If a girl doesn't get it right the first go-round, here's to the next, Aunt Weepie always said with a martini toast. And I fully believe a lot of second marriages work because they're not solely built on a pyre of lust. A good many of the same women who once equated heat and passion, pain and anguish with real love, have learned differently. We've got the bruises on our hearts, the dents in our chests to prove it. All we want is someone to love us, treat us with a few ounces of compassion and be good to our kids. That's really not much to ask.

And all those "nerds" we tossed out in our youth, as if they were the amoebae of the men-pool . . . well . . . we know better now. Those are the ones we should have hooked in the beginning. Look around. The girls who married the nerds, chances are, they're in the 50 percent who don't have to spend years in court arguing over who gets the Oneida and who gets the Mikasa, who pays support and which child sleeps with which parent on what nights.

I pondered all of this as I flipped through the various sections of the paper, ads and inserts flying out and fluttering to the floor. I wondered as I saw all those brides and brides-to-be in those glorious photos, if they had that ache-and-hunger kind of love, or the slow mellow version that lasts. As I hurriedly scanned pages, my stomach twisted into a jangle of nerves and noises. And then . . . then . . . I saw it.

The photo. Our engagement announcement.

I began to laugh, picturing sweet Mama drinking her Maxwell House Lite, trying to cop a java high off the reduced caffeine while peering into her favorite section of the *Herald* and seeing our huge announcement, which she had no idea was running. I paid big money to have the picture blown up, a beautiful photo of Croc and me not as we appear now, but as we were then, senior year in high school.

I had an enormous pair of Farrah Fawcett wings going, and Croc was wearing a blue tuxedo from our Homecoming Court picture, same one that appeared in the yearbook. The photo was a perfect backdive through the decades, straight into my virginity, which I'd managed to hang onto for eight additional months after the flash popped and mottled.

I pried myself from the floor and hauled the newspaper to my big comfortable bed and climbed in just as the sun stuck its first morning fingers through the mini-blinds, giving me enough light to read the words I'd chosen so carefully the week before.

> *Mr. and Mrs. Parker Millings unofficially and unknowingly announce the engagement of their daughter, Prudence "Dee" Faith Millings to Edward Brooks "Croc" Godfrey, son of Mrs. Barbara Louise Godfrey and the late Edward Brooks Godfrey, Sr.*
>
> *The couple were high school sweethearts, reuniting after two decades. Both have baggage to*

*bring into the future marriage, but none is expected to pose problems for a long-lasting union. They both like a lot of luggage, anyhow.*

*As for setting an official date, this is still under a considerable amount of fair and gentle debate. Be sure of one thing, the bride WILL wear white and the reception will feature delicious food and spirits. Both parties firmly believe buttermints and 7-Up punch aren't going to cut it. In addition, the bride and groom are educated and have degrees, but won't bother readers with that overdone piece of information. It may be worth a note to say that the couple, while living together, is abstaining from "relations" until their wedding night, firmly believing virginity is a commodity as recyclable as paper and plastic.*

*The future groom has retired from the real world and will now concentrate on his many musical talents. The bride is returning to college to finish a long-awaited career in Beginnings and Endings.*

I shivered with pleasure, rolled over and fell into a deep satisfying sleep, dreaming of my bridesmaids, picturing Annie Sue and Aunt Weepie, Amber and a few others in a pink silk with dyed-to-match shoes. I didn't stir until I could not ignore the jangling phone any longer.

I'd forgotten to cut off the ringer or slide the volume to "Low."

**MAMA:** *"Prudy? Prudy! I know you're there. You pick up the phone right this minute, young lady. Make that Middle-Aged Lady.*

*PRUDY! Pick it up now or I'm going to have to check myself into the hospital for a pre-meditated stroke.*

*This . . . this . . . announcement is in the poorest of taste. Did you even consider my bridge biddies? I'm going, Prudy. I'm hanging up and heading to Eckerd's as soon as they open. My blood pressure is sky-rocketing. I don't believe in a million—"*

I fumbled along the nightstand until I grabbed what felt like a phone. "Mama," I said, groggily. "It's okay. Everything's going to be all right. I promise."

And as I said it, I felt the words sinking in, settling near the torn corners of my heart, the old hurts at last closing, stitched and embroidered with the thickest red threads of love. Threads that weren't likely to break. Not this time.

# *Author's Note*

While the photo on the front cover of this novel may (or may not be) of me, the book has nothing to do with my life. Well, except my mother is a bit like Lucinda Millings.

All other plot lines and characters are fictional. However, Annie Sue truly was a 104-year-old woman I knew who actually drove me in her car to the DMV to try to get her license renewed. And yes, I almost didn't survive the drive. Bless her dearly departed heart.

The rest, I promise, are people perhaps in my subconscious.

The premise of the novel arose from an incident in which a woman was mowed down by a church van driven by her crazed preacher husband. This actually happened near my hometown of Asheville, North Carolina.

I met this heroic domestic abuse survivor fifteen or more years ago and never forgot her courage and capacity to endure what would have put most women in their graves. I don't remember her name, but will never forget her grace and wisdom.

# *About the Author*

Susan Reinhardt, a well-known, award-winning columnist from Asheville, North Carolina, is author of six books and has collaborated on many best-selling anthologies. Her Amazon and Barnes & Noble best-selling book of humor, *Not Tonight Honey, Wait 'Til I'm a Size 6*, is now in its seventh printing. This was followed by *Don't Sleep with a Bubba,* A Book of the Year winner, and *Dishing with the Kitchen Virgin*, a collection of hilarious culinary disasters with a dash of PG-13 humor. All were published by Kensington in New York City. Her recent books include participating in the Malaprop's Bookstore/Café best-seller, *Naked Came the Leaf Peeper,* in which a dozen of Western North Carolina's most well-known authors went wild with a serial novel, each taking a turn with his or her own chapter. The book was highly praised by Charles Frazier, author of *Cold Mountain*, along with *Eat Pray Love*'s Elizabeth Gilbert. In November 2012, she and co-author and editor DC Stanfa released *Fifty Shades of Funny: Hook-Ups, Break-Ups, and Crack-Ups*, featuring some of the most famous authors and bloggers around.

In addition to writing, she's a stand-up comedian, public speaker, public servant, taxi driver to her teen daughter, debit card to her 21-year-old son and a borderline candidate to appear on *Hoarding: Buried Alive* if you saw her bedroom/office and the amount of books and stacked papers.

She is mother of two: daughter Lindsey and son Niles. They are her true loves and open pockets of her heart and wallet.

Reinhardt is involved in many charities, including child and animal welfare groups and is a community volunteer.

To book her for speaking, comedy or book club events, go to her website www.susanreinhardt.com or contact her through Facebook at Susan Gambrell Reinhardt. E-mail her at reinhardtnc@yahoo.com.

CPSIA information can be obtained at www.ICGtesting.com
Printed in the USA
BVOW08s0841160714

359338BV00008B/225/P

9 781935 130628